The American Idea

The American Idea

Idea

The Literary Response to American Optimism

by Everett Carter

The University of
North Carolina Press
Chapel Hill

68588

Library of Congress Cataloging in Publication Data

Carter, Everett.
  The American idea.
  Bibliography: p.

  Includes index.
  1. American literature—History and criticism.
  2. United States—Civilization. I. Title.
  PS88.C39   810'.9   76-13867
  ISBN 0-8078-1279-X

Contents

Preface

The literary historian who interprets American writers from the standpoint of their interaction with their culture must have certain faiths. He must believe that there is an American culture; he must believe that it has been a valuable addition to humanity; he must believe that significant and pleasing literature has been shaped by—and in turn has shaped—this culture. I believe these things.

Yet after affirming these faiths, I avow the doubts that should occur to anyone who says that *this* is American culture, *this* is how our poetry and prose took their shapes, *these* are the writers in whom we best see the interplay of social and individual artistry. So various have been the ways of Americans that it seems safer, if not truer, to deny the existence of an American civilization and to tell instead the variety of its paradoxes; so pervasive has been the modernist conviction of its failure that it seems strange to respect its achievements; so blessedly, humanly contradictory are the best writings of its best writers that to evaluate them as parts of a pattern seems reductive. The following pages, I hope, are respectful of these doubts at the same time that they argue that many of our writers were products of a controlling social consciousness, a common *idea*, which constituted the reality of American sensibility, especially in the nineteenth century, and that the forms of these writers were metaphors of their affirmation or rejection of that idea. *Many*, not *all*. Not Emily Dickinson, not Stephen Crane, not a few other important poets and novelists whose work, even more than that of other major writers, resists my possibly procrustean synthesis.

The perspective of this study compels a further deference. My conception partakes of one version of post-Cartesian uncertainty about the separation of subject and object—a version best represented by William James and Robert Frost, who both saw reality as a relation between perceiver and thing perceived without losing their respect for the world "out there." This perspective suggests that the perceptual world of many modern observers is so different from that of the nineteenth century that they are unable to see the artifacts of this great age. I am conscious of both the irony and presumption of my conviction that the objects *I* have seen— the prose and poetry of the American past—are probably the true objects. Nevertheless, I hope to show that my perceptions, sympathetic to the optimism that was the controlling tone of the nineteenth century, can illuminate the significance and appreciate the value, not only of the currently fashionable writers of rejection—Melville, Hawthorne, James —but of the major affirmative writers—Emerson, Thoreau, Whitman, and, yes, Mark Twain—and of the minor worthy voices of Lowell, Holmes, and Longfellow. The latter are voices we are in danger of losing in the current revulsion against forms of affirmation, and this danger explains why some of these writers receive more attention from me than their rank would seem to warrant.

In making this synthesis between the idea of America and literary forms, I started at the beginning with an examination of the writers of the seventeenth and eighteenth centuries to show how early literary forms expressed the variety of responses to the growing public faith in goodness and progress. My major concern, however, was with the century when our greatest literature was written and when, with few exceptions, the styles of our writers might be seen as functions of their involvement with the official style of the nineteenth century. My study ends with the beginning of the twentieth century, save for some afterwords about one of our most respected contemporary novelists that suggest that, despite the exhaustion of nineteenth century faiths, the ghosts of the optimism that constituted the cultural meaning of

America continue to haunt the American literary imagination and to shape American literary forms.

My views are the result of the research and criticism of more writers than I can possibly name. The formulations of Oscar Cargill, Merle Curti, Ralph Gabriel, Henry Bamford Parkes, Max Lerner, and Daniel Boorstin about American intellectual history and the specific studies of the idea of progress in America by A. A. Ekirch and W. Warren Wagar are among the works that provided the backgrounds for my interpretation. Previous observers who have been concerned with the literary aspects of this history are more numerous; some, but necessarily only a small proportion, have been acknowledged in my text. My colleagues in the American literature group at Davis, especially James Woodress and Brom Weber, have cheered me by their continuing interest in literary history. I have come to realize that my early teachers —Dixon Wecter, Louis Wright, and Leon Howard—always brought idea and form together in their masterful writings about our literary past. It is from an essay on Oliver Wendell Holmes written for the celebration of Leon Howard's contributions to our profession (*Themes and Directions in American Literature: Essays in Honor of Leon Howard*, edited by Ray B. Browne and Donald Pizer [West Lafayette: Purdue Research Foundation, 1969]; reprinted by permission of the publisher) that the present work in large measure stems. I have also used parts of my essay written as the introduction to Harold Frederic's *The Damnation of Theron Ware*, (Cambridge: Harvard University Press, 1960, © 1960 by the President and Fellows of Harvard College; reprinted by permission of the publisher), in my present treatment of that writer. I am grateful to the John Simon Guggenheim Memorial Foundation and to the Research Committees of the University of California, Davis, for their generous aid. And I wish to thank my wife, Cecile Doudna Carter, who is reason enough for sympathy with American optimism.

The American Idea

I ~ The American Idea

This is a view of American literature from a perspective familiar[1] to aging readers of Vernon Louis Parrington's *Main Currents of American Thought*. Forty years ago Parrington identifed an optimistic belief in human possibility as the flow of social faith that sustained American writers from Roger Williams through Emerson and Howells and against which Poe and Melville and James swam with varying degrees of desperation. Parrington's insight has been submerged under the negations of a "modernism" that has become the orthodox academic position toward the arts. Turning away from society, first under the impact of new critical formalism and then under the influence of a variety of metaphysical pessimisms, the new orthodoxy has had little but scorn for a view of literature that sees art as a function of society and little but contempt for visions of life in America as anything but a disaster.

Yet the past forty years have not only produced the orthodoxies that have obscured Parrington's accomplishment, they have also witnessed a body of thought[2] and a new terminology that permit us to reexamine our major writers from the standpoint of their interaction with society. F. O. Matthiessen and Harry Levin have shown the interplay between private and public metaphors. Howard Mumford Jones studying the "history of sensibility," Perry Miller describing an "official faith," Frederick Ives Carpenter anatomizing a national "dream," Roy Harvey Pearce working with a new "historicism" have joined with Raymond Williams in the exploration of culture as a "structure of feeling." The key terms in Williams's description are the common denominators of the work of a variety of French observers, chief among them Lucien Goldmann, whose view of culture as a system of metaphoric belief suggested a method of identifying the meaning of a literary work and of providing some clues concerning its value. Kenneth Burke has provided the insight through which structural analysis may be related to social ideology, which enables us to distinguish between radically opposite kinds of literary symbolism that arise out of opposite attitudes toward the beliefs of a culture.

The point of departure of these views, and for this study, is that art is the making of form and order out of the stuff of experience and that all social activity is therefore art: the ordering and arranging of the raw stuff of nature. The fine arts, the refined essences of a social style, are a part of the larger arts of a culture's way of life. They are functions of the grosser arts of daily living that constitute familial and social organization: the arts of tilling the soil, making love, building houses, eating dinners, forming laws and learning to live by them. All men are artists; the "fine" artist is he who deals with form, the one common denominator of all the other arts. The basic stuff of all literature is the form and order by which all the other arts—those summarized by the term *culture*, or civilization —have made sense of the universe. Unexpressed, a function of the human behavior whose outlines it determines and whose texture it permeates, this form is the *soul* of a culture, the feature that distinguishes it from other cultures. It is the set of beliefs that constitutes the *style of life* or the *structure of feeling* of a civilization. It is the medium in which the aesthetic consciousness of the individual artist is suspended.

The point of critical perception in this sociological point of view is the junction of the artist's private metaphorical world with the public world of his society's beliefs about the meaning and significance of the universe. The task is to risk an identification of the larger cultural style and then to examine the little styles—the poems and the stories created by American artists—and to describe the varying ways in which these styles and structures are affected by their attitude toward their culture's organizing beliefs. It is a task that needs to be done because forty years of post-Parrington studies have usually rejected Parrington's insight; indeed, a history of American letters that virtually ignored Henry James, Edgar Allan Poe, and *The Education of Henry Adams* was an incomplete history. Parrington was right in treating literature as a function of controlling cultural convictions. Yet he was wrong in failing to see that great art not only comes from the expression of a dominant social certainty but as often comes out of the anguish of rejection of a society's central beliefs and the attempt to create an order to fill the void left by the withdrawal of the sustaining faith.

Was there indeed such a sustaining faith, such a pattern of beliefs, such a controlling assumption about men and history, that has been generally held by most Americans? With Parrington, we can run the risk of oversimplification by agreeing with the overwhelming testimony of writers, travelers, historians, philosophers that the article of faith identified with America is its optimism, a complex tone of which the primary ingredients are hopeful views of man's experience in this world and a sanguine regard for man's intrinsic value. The first part of this optimism is its attitude toward human history: its rejection of the past, its acceptance of the present, its hopes for the future; the second part is the basis for these hopes: a belief in the value of man and in his fundamental virtue.

The first ingredient, the attitude toward history, is summarized by one of the controlling ideas of Western civilization, the idea of progress. The idea, of course, was not, and is not, peculiarly American. Its historian, J. B. Bury, has described its rise in Western civilization after the otherworldliness of the Middle Ages was replaced by the "this worldliness" of the Renaissance. He has narrated how, with the publication of Bacon's new instrument for inductive reasoning and his rejection of the idols of the past, there came to be a looking forward rather than a looking backward to the golden age.[3] R. F. Jones told the story of the development in the seventeenth century of the new conception that the moderns were not necessarily inferior to the ancients and even, if we are to see them as dwarfs on the necks of giants, may be able to see farther and better.[4] And finally the flood of Enlightenment in eighteenth-century France and then in England swept away most of the pessimisms and replaced them with hopes for the future. "The object of the work I have undertaken," wrote one of the contributors to the *Encyclopédie*, is "to show that the perfectibility of man is absolutely indefinite . . . that the progress of this perfectibility has no other limit than the duration of the globe upon which nature has placed us."[5]

By the nineteenth century "the general idea" of progress "became part of the general mental outlook" of people of England and western Europe, and for many it became "a working faith of great vitality."[6] In England, Godwin and Mill enunciated the utilitarian creed of the progress of social usefulness, and their disciple, Herbert Spencer, developed a science of sociology which would study how "the primary process of evolution . . . will eventually reach a still higher stage and bring yet greater benefits."[7] In Germany, Hegel described the necessary and inevitable pulsing of thesis and antithesis of historical process under the direction of God, and with enormous persuasiveness Marx outlined the same movement under the pressures of materialistic necessities. Auguste Comte made the most elaborate schematization of the idea when he described the rise of man through infant beliefs in the supernatural, through adolescent convictions about metaphysical principles to the full, glorious maturity of the scientific method.

Although in Europe the idea had great vitality, in America it became an article of faith so widely and pervasively held that it could be called "official."[8] The very word itself, in its verbal form, was an Americanism; it is so described in the Oxford English Dictionary. In the eighteenth century, the editors remark, the word became obsolete in England but was apparently "retained (or formed anew) in America, where it became common c. 1790 . . . thence readopted in England after 1800 . . . but often characterized as an Americanism, and much more used in America than in Great Britain." In 1803 a Yale student sitting in the class of Dr. Timothy Dwight recorded in his notes: "The doctor remarks that the verb 'Progress' is not an English word, but coined in America."[9]

Not only the word itself is typically ours; the concept in its complete vigor is peculiarly associated with our national history and character. Americans are children of a Western culture that begins with Bacon and his new instrument of scientific induction: the first year of our continuous history is the year that Bacon published the work that ushered in the era of scientific development and the concomitant conviction about an improvable future. The years of our growth as a colony parallel the gradual growth of theoretical and applied science and the development of the Royal Society in England and of the *Encyclopédie* in France. The forces in Western culture that nurtured the ideas of contractual government and of natural rights were identical with the forces that proclaimed the existence of these rights by virtue of the possibilities of man and of his future development. And just as our birth as a colony was simultaneous with the birth of the theory of scientific induction, so was our birth as a nation associated with the spirit of the Enlightenment and its belief in possible improvement. By the beginning of the nineteenth century, Thomas Jefferson could suggest for the design of the great seal of the United States the children of Israel walking out of the wilderness toward the New Jerusalem, and by 1818 he could write to Benjamin Waterhouse: "When I contemplate the immense advance in science and discoveries in the arts which have been made within the period of my life, I look forward with confidence to equal advances by the present generation, and have no doubt they will consequently be as much wiser than we have been as we than our fathers were, and they than the burners of witches."[10]

Ralph Waldo Emerson, traveling in England thirty years later, reported that his English friends asked "whether there were any Americans?—any with an American idea,—any theory of the right future of that country? Thus challenged, I bethought myself . . . only of the simplest and purest minds; I said, 'Certainly, yes;—but those who hold it are fanatics of a dream which I should hardly care to relate to your English ears, to which it might only be ridiculous,—and yet it is the only true.'"[11] In calling his country's cluster of beliefs the "American idea," Emerson was invoking more than a mere mental construct that was outside of and apart from the things observed; his theory of perception fused the outer world with the world of the mind and made "idea" the form-giving force of reality. Emerson's "idea" of America was the term for the central organizing perceptual catalyst that would pattern the chaos of impressions. Why should it sound strange to his overseas listeners? The peculiarly "American idea" might have sounded "ridiculous" to some English ears because it was invariably yoked to another belief to which it seems contradictory: the belief in the essential goodness of natural man. This combination of beliefs not only seemed illogical to Emerson's English friends; it has continued to cause difficulties for subsequent American critics who have averred that the assumption of the truth of both primitivism (the usual term for a belief in the natural goodness) and progress constitutes a paradox, a clash of irreconcilable values that could lead to "an interpretation of American history" as "potentially tragic."[12] Primitivism, however, is not an historical but a moral position. There is in the American idea no longing to go back to a primitive state of innocence, no yearning to turn back civilization's clock. Quite the contrary: there is the yearning to go forward, to conquer the forest, to make the plains social, to harness the rivers and the tides.

The American idea made primitivism and progress into one belief by adopting the middle-class optimism of eighteenth-century Scotland, an optimism that combined a commitment to the advancement of the race with a commitment to the natural goodness of man. Through its American disciples the commonsense school of philosophy, whose major Scottish figures were Dugald Stewart and Adam Ferguson, dominated the philosophical faculties at Harvard, Yale, and Princeton for the first three decades of the nineteenth century and formed the thought of two generations of preachers and social leaders at a crucial time in the formation of American beliefs. This pervasively influential school[13] confronted that apparent discrepancy between primitivism and progress, which has disturbed some of our modern historians. How can we believe that "natural" man is essentially good, that his "nature" tends to actions that are virtuous and valuable, and at the same time be convinced that increasingly complex social organizations and developments of techniques for manipulating nature are also good? The commonsense school answered that the resolution of this apparent paradox lay in the definition of *nature* and *natural*. It is in the nature of man to be social; to form societies is part of the natural propensities of human beings. Finding his way upward from primitive isolation and clannishness, man progressively realized possibilities already in his nature. Furthermore, the tendency to manipulate his environment is also part of the nature of man; to be an artist, in the widest sense of the term, is to be a man; to desire to affect the natural world about him is one of the defining characteristics of the species. Therefore, the belief in progress and the belief in primitivism were fused in affirmation, not caught in a paradox potentially tragic. In a work published in 1793, which went into eight American editions before 1819, Adam Ferguson put this affirmation most clearly: "If we admit that man is susceptible of improvement and has in himself a principle of progression, and a desire of perfection, it appears improper to say, that he has quitted a state of nature, when he has begun to proceed; or that he finds a station for which he was not intended, while, like other animals, he only follows the disposition, and employs the powers that nature has given."[14]

The clue to the resolution of the "paradox" of primitivism and progress lay in the one absolutely necessary ingredient in both the eighteenth century's interest in primitivism and the eighteenth century's conviction of progress: in both there is the belief in the essential goodness of man and the essential value of nature. This faith in the goodness of man and nature is what makes primitivism and progress, not opposites, but logical and even necessary complements. Believing that man is essentially good (or at the very worst morally neutral), the American believer saw the natural man—the nonexistent but necessary fable of man before environment begins to influence him—as a reservoir of potentially beneficent natural energies and powers that civilization must realize. The "American Adam" was no goal for the future;[15] he was simply a metaphor for a belief in the goodness of man, which then makes the progress of nations possible. Goodness of man, goodness of nature—these were the binding elements of the faith in primitivism and progress. Indeed, this combination is essential to the democratic belief wherever it is held. For a Hobbes there could be a definite opposition between belief in law and belief in man's goodness; an autocratic civilization is designed to control radically evil man. Democratic government and civilization, however, must be founded upon some form of *primitivism*: naturally good man can be trusted to make a civilization that will be good and that can be continually improved by the naturally trustworthy members of that civilization.

The possibilities of the future based upon an assumption of the goodness of man and nature—this, then, is the "idea" of America: the way in which Americans themselves, and the rest of the Western world, have made sense of the American experience. Through the encounter of the American writer with this idea was formed much of our significant literature. The following pages are a study of the results of that encounter and of the particular forms and styles that American writing took when it either accepted or rejected or modified the basic structure of feeling of its culture. Most of our major literary imaginations found themselves at one pole or the other of acceptance or rejection of the American idea; many took their position somewhere between; but whether accepted or rejected or modified, the idea of America has shaped the literature that Americans have created.

II ~ The Making of the Idea

The American idea of progress was a nineteenth-century shibboleth, the interaction with which formed the literature of that most fruitful age in our literary history. However, since the elements of the idea were implicit in writers of the seventeenth and eighteenth centuries, an examination of these earlier authors will suggest how literary forms shape themselves to express the variety of private responses to the public faith of their day. Puritan ideology, though mixed, was antipathetic to an optimism that predicted man's advancement through works, and Puritan rejections were invariably fashioned in an emblematic style where the images and figures were subordinated to a higher truth that the emblems attempted to express. On the other hand, the prose and verse of the writers of theological optimisms, the Quakers or the eighteenth-century deists, were invariably "realistic" in the sense that their images of the world of appearances were self-sufficient; finally, at the end of the eighteenth century, the secular optimism of Jefferson and Franklin was embodied in the classic prose of the Declaration and the *Autobiography*. In these centuries, then, there was already suggested the division in American styles between *objective styles*, where the objects are valued for their own sake, and *subjective styles*, where the objects were symbols or emblems of a world other than the world of appearances; this division would persist throughout the next two centuries.

1. Puritan Images

One of the seedbeds of American ideology, Puritanism had a double attitude toward man's hopes built into its peculiar combination of theology and historical circumstance. Historically, the Puritans were part of a movement toward the future; they were part of the first wave of the transatlantic migration that turned its back on Europe and hoped for an improvement in the New World. Filled with a sense of mission, these migrants felt themselves a chosen people building a New Jerusalem in the wilderness. Theologically, too, their beliefs, for all their worldly darkness, were pervaded by what Perry Miller described as a "cosmic optimism." As their spiritual heir, Nathaniel Hawthorne, later put so nobly, they knew that the universe wears a frown, but not a sneer; they believed it to be an ordered cosmos directed by an omnipresent and wrathful—but just—God, who had chosen them to build his kingdom in the wilderness, dedicated to his absolute worship.

This was a thoroughgoing belief in a kind of progress, a belief full of the apocalyptic fervor of otherworldly medieval Christianity that brought the spirit of millennialism to the New World. This belief was the legacy of the Puritans to one kind of progressive faith in America: Americans had entered into a covenant of grace with God; inevitably the ocean would be crossed, inevitably the wilderness would be conquered, inevitably the Indian—scion of the devil—would be subdued, inevitably would all heretics be scourged and cast out, inevitably would the city of God be established: "Whatever their sufferings . . . Puritans could take heart through the darkest moments in the confidence that all things are ordered after the best manner, that serene and inviolate above the clouds of man's distress shines the sun of a glorious harmony."[1]

Often in the eighteenth and nineteenth centuries the residue of this Puritan confidence, drained of its rich theological justification, would exist as one of the varieties of American optimism. Long after many Americans ceased to believe literally in the rapturous and immediate presence of God, they clung to a belief in an absolutely determined march of events in a closed universe that must inevitably progress toward perfection, with America as the chosen instrument for this divinely ordained progression.

Although American Puritanism, in its seventeenth-century expressions and in its revival in the eighteenth century by Jonathan Edwards, contributed a belief in necessary God-ordained progress, it denied the possibilities of man in the physical universe. The Flemish artisans who fled the Inquisition brought to England their looms, their skills, and an invincible devotion to the doctrine of Calvin; it was this doctrine, with its emphasis upon an Old Testament God of wrath and an Augustinian sense of original and pervasive sin, that formed the theology of the group of English Protestants who provided the stock from which the American Puritans came. Not for them would be the liberalism and the tolerance of the Puritans who would also develop a John Milton. Instead they sternly insisted upon the purification of the church, not only of idolatries, but of the least suspicion of a pride in man. A fervently God-centered creed, it derided and denied the essential goodness—or even the moral neutrality—of natural man and counterposed a fervent belief in human depravity. It constituted, then, from the very beginning, a mighty opposite to the strong tide of humanistic faith that flooded into the eighteenth century and created the conditions for the Declaration of Independence, for the *Autobiography of Benjamin Franklin*, and for the poems of the Republic.

And this dark Puritan vision produced a small but powerful literature whose content was deeply religious and whose form was one with that content. The interaction between Puritan form and content demonstrates the way in which public and private styles of life intermingle. The forms of Puritan prose and poetry were embodiments of Puritan otherworldliness and provided the basis for later styles fitted to a sense of the rejection of the American idea. It was an intense, frenetic style whose images were either a denigration of the material world of things or were images of dread—perfect examples of the "negative mythology,"[2] the emphasis upon mythological forms of threat and disaster of cultures involved in untoward historical circumstance.

The Puritan writer used images of worldly things, not as symbols of the meanings and values that lie within this world, but as allegories of the next world. Material objects—a spinning wheel, a caged bird, a map, a spider, the love between man and wife—these were evoked, not for themselves, but because they provided paltry, inadequate, but indispensable means of celebrating one or another of the aspects of the unseen world. Even one of their "more worldly"[3] clergy began his book on the conduct of Puritan life with a startling, violent metaphor—comparing religious faith with an apoplectic seizure and describing the true Christian's world as a world of apocalypse—prescient of Poe's "City in the Sea" or Melville's London, the City of Dis: "Either I am in an apoplexy, or that man is in a lethargy who does not now sensibly feel God shaking the heavens over his head and the earth underneath his feet—the heavens so as the sun begins to turn into darkness, the moon into blood, the stars to fall down to the ground so that little of comfort or counsel is left to the sons of men; the earth so as the foundations are failing, the righteous scarce know where to find rest, the inhabitants stagger like drunken men."[4]

Another, telling his congregation the nature of "A True Sight of Sin," used a similar series of characters and events to illustrate the need to acknowledge the vileness of the human condition: an artisan testing the quality of his metals and a traveler trying to know truly the contours of a country; then, when he wished to demonstrate the ultimate meanness of man, the Puritan writer turned to that favorite object of Puritan disdain, the worm. With the first of these images, the Puritan divine described the activities of the goldsmith as the way in which every man must assay his moral being: he must "search the very bowels of the Mettal, and try it by touch, by tast, by hammer, and by fire; and then he will be able to speak by proof what it is." In the agony of his fallen spirit, man must have direct knowledge of his frailty; to do otherwise would be to know a country only by its charts: "There is a great ods betwixt the knowledg of a Traveller, that in his own person hath taken a view of many Coasts . . . and by Experience hath been an Eye-witness of the extream cold, and scorching heats, hath surveyed the glory and the beauty of the one, the barrenness and meanness of the other . . . and another that sits by his fire side, and happily reads the story of these in a book, or views the proportion of these in a Map . . . the one saw the Country really, . . . the other only in the paint of the Map drawn." And soon in the same sermon came the scathing alliteration, lending sharp point and awful weight to the image of the physical world most suited to the meanness of man: "Dost thou not wonder that the great and Terrible God doth not pash such a poor insolent worm to pouder, and sent thee packing to the pitt every moment?"[5]

The whole grim sense of the smallness and meanness of the physical universe and of man's place in it was thus at every point emphasized by the direction of Puritan metaphor: there was little sense of the glory of the spiritual, flowing toward and filling with immanence the physical world; instead there was the use of physical images, the exploitation of the corrupt and deceptive material universe as the material out of which might come the admittedly poor and inadequate suggestions, tarnished and misleading emblems of the spiritual realities from which we are cut off by our radical imperfection.

The emblematic quality of metaphor was at the heart of the best poetry produced by the Puritan mind; indeed, the use of the physical world as emblem was the basic style of the Puritans. There is a humbling of the material universe in the metaphysical verse of the Puritans as well as in their sermons. The movement of Anne Bradstreet's metaphor was, without exception, first a tentative exploration of the world of the senses, then a quick rejection of this sensual world as at best an inadequate shadow of divine beauty and at worst a distraction from our sense of sin and human depravity. In "The Flesh and The Spirit" she described sister Flesh chided by her sister Spirit, who tells her: "Be still, thou unregenerate part,/Disturb no more my setled heart." Spirit adds that the celestial "City pure" is not for Flesh,

For things unclean there shall not be.
If I of Heaven may have my fill,
Take thou the world, and all that will.[6]

Even when dealing with more specific matters that are less concerned with the general idea of contempt of the flesh, Anne Bradstreet showed the same fusion of form and idea to produce a sense of the inadequacy of this world. She began her poem "Contemplation" with a warm appreciation of the trees, the bird, the sun, the vigorous burgeonings of nature; but she used these only as examples of the "fatal wrack of mortal things" and saved her praises for the glories that lie beyond the oblivion. In her tender poem to her husband, she came close to an acceptance of the physical world on its own terms: "If ever two were one, then surely we;/If ever man were loved by wife, then thee." Yet she ended her warm human reverence for a physical fact with a couplet that makes it clear that this love must only be viewed as an emblem of another kind of love in another world: "Then while we live in love let's so persevere/That when we live no more we may live ever."[7]

The most accomplished of the Puritan poets was Edward Taylor, who wrote in unpublished solitude metaphysical verse worthy to be placed alongside that of Crashaw, Marvell, and Vaughan. Like them and like Anne Bradstreet, Taylor humbled the physical world by treating its manifestations as emblems of spiritual truths. In "Meditation Six" he worked out the correspondences between a minted coin and a soul whose worth is a direct function of a king's imprimature. Just as the coin has no intrinsic value but only the value that accrues to it because of the king's image stamped upon its face, so does worthless man achieve significance only because of the seal of faith that the Lord fixes upon him. In "Huswifery" Taylor transformed the process of the spinning of yarn into an extended conceit, with every part of the spinning process emblematic of the relation of the soul to God: the distaff emblematic of the Bible; the desires of man representative of the flyers that guide the yarn on to the bobbins; the soul, the spool on which the yarn is wound; and, finally, the whole cloth, a suitable apparel for the worshiper on Judgment Day. Taylor subjugated the physical to the spiritual and justified the existence of material things in terms of their ability to represent dimly a religious mystery.

This major Puritan poet carried the emblematic representation of mystery to its most artful lengths in "Meditation

Eight," which began with a rejection of the possibility of finding the meaning of the cosmos or of understanding God by reasoning from nature: the poet's "Pencill" could not trace the path from the astronomer's heaven to a meaning in the universe; his reason was no guide to knowledge. Instead, he found the answer in the loaf of bread at his door, the bread that is the Body of Christ. With passion and precision Taylor elaborated the meaning of the emblem: the bread of faith became "the truth"; the fruit of knowledge, a false nourishment that denied any comfort to the pitiful bird of the soul, locked in its wicker cage. Filled with a sense of the unimaginable awfulness of the Lord's will, Taylor described Him grinding and kneading the meal into the bread of life; then in a marvelously homely touch the Lord became "Heavens Sugar cake" that filled the world with ecstatic repletion. Human rapture, enormous as it is, is far too petty truly to enjoy the celestial banquet; so the poet cries:

Ye Angells help: This fill would to the brim
Heav'ns whelmed-down Chrystall meele Bowle,
        yea and higher
This Bread of Life dropt in the mouth doth Cry:
Eate me, Soul, and thou shalt nevery dy.[8]

2. Jonathan Edwards

This cry of religious fervor—and the style in which it was phrased—was echoed in America fifty years later, in the midst of the eighteenth century, when a quite different set of beliefs—beliefs that would lead to the formulation of the American faith in progress by Jefferson and Franklin—was developing. In 1721, at the age of eighteen, studying theology in an atmosphere of an increasing religious liberalism that was changing the hard rigor of Puritanism into the comforts of Unitarian belief, Jonathan Edwards was seized with a transport of mystical awareness that turned him away from the future and back toward the stern Calvinism of Winthrop and John Cotton and to the literary style of Ward and Brad-street and Taylor. In his "Personal Narrative" Edwards described his awakening to the vileness of nature, to his "feebleness and impotence, every manner of way; and the bottomless depths of secret corruption and deceit"[9] in his heart. He "panted after this, to lie low before God, as in the dust, that I might be nothing, and that God might be All."[10] Like Emerson, a hundred years later, he felt himself part and parcel of the deity; unlike Emerson, he felt obliterated and humbled by this obsession. Emerson felt his soul expand to the dimensions of God; Edwards, convinced of his "sinfulness and vileness,"[11] felt himself reduced to a worm, or to a nonexistence. "My wickedness," he wrote, "has long appeared to me perfectly ineffable, and swallowing up all thought and imagination; like an infinite deluge, or mountain over my head. . . . When I look into my heart, and take a view of my wickedness, it looks like an abyss infinitely deeper than hell."[12] However, Edwards preached to an America that was to be Benjamin Franklin's, not his; when he insisted upon crying his message of the infinite evil of man and nature and the infinite grace of God, he was banished to the frontier and to an Indian congregation—there to write his great tracts on the limitation of the freedom of the will, to become America's first alienated intellectual, and to begin a tradition that stretched through Melville and Poe, Henry Adams, and T. S. Eliot.

One of the best minds America has produced, Edwards, knowing fully the implications of the science of Newton and the psychology of Locke, used the most recent advances in knowledge to prove the inadequacies of the human mind and of the physical world that it perceived. The Newtonian universe with its laws of light and gravity was not, as it was for the deists, proof of the self-sufficiency of the ordered universe; rather it became, as Edwards put it, "a type of love or charity in the spiritual world."[13] He turned the Newtonian discoveries about the true nature of color into a demonstration that beauty delights the mind because it is an emblem of the hidden harmony of God. "That mixture we call white," he wrote, "is a proportionate mixture that is harmonious, as Sir Isaac Newton has shown, to each particular colour, and contains in it some harmony or other that is delightful."[14] As well as the cosmology of Newton, he understood Locke's new psychology of sensationalism, the formulations about the mind that gave the Enlightenment the basis for its rejection of absolutes and its affirmation of the material world of flux and change. Yet just as he used Newton to support his theism, Edwards used Locke to support, not the growing American belief in progress, but the doctrine of Calvinistic determinism—not the conviction that man could save himself through his deeds, but the belief that salvation could come only through faith. He could agree that "one born blind"[15] has no conception of pleasant and beautiful colors—a denial of the existence of innate ideas that proved an emancipation to the thinkers of the Enlightenment, who argued that since man's notions are formed by experience, one could hope for infinite improvement by manipulation of his environment. For Edwards, though, sensational psychology proved that man was locked in a prison of his senses with absolutely no way of forming abstractions save through the power of some other, suprasensual agency—the grace of God.

Just as he turned Lockian psychology to the purposes of a Puritan vision of man, so did he make both Baconian and Newtonian logic serve the purpose of Calvinistic theology. The Enlightenment found in these scientific philosophers the basis for its beliefs in the truth and reality of the marvelously ordered physical world. Edwards used them to demonstrate that man's actions must be completely determined and hence to argue that the conception of freedom of choice was a direct contradiction of the most advanced science of his day. As Bacon had theorized and Newton had proved, the key to the physical universe was a system of causality: every effect must have a sufficient cause. Since all men's actions are caused and since each effect has only the qualities and materials of the sum of its causes, then all of man's actions must be effects; hence there must be severe limitations to, if not a complete denial of, man's freedom of will.

Edwards's writing was an embodiment of this Calvinistic interpretation of Lockian psychology and Newtonian cosmology, an interpretation that reduced man to an effect and the physical universe to a shadow of divine things. Indeed, this latter phrase is the title of one of Edwards's works. For him, as for Anne Bradstreet and Edward Taylor, the things of the world are emblems, or—to use his own term—"types" of spiritual reality. Taylor could not "line" with his "Pencill" the knowledge of astronomy; Edwards was perfectly capable of using astronomy, but like Taylor he would insist upon seeing this kind of knowledge only as "a type and forerunner of the great increase in the knowledge of heavenly things."[16]

This conception of *type* is exactly the conception of the Puritan *emblem*: a worldly object that is described only because it stands for some theological doctrine. Edwards's use of typical, or emblematic, imagery in all his prose was a function of a conviction that the physical world is shadow, and his autobiography, "Personal Narrative," is an effective example of his fusion of style and belief. The principal image in the narrative is the private individual—Edwards himself. Yet Edwards was interested in himself only as a proof of religious doctrine. The intent of the autobiography is to reduce this personality, to humble this creature, to destroy its feeling of self-sufficient existence. In American writings that express the American idea, there was a sense of joy in pure *being*—the joy of Franklin, Jefferson, Holmes, Howells in the Smiths and the Joneses of America or a rhapsodic delight in the simple state of existence, such as the transports of Emerson, Thoreau, and Whitman. Edwards's mode was an embodiment of an opposite spirit, the spirit of dread in face of the emptiness of man without God. In a note to "The Nature of True Virtue" (1765), Edwards, talking of degrees of "existence," observed that great things have more existence than small things; an archangel, therefore, "must be supposed to have more existence, and to be in every way further removed from nonentity, than a *worm*, or a *flea*."[17] In this scale from flea to archangel, humans would presumably fill a middle place. Yet Edwards tried to prevent man from feeling even the moderate sense of pride in this modest station through his favorite device of comparing man to an insect, most notoriously the spider, and challenging man's sense of being by making this comparison. Comparing humans to insects, he implied the worthlessness of man.

This worthlessness was not only a function of man's lowly place on the scale of existence; it was also a function of the delusiveness of the world of appearances itself. In a key sentence of "Personal Narrative," Edwards spoke of the next world, "where those persons who appear so lovely in this world, will really be inexpressibly more lovely."[18] The compelling words are "appear" and "really"; things of this world *appear* beautiful; in the spiritual world they really *are*. The autobiography was the story of Edwards's realization that the world of things is a world of shadows; that emotions and intuitions must supplant reason; that faith is superior to analysis; and that emotions, intuitions, and faith combine to tell us the infinite smallness of man, who must place his only hopes upon a possible absorption into the infinite greatness of God.

All the apparatus of a powerful mind working through an equally powerful prose was bent to this task of humbling personality. His early attention to worldly delights he described as the returning of "a dog to his vomit."[19] When he told of the first seizure of insight through which he knew the truth, he described an intense desire to be destroyed, annihilated, amalgamated; his images brim with the acids of digestion: "Swallowed,"[20] he cries, and he repeats, "wrapt and swallowed up in God." His experience taught him "his extreme feebleness and impotence . . . and the bottomless depths of secret corruption and deceit there was in [his] heart."[21] He came to know the "mire and defilement" of the human condition. Looking back over his exceedingly pure life, he wrote, "My wickedness . . . has long appeared to me perfectly ineffable, and swallowing up all thought and imagination; like an infinite deluge, or mountain over my head."[22] And finally, in an extremity of self-abasement, he turned once more to images of digestion: "The very thought of any joy arising in me, on any consideration of my own amiableness, performances, or experiences, or any goodness of heart or life, is nauseous and detestable to me."[23] Here indeed is the mighty opposite to the public style of eighteenth-century America—joy in accomplishment was hateful to him, and the repugnance was expressed in images of physical revulsion. The possibilities of man's goodness of heart, the possibilities of a better future through performances and experience—these were "nauseous and detestable."

Edwards's belittling of the body of man and the things of the earth was accompanied by a corresponding emphasis upon God-inspired emotions rather than on reasonable analysis. If we are to believe him, he alternated between fits of weeping and periods of "ejaculatory prayer."[24] The truths revealed to him were incapable of rational communication. He could only turn to images of physical disasters to convey his amorphous spiritual dread and to rhythmic incantations to project the meaning of his self-discoveries: "Often, since I lived in this town, I have had very affecting views of my own sinfulness and vileness. . . . My wickedness, as I am in myself, has long appeared to me perfectly ineffable, and swallowing up all thought and imagination; like an infinite deluge, or mountain over my head. I know not how to express better what my sins appear to me to be, than by heaping infinite upon infinite, and multiplying infinite by infinite. Very often, for these many years, these expressions are in my mind and in my mouth, 'Infinite upon infinite. . . . Infinite upon infinite!' "[25]

These attitudes found extreme expression in the sermon that has come to represent Edwards for posterity. "Sinners in the Hands of an Angry God" is a hyperbolic statement, uttered at the height of the great awakening, calculated to overwhelm the unregenerate man with a sense of personal depravity so that he might hasten to accept the small chance of salvation open to him under the Calvinistic covenants; but it is typical nevertheless and demonstrates the literary forms taken by Puritan distaste of the world. "The God that holds you over the pit of hell," he told his congregation, "much as one holds a spider, or some loathesome insect over the fire, abhors you, and is dreadfully provoked: his wrath towards you burns like fire; he looks upon you as worthy of nothing else, but to be cast into the fire." Then, in rising cadences of ritual incantation, Edwards battered the humanistic pride of Renaissance man:

It is nothing but his hand that holds you from falling into the fire every moment. It is to be ascribed to nothing else, that you did not go to hell the last night; that you was suffered to awake again in this world, after you closed your eyes to sleep. And there is no other reason to be given, why you have not dropped into hell since you arose in the morning. . . . There is no other reason to be given why you have not gone to hell, since you have sat here in the house of God, provoking his pure eyes by your sinful wicked manner of attending his solemn worship. Yea, there is nothing else that is to be given as a reason why you do not this very moment drop down into hell.[26]

3. *From Williams to Franklin*

It was too late. If, as Edwards insisted and Reinhold Niebuhr has emphasized in our own day, the road of the dream of human perfectibility was the road to damnation, America had firmly set its foot on the path to hell. Edwards, rejected by his congregation and his church, went off to Stockbridge to preach in exile and to write his major philosophical works. As the first of a series of American artists and intellectuals to be repelled by Western man's devotion to progress and to the quest for material betterment, he was the first member of the "adversary culture," for optimistic meliorism was already the dominant tone when Edwards preached his sermon on the inevitability of hell-fire. The Puritans were but one breed of Reformation men: there were others who carried to their logical conclusions in the social and religious sphere the Protestant principle of the right of private inquiry untrammeled by authority and who used this principle to develop a belief in the rights and dignity of man.

Roger Williams was one such man, and he became, for later interpreters of the American style such as Vernon Louis Parrington, the best example of the way in which the religious fervor of the Reformation, with its emphasis on individual interpretation of divine law, could lend itself to a corresponding exaltation of private man and of his capacities for self-government. Invariably—and more important for our present study—this social affirmation was embodied in a literary style that used the things of this world not as emblems, but as valued and self-justifying existences. Although Williams was careful to set the bounds that he knew must circumscribe unrestrained liberty if it were to be true freedom and not degenerate into anarchy, he nevertheless told the authorities that the "*Sovraigne, originall*, and foundation of *civill power* lies in the *People*."[27] Governments, therefore, are truly "commonweales" and have no more power than men's "consenting and agreeing shall betrust them with."[28] Then with significant emphasis upon the reliability of the physical world, he rested his case for government by consent upon "the experience of all *commonweales*,"[29] which demonstrated the difference between respect for this world and the Puritan contempt for deeds and works.

Williams had been goaded into these words by the orthodoxy of John Cotton; a generation later, the rigidity of Cotton's spiritual descendant and namesake, Cotton Mather, caused another New England Protestant to give expression to ideas that became part of the dominant American creed. John Wise, in his "Vindication of the Government of New England Churches," went much further than Williams along the path to Edwards's hell, for he based his argument for church liberty on the laws of nature—laws that by strong inference were assumed to be good and beneficent. Wise was conformist enough to admit at the beginning of his argument that "revelation is nature's law in a fairer and brighter edition."[30] However, once having paid his respect to the supremacy of a transcendent world, he then confined himself to the knowledge of these laws by "the light of reason."[31] For him the rational faculty was a thing of light and beauty; at least one cardinal human sin was transformed by similar alchemy to a virtue. Winthrop, Cotton, Mather, and Edwards knew that the spirit of individual freedom was evidence of the workings of that deadliest of sins: human pride. For Wise, man's "high valuation of himself"[32] had its foundation, "not in pride, but really in the high and admirable frame and constitution of human nature." The word *man*, Wise observed, "is thought to carry somewhat of dignity in its sound."[33] The Puritan sin of pride has here become the democratic virtue of dignity, along with the change in the form of polemical expression from incantation to a sober, reasonable appeal to the "light" of human understanding and from a metaphorical mode that used physical experiences as emblems to one that used material objects as realities to be treasured for their own sake and not as shadows of divine things.

Williams and Wise wrote within the framework of the Puritan hierarchy; modifying Puritan doctrine by an appeal to human dignity, they were heretics of one kind. More radical heretics were the Quakers, whose fundamental convictions were diametrically opposed to the Puritan creed of evil in man and the wrath of God. Deriving their creed from a mysticism of love, not fear, the Quakers brought to America a devout sense of the spiritual worth of man and a conviction that his physical universe was formed, not in fright, but in love. The commonwealth of Pennsylvania was erected on this conviction; the works of its founder were everywhere imbued with this optimistic faith; and the words of the Quakers were one with their beliefs, for they demonstrated the same sense of the value and meaning of common man and his physical world. When William Penn described the land that lay about him and its inhabitants, he portrayed them in loving detail, with an obvious conviction of their inherent, rather than their emblematic, worth. The world was worthy of a meticulous and reverent catalogue:

Of Living Creatures: Fish, Fowl, and the Beasts of the Woods, here are diverse sorts, some for Food and Profit, and some for Profit only: For Food as well as Profit, the Elk, as big as a small Ox, Deer bigger than ours, Beaver, Racoon, Rabbits, Squirrels, and some eat young Bear, and commend it. Of Fowl of the Land, there is the Turkey (Forty and Fifty Pound weight) which is very great; Phesants, Heath-Birds, Pidgeons and Partridges in abundance. Of the Water, the Swan, Goose, white and gray, Brands, Ducks, Teal, also the Snipe and the Curloe, and that in great Numbers; but the Duck and Teal excel, nor so good have I ever eat in other Countries.[34]

Far from viewing the Indians as emblems of evil, Penn looked upon them as valued human beings and observed their customs and traditions with a reverent, if somewhat amused, eye: "Their postures in the Dance are very Antick and differing, but all keep measure. This is done with equal Earnestness and Labour, but great appearance of Joy."[35]

His fellow Quaker, John Woolman, whose *Journal* is the best expression of eighteenth-century Quaker attitudes, similarly described both the nature of the New World and of its inhabitants. His views of the Indians were, like Penn's, motivated by an essential optimism about humanity. Having for many years felt love in his heart "towards the Natives of this Land," he could try to understand even their most violent actions as a result of reasonable causes, rather than of inherent wickedness. "I perceived that many white People do often sell Rum to the Indians, which, I believe is a great evil. First, they being thereby deprived of the use of their reason and their Spirits violently agitated, quarrels often arise which ends in mischief."[36] Woolman's beliefs in the essential goodness of the physical world caused him to extend his sympathies to the whole range of creation, animal as well as human, and one of the most moving parts of his narrative describes his anguish after killing a robin and then forcing himself to the further necessary cruelties of destroying its young. His horror at the act convinced him that "he, whose tender Mercies are over all his Works, hath placed a Principle in the human Mind, which incites to exercise Goodness towards every living creature."[37] Such universal sympathy inspired Emerson, a half century later, to say that if he had a creed it would be that of the Quakers. He could have added that his literary style owed much to their exuberant naming of the things of this world and their ecstatic sense of a self-sufficient significance of the world of things.

4. The Enlightenment

These were the religious strains, and the language that embodied them, that helped to form American style in the eighteenth century. Equally important were secular trends: convictions about the order and significance of the natural world, whose regularity and beauty had been defined by Newton; beliefs in the essential goodness of man that had been made possible by Locke, proposed by Shaftesbury, and erected into an article of faith by Rousseau; and claims that this essentially good being in an ordered universe had natural rights, some of which he gave over to the trusteeship of temporal authority so that other unassignable rights could remain inviolate. In brief, these were the ideas of the British and French Enlightenment, and they combined with the beliefs of the more optimistic theists to give the new nation its basic creed.

The ideas of the Enlightenment were natural outgrowths of the Renaissance spirit against whose worldly aspects the Puritans had set their faces. The South and the central colonies, however, were from the beginning of their history havens for the humanism of the Renaissance—for both its wonder at the "piece of work" that is a man and a reverence for "this magestical roof fretted with . . . fire." This was the tone of John Smith as he told of his voyages to the New World. The motive for his travels was the hope of man's progress, and the purpose of his voyages was the making of a better life for his children. His rhetorical question summarized Renaissance values: "Who can desire more content, that hath small meanes; or but only his merit to advance his fortune, than to tread, and plant the ground he hath purchased by the hazard of his life? If he have but a taste of virtue and magnanimitie, what to such a minde can bee more pleasant, than planting and building a foundation for his Posteritie?"[38] Spokesmen for the planters and builders of the southern colonies continued to revere worldly, not otherworldly, values. A squire like William Byrd, who has left us the best record of the mind of the Virginia colonial gentleman, was devoted to the daily round of living, for which he gave thanks each night with "good health, good thoughts, and good humor."[39] He would record the homeliest of details of his day with its sequence of worldly events, into which a thought of God slipped as an afterthought: "I rose about 8 o'clock because my wife made me lie in bed and I rogered her. I read nothing and neglected to say prayers but had boiled milk for breakfast."[40] His *History of the Dividing Line* showed an admiration for the Indians equal to that of a Penn or a Woolman, but unlike the two Quakers this Virginia gentleman approved of them for their physical attractions: they were, he wrote, "generally tall and well proportioned . . . healthy and strong, with constitutions untainted by lewdness, and not enfeebled by luxury." Then with a blitheness that must have rankled in more puritanical breasts, he added: "Besides, morals and all considered I cannot think the Indians were much greater heathens than the first adventurers, who, had they been good Christians, would have had the Charity to take this only method of converting the natives to Christianity. For, after all that can be said, a sprightly lover is the most prevailing missionary that can be sent amongst these or any other infidels."[41]

A worldly, moderate man of good estate, Byrd was a neoclassical ideal, the kind of man that American poets of the eighteenth century—frankly copying style, tone, and subject from Prior, Pomfret, and Shenstone—often celebrated in measured, restrained Augustan verse. Minor writers like these were popular in eighteenth-century America, but the most influential figure of them all was Alexander Pope, the guide and model for much of the content and all the form of American pre-Revolutionary poetry and the poetry of the early Republic. The proper study of man was mankind for the colonial versifiers, as it was for the poets of Augustan England; and *An Essay on Man* was the most celebrated and imitated poem. Yet the single great exception American poets took to the doctrines of Pope is highly significant. American writers invariably objected to only one aspect of Pope's ideas—his pessimism and his looking backward to the ancients rather than forward to the possibilities of the future; this reaction "suggests, at least, that a widespread belief in progress through purely human efforts was one of the most important elements in the emotional and intellectual climate of the early United States."[42]

The best of the poets of the Revolution (the competition for this title is not keen), Philip Freneau, chose his subjects from among the group sanctioned by Augustan beliefs: the values of the natural world, the surmounting of death by life, the glories of the rights of man, the praises of great men who embodied them. His style was completely consistent with the vision of reality that was the American idea. Not for him was the emblematic mode, which used nature as the shadow of divine things. Quite the opposite. Like his English counterparts he employed generalized diction to express the universal truths contained in natural experience: "All that we see about, abroad/What is it all, but nature's God?"[43] In nature, which is itself the body of God and hence completely good, there is ultimate significance: "In meaner works discovered here/No less than in the starry sphere."[44] The world for Freneau was formed in love:

No imperfection can be found
In all that is, above, around,—
All, nature made, in reason's sight
Is order all, and *all is right*.[45]

In a universe of order, man may look forward to the future with joy, not with dread; it will be a future that he will help to make and a world that he can help to complete:

Joy to the day, when all agree
On such grand systems to proceed,
From fraud, design, and error free,
And which to truth and goodness lead.
Then persecution will retreat
And man's religion be complete.[46]

The dignity of man, the worth and value of the American individual—it was this humanistic creed to which both religious and secular tendencies contributed, a creed that received its noblest expression in the words of a Frenchman who came to America and then returned to his own country to write the *Letters from an American Farmer*. Hector St. John de Crèvecoeur expressed his reverence for the simple joyous acts of common life, which was at the heart of this secular faith: "When I contemplate my wife, by my fire-side, while she either spins, knits, darns, or suckles our child, I cannot describe the various emotions of love, of gratitude, of conscious pride, which thrill my heart."[47] These physical acts are no emblems; they are worshipped for their inherent and intrinsic values. This kind of reverence led inevitably to a corresponding belief in the things and forms of man's physical and social world and in the probabilities of man's making a better future for himself: man will "change in a few years that hitherto barbarous country into a fine fertile, well regulated district. Such is our progress, such is the march of the Europeans toward the interior part of the continent."[48] Above all, there is the echo of Shakespeare's "what a piece of work is man" and Wise's convictions of "the high and admirable frame and condition of human nature" in Crèvecoeur's famous definition of an American: "*He* is an American, who, leaving behind him all his ancient prejudices and manners, receives new ones from the new mode of life he has embraced, the new government he obeys, the new rank he holds. He becomes an American by being received in the broad lap of our great *Alma Mater*. Here individuals of all nations are melted into a new race of men, whose labours and posterity will one day cause great changes in the world."[49]

The language was mythical, but the myth was of a healing mother and not an angry God. Columbia had replaced Jehovah; men were no longer emblems and shadows but significant participants in a significant world of appearances.

5. *Jefferson and Franklin*

To this sense of the meaning and value of man in his physical and social world, Thomas Jefferson and Benjamin Franklin gave the principal imaginative expression and shaped the style suitable to the idea. From this point on, all other American styles would have to measure themselves against theirs. Some American writers—Cooper, Holmes, Lowell, Howells, Mark Twain, Sinclair Lewis—would accept the terms of the official faith to a greater or lesser degree; some—Emerson, Whitman, Steinbeck—would find it necessary to reinforce the official faith with a strong sense of its mystical and spiritual significance. Some—Poe, Hawthorne, Melville, Adams, James, and Faulkner—who were among our most sensitive makers of imaginative worlds would test the creed and find it wanting and, in the agony of the emptiness left by the withdrawal of this faith, would try to build some other system of illusions to satisfy the basic requirement of man: to make order and meaning of this universe. Yet all of them, without exception, would be forced to take account of the attitude to which Benjamin Franklin and Thomas Jefferson, representatives of their times, gave definitive expression. Jefferson's brief masterpiece, the Declaration of Independence, was the public statement of the complex of ideas and feelings that comprise the American idea; Franklin's *Autobiography* was the form the idea took when it was embodied in the story of an individual's life. The Declaration summarized the colonist's belief in the essential goodness of man and nature, in the value of common sense, in the ability of men everywhere—after having been put in possession of a correct knowledge of the facts—to know the truth; Franklin's *Autobiography* proclaimed the possibilities of the individual as he is organized into societies of his own making and his own choice. Together, Jefferson's Declaration and Franklin's *Autobiography* constitute the classic statements of the way in which American culture has generally made sense of the universe and of man's place in it: the *style*, the *myth*, the *dream*, the *official faith*, or whatever other terms we choose to depict the "imaginative idea which— whatever its truth— induces men to feel and act."

The very lack of originality of the Declaration of Independence is in itself proof of its dethronement of intuition and revelation as the principal instruments of knowledge and proof of the corresponding exaltation of the common sense of humanity. In complete accord with Pope's definition of neoclassical literary virtue—"what oft was thought, but ne'er so well express'd"—its ideas and most of its phrases were outgrowths of a hundred years of enlightened thought. Rousseau, Montesquieu, Burlamaqui are some of the authors Jefferson had in mind when he wrote "etcetera" at the end of a list of some of the originators of its ideas; the document, he said, consisted of "the harmonizing sentiments of the day, whether expressed in conversation, in letters, printed essays, or the elementary books of public right, as Aristotle, Cicero, Locke, Sidney, etc."[50]

Born into fortunate circumstances, moving with ease through a classical education that taught him, as it taught the Augustans, that reason, moderation, decency, and civil behavior were the highest goods of social man, Jefferson was a summary of the neoclassical virtues, and his literary expression, in turn, was an effective embodiment of his system of beliefs: "We hold these truths to be self-evident, that all men are created equal, that they are endowed by their Creator with certain unalienable Rights, that among these are Life, Liberty, and the Pursuit of Happiness."[51] The measured, calm periods of the Declaration recalled the Roman orator; prudence—restraint—was in its quiet and stately structure: the statement, then the threefold analysis of the statement; its style demonstrated the "prudence" that, he would say later, dictated the need for the Declaration. Describing with patrician sadness the necessity for renouncing the ties of kinship with Englishmen, the Declaration expresses balance and toleration even in this renunciation of consanguinity: "We must therefore endeavour to forget our former love for them, and hold them as we hold the rest of mankind: enemies in war, in peace friends." Just as the general tone was one of reliance on common sense, so was the relation established between man and God, a relation humanistic in its emphasis. "Man" was mentioned first; his creation was expressed in the passive, rather than active, mood: as if he grew out of the inner necessities of the universe and not out of a spontaneous act of an anthropomorphic deity. The verb "endowed" was a telling one in this connection. Natural rights, the metaphor implied, were an irrevocable gift to man; man was given these rights in perpetuity. The term "unalienable," which seemed to deny to temporal authority the power to take these rights away, hinted, at least, that a similar restriction was imposed upon the Creation itself; it is significant in this connection that Jefferson had written "inherent"[52] as well as "inalienable" in the original draft, for it emphasizes that there are rights that inhere in man's very condition of being human. And then the rights that were singled out for mention were the secular, humanistic triumvirate: "Life, Liberty, and the Pursuit of Happiness."

The last phrase was the most influential statement of the American idea. Here, frankly and openly, human well-being—by implication the basic fleshly, as well as spiritual, delights—was idolized as the end and object of all human organization. Like the other parts of the Declaration, this, too, had been part of the "harmonizing sentiments" of the day and had, indeed, been very close to the language of the Virginia Bill of Rights, sent to Congress for its study a month before the Declaration. There, the farmer George Mason had written of certain inherent rights of which men could not, by any contract or compact, deprive their posterity; the fourth right, according to Mason, was the right of "pursueing and obtaining Happiness and Safety."[53] With the change of the verb to the noun, Jefferson gave America its most persuasive image, as well as a summary of American optimism. It is a compendium of the American sense of the unfinished, po-tentially perfectible world, for it refers, not to happiness in an already achieved world, but to an ideal that men must be given the freedom to attempt to achieve. In Mason's phrase the verbal form *"pursuing"* had a transitory quality that was ill-suited to bear the burden of a culture's dream. "The pursuit"—an activity so completely believed in that it takes on the density of a substance—this is the stuff of which enduring myths are made, and it is what Jefferson fashioned out of the depths of his culture's consciousness. As he said of his masterpiece in retrospect, it was neither original in principles nor in sentiment; nor was it copied from another author: it was an attempt to express the American mind.[54]

Jefferson framed the Declaration with some help from a committee of which the most active member was Benjamin Franklin, the elder statesman of the Revolution. Franklin made at least one revision of Jefferson's draft: where Jefferson had written, "We hold these truths to be sacred," Franklin crossed out the word "sacred" and substituted "self-evident."[55] The implications of this change have been pointed out by a historian of science: "Jefferson implied that the principles in question were holy, of divine origin, and were to be respected and guarded with reverence for that reason. . . . But 'self-evident' was a technical scientific term applied to axioms. . . . This is the sense in which Franklin's phrase represents the summit of excellence."[56] Franklin's devotion to the experimental method, his insistence that all truths be tested by experience and by experiment, brought to the American idea its strong scientific bias. From Franklin's time on, the official American creed regarded science and the scientific method as man's principal ally in achieving progress; writers who aligned themselves with the creed almost invariably accepted the truth that the experimental method is a boon to mankind and based their art and their philosophies on that method: realism in art and pragmatism in philosophy would be the reflections of a basic faith in the scientific method of observation, experiment, and induction. After Franklin writers who believed in the American idea made novels and poems that demonstrated "how being a good scientist and being a good neighbor, friend and citizen were but different aspects of a . . . fundamental quality of mind."[57]

The summary of Franklin's empirical optimism was his *Autobiography*, which gave the American idea its classic prose form—realistic in its depiction of the life the author knows and in its attention to the details of the physical surface of the world, scientific in its attention to reasonable causality and in its firm rooting in a historical time and place, optimistic in its reverence for the stuff of the immediate, common-sensual universe and in its movement toward a happy ending. A comparison with Jonathan Edwards's *Personal Narrative* is a comparison between polar views of the American idea. Edwards's story of his life, written to demonstrate the need for a dissolution of personality in God, scorned the flesh and the physical world by treating the body of man and the structure of things either as shamefully low orders in a scale of "being" or as "shadows" of a spiritual reality. Franklin's *Autobiography* was exuberantly fleshly: a hymn of praise to dinners and easy chairs, buns and ale and good conversation. He wrote from the perspective of satisfied, secure age and treated his life both as a valuable thing in itself and as useful experimental data in the formulation of other experiments in living. So successful was his particular experiment that he would have "no Objection" to its repetition from the beginning, "only asking the Advantages Authors have in a second Edition to correct some Faults of the first."[58] The accent was on life and on the liberty of free men to choose one or another of the courses of action that would lead either to failure or to success. The course he had chosen—that of industry, prudence, common sense—had led, not inevitably, but with some degree of probability to happiness, for this is a world, as he said at the outset, framed by a Providence that is kind and that blesses us even in "our Afflictions."[59]

Franklin loved his world; it was the scene of the only drama of salvation he could comprehend. George Whitefield, the evangelical preacher of the great awakening, "us'd, indeed, sometimes to pray" for him, Franklin remembered, "but never had the Satisfaction of believing that his Prayers were heard." On one occasion, Whitefield had no place to lodge. "You know my House," Franklin told him, "if you can shift with its scanty Accomodations, you will be heartily welcome." Whitefield replied that if he had made that kind offer for Christ's sake, he would not be "miss of a Reward." Franklin answered: *"Don't let me be mistaken; it was not for Christ's sake, but for your sake."* He then added that one of their common acquaintances "jocosely remark'd, that knowing it to be the Custom of the Saints, when they receiv'd any favour, to shift the Burthen of the Obligation from off their own Shoulders, and place it in Heaven, I had contriv'd to fix it on Earth."[60]

A good deed, then—and everything else in this physical world—was no emblem for Franklin but a value in itself. The events of the *Autobiography* have their own inherent meaning without reference to a transcendent world. This is the governing spirit of the realistic method, the essence of a representationalism that was the inevitable and natural style for the American idea of progress, a realism that emphasized the small and seemingly insignificant as well as the large and portentous. Franklin described his contribution to the highest moments of American history but was proud as well of his pioneering suggestions about ways of warming houses and cleaning streets. After describing in some detail his plans for organizing a sanitary corps, he observed that "some may think these trifling Matters not worth . . . relating," but, he insisted, "Human Felicity is produc'd not so much by great Pieces of good Fortune . . . as by little Advantages that occur every Day."[61]

The small, as well as the large, events of ordinary life are the materials of Franklin's homely art. To tell us these events directly and clearly so that we may use them as the data of experience and, by exercising our reason upon these data, increase the store of private and public happiness—this constituted the method and the motive of Franklin's literary form. The tone and attitude he assumed were the tones and attitudes of the Augustan age: calmness and moderation. He quoted Pope admiringly on the need for modesty and restraint; he decried excess, even an excessive devotion to reason or the scientific method. One of the Junto, his group for mutual improvement, was "Thomas Godfrey, a self-taught mathematician, and afterwards inventor of what is now called Hadley's Quadrant. But," Franklin complained, "he knew little out of his way, and was not a pleasing Companion; as, like most . . . Mathematicians I have met with, he expected unusual Precision in every thing said, or was forever denying or distinguishing upon Trifles, to the Disturbance of all Conversation. He soon left us."[62]

This dislike of passion or excess was part of a total personality whose attitude toward the world, whose way of feeling "the push and pressure" of the universe, has increasingly been felt to be the American idea. Franklin instinctively rejected extremes and absolutes. He saw all virtue and truth to consist of action and regarded the test of virtue and truth to be the results that accrued to a given mode of behavior. The world of social appearances was for him the only place where these results could be realized. The "appearance" of the virtue of humility, for example, a virtue that Franklin was constitutionally unable to feel inwardly, was for him quite as satisfactory as the actuality. This commonsensical attitude would later receive a technical philosophical name, but *pragmatism*, as William James later said, was after all but a name for an old way of thinking, one that James traced back at least as far as Locke and one that certainly included Franklin. Although pragmatism provided the strength of Franklin's homely and practical attitude toward society, it also produced the least attractive sections of the *Autobiography*—the description of his calculated approach to love. He wooed a Miss Godfrey but told her mother that he "expected as much Money with their Daughter"[63] as would pay off his debt. When the mother announced that they had no such sum to spare, he said, "They might mortgage their House in the Loan Office."[64]

This unlovely disinterestedness, the aspect of Franklin that was to prove so repellent to Herman Melville, was the price to pay for the major contribution that Franklin made to his country's official faith. The *Autobiography* was written to prove that reason must always govern passion for the good of man and his society. It put this argument simply and clearly. The American public style has had no better private voice. His countrymen later recognized the supreme expression of their national style in the person of the sage of Philadelphia by putting his name on their elementary schools, their post offices, and their one-cent stamps.

III ～Nineteenth-Century Styles of Affirmation

"If we admit man is susceptible of improvement . . . , it appears improper to say he has quitted a state of nature, when he has begun to proceed." Adam Ferguson's words might serve as a text for those works of early nineteenth-century American writers that embodied the American idea: the Leatherstocking romances of Cooper; the poems of Bryant, Longfellow, and Lowell; the essays and poems of Oliver Wendell Holmes. Celebrating the unexpressed assumptions by which most Americans ordered their universe, these writers owed their immediate acceptance to their appeal to the beliefs that constituted their culture's official faith. In their works we find the American public style at one with American private styles, and we observe in its clearest form the connection between the private styles of the makers of our literature and the public style of our culture. They shared an allegiance to the commonsense world of the eighteenth century and to its vision of reality, and they made this vision a part of their minor, but substantial, art.

1. Progress and Primitivism in the Deerslayer Romances

Cooper's works have quite understandably taken their place among our most popular public daydreams, for they blended the twin doctrines of primitivism and progress in fantasies completely reassuring to American culture. The symbiotic relationship between the two beliefs was dramatized by the relationship between the cultural levels of Cooper's characters. Uncas, Chingachgook, and Natty Bumppo were primitives, embodying the proposition that man in his natural state is potentially good and actually good if he lives according to the principles of nature's God. Yet in most romances in which the Deerslayer and the "good" Indians appeared, they were servants, helpers, and guides to another group of civilized and refined characters whose fates were the principal concern of the fable and whose inevitable happy ending in suitable marriage testified to the essentially optimistic tone of the fiction. The primitives supplied the energy, the strength, the craft; but the triumph of the civilized heroes and heroines over the more dangerous aspects of nature—the wilderness, the savages, the prairie, the squatters—supported the central fable. When one of these lower characters, representing one side of the primitivism-progress duality, is involved in a love affair, the affair is either doomed (as is Uncas's love for Cora) or frustrated, as is Leatherstocking's for Mabel Durham. Only when the frontiersman has become tamed—when he has taken his steps up the ladder of civilization—can he be part of the main fable of rescue and marriage. First he moves from hunter and fisher to the slightly more civilized art of bee hunting; and then it is made clear that his final triumph will be his taking a higher position in organized society as a respected member of its processes. In *The Prairie* Paul Hover marries Ellen Wade and through the efforts of characters higher on the scale of social advancement, progresses even further from the primitive. We are told that "in the process of time" Middleton and Inez succeeded "in working a great and beneficial change"[1] in Paul's character. Then follows one of that century's most forthright fictional statements of the American idea of progress: "He soon became a landowner, then a prosperous cultivator of the soil, and shortly after a town-officer. By that progressive change in fortunes, which in the republic is often seen to be so singularly accompanied by a corresponding improvement in knowledge and self-respect, he went on, from step to step, until his wife enjoyed the maternal delight of seeing her children placed far beyond the danger of returning to that state from which both their parents had issued."[2]

That this is no idiosyncratic position but rather a general attitude in all of Cooper's romances of the frontier can be seen in the consistency with which he pursued this pattern over the course of twenty-five years. His own political and social convictions underwent severe modifications, but his acceptance of the dual and paradoxical values of both primitivism and progress remained. In the first of the frontier tales, *The Pioneers* (1823), which introduces Natty Bumppo, Elizabeth Temple proudly proclaims that her father, Judge Temple, is "taming the very forests"; her praise is given in the context of a plot that clearly shows the need for society and for law: "How rapidly is civilization treading on the footsteps of nature!"[3] Elizabeth exclaims admiringly. In the last of Cooper's long fictions about the frontier, *The Oak Openings* (1848), Ben Boden, another bee hunter, reenacts Paul Hover's progress through the ranks of society. After a series of adventures in the wilderness of Michigan in which he rescues his beloved from the savages, Ben rises to become a landowner. Neither he nor Paul, however, is permitted a seat in Congress; these are reserved for men like Captain Middleton, for they are better "suited to the difference in their educations."[4]

All this, of course, is not to take away from the overriding vitality and interest of Leatherstocking and his fellow primitives. This is precisely the point—the vitality was theirs, just as the vitality of the democratic faith in progress lay in its convictions of the goodness of natural man. There was sadness in the inescapable fact that simplicity had to give way to the advancement of the race, but the primitives could and did receive their apotheosis in the simple epics and the popular fables that celebrate their vigor and powers. Modern primitivists like D. H. Lawrence, detesting the nineteenth century's belief in progress, have revised Cooper by assigning to Natty Bumppo, not only the important ritualistic part in the religion of progress, but the overwhelming emphasis in the romances; they have made him the sole "hero" of the tales rather than the most effective of the lower characters who make possible the movement of the principal fable—a revision parallel to the modern reinterpretation of *Henry IV* that makes Falstaff its hero.

Natty himself knew his place. Although he eloquently stated his sorrow at the way civilized men "scourged the very 'arth with their axes" and deformed "the beauty of the wilderness," he regarded himself as part of the pattern of development, which was necessary and, on the whole, beneficial and which meant his inevitable demise, just as it previously had meant the demise of the Indian. The frontiersman was not the most primitive, the nearest to nature, of the characters in the American fable of progress. Ranged on the other side of him were the red men, whom he supplanted and over whom he had advanced in technique as well as religion. Leatherstocking was fanatically proud of the fact that he was part of this advance; he repeated continually that he had "no cross"[5] in his blood and that the worst enemy he had on earth could not deny the purity of his blood. When, in *The Last of the Mohicans*, Chingachgook bewailed the fate of the Indian and complained of the white man's triumph, Leatherstocking vigorously defended the conquest as part of the natural order of things. It was right, Leatherstocking insisted, that the white man replace the Indian, even though he felt a genuine sadness at the passing of the red man. And this attitude inevitably led to the next step in progress—the supplanting of the frontiersman by the settler—the stage described in *The Prairie*, where Leatherstocking, by that time an octogenarian, stood "colossal . . . musing and melancholy"[6] with his old dog and his old gun at the last frontier. Indeed, in his preface to the romance, Cooper summarized the American idea: the affirmation of progress combined with reverence for the primitive. First the glorification of progress: "The power of the republic has done much to restore peace to these wild scenes, where civilized man did not dare to pass unprotected five-and-twenty years ago." Then the note of sadness for the passing of Leatherstocking: "Pressed upon by time, he has ceased to be the hunter and the warrior, and has become a trapper of the great West. The sound of the axe has driven him from his beloved forests to seek a refuge, by a species of desperate resignation, on the denuded plains that stretch to the Rocky Mountains. Here he passes the few closing years of his life, dying as he had lived, a philosopher of the wilderness, with a few of the failings, none of the vices, and all the nature and truth of his position."[7] Leatherstocking's last word in the book was the same as the one he spoke when we first met him in *The Pioneers*; in that earlier romance he had answered his earthly superior in the scale of being, Judge Temple, with the dignified yet thoroughly acquiescent monosyllable "here." In *The Prairie* he met the master of his universe, as he had met the master of his settlement, with the same reply.[8]

Both of the elements of the controlling idea, both progress and primitivism, are bound up with youth and newness, with a retrospective nostalgia for the country's adolescence and a forward-looking optimism to its nascent future. And so it was not *The Prairie* but *The Last of the Mohicans*, a work about the younger Leatherstocking, that was and is Cooper's most popular novel. In talking about a writer like Cooper, we defer to popular taste, for it is in its relation to popular reception that his work can be seriously discussed. It is a species of public daydream, a dramatization of the dominant ideas and the unexpressed commitment of a society. The characters, events, and objects of these romances were not "emblems" or "allegories" of the kind that the Puritan writers used or that Hawthorne devised; neither were they symbols in the sense that they would become, in two different ways, in Whitman or Melville. Rather they were accurate reflections of popular beliefs. In this *The Last of the Mohicans* resembled the sagas and the medieval romances, for it created a simplified world that gained its force from its expression of profoundly pervasive cultural beliefs.

The Last of the Mohicans tells of a series of three adventures encountered by the daughters of Major Munro in their efforts to reach Fort Henry just before its fall to the French and the Indians and then in their efforts to escape the marauding Indians. Their destinies are guided by the keen-eyed trapper and hunter Natty Bumppo and by his two Indian friends, Chingachgook and Uncas, the "last of the Mohicans." In telling this simple story of danger, chase, and rescue, Cooper created an ordered natural world, entirely regulated to the scale of man. Like the lawlessness of men, the tangles of trees and the turbulence of waters were pictured as proofs of the dangers of anarchy. For Cooper the apparent chaos was superficial. Underneath lay the order of nature's God. Although the forests of New York State were, at the time, immense and the prairies even larger, Cooper's characters populated the scene densely and gave something of the effect of a map on which human figures have been drawn larger than life. "Though the arts of peace were unknown to this fatal region," Cooper declared near the beginning of the narrative, "its forests were alive with men." Then he described how "its shades and glens rang with the sound of martial music" and how "its mountains threw back the laugh, or repeated the wanton cry, of many a gallant and reckless youth."[9]

In this Nature, reduced to human scale to match the humanism of the Enlightenment, Cooper places characters who, as we have seen, are arranged on the scale of civilization and whose lives testify to the regularity of society and of the universe. Duncan Heywood, a handsome, educated officer, loves Alice Munro, and their union is the primary concern of the plot. Alice's half sister, Cora, almost as beautiful and as highly placed, is nevertheless potentially available to Uncas, for there was a "curse"[10] of dark blood in her birth. So strong, however, is the belief in natural hierarchy that while this taint could make her eligible, it could never bridge the gap between her and the Indian; and Leatherstocking declares at the end that they might not be joined, even after death.

These one-dimensional characters in their idealized setting participate in a series of actions of the most primitive variety: a movement through space with a corresponding series of rescues of endangered and ineffectual innocence. At the beginning Major Munro, in one of the absurd deviations from common sense that was frequent in Cooper's tales, sent for his daughters to come to the besieged Fort Henry, and—accompanied by David Gamut, a low, comic, psalm-singing frontier preacher; Leatherstocking; his good Indian companions Chingachgook and Uncas; and the bad Indian, Magua—they set out. Their adventures in reaching Fort Henry—the capture of the lovers by the Hurons and their rescue by Leatherstocking and his Indian allies—comprise the first section of the plot. Fort Henry falls before

Montcalm and, as could have been predicted, becomes no place for two well-born young ladies. Separated from their protectors after the surrender, they are again captured by the Hurons, who are pursued by Leatherstocking, Uncas, Chingachgook, Heyward, and Major Munro. After a series of muddled stratagems in which, among other absurdities, Leatherstocking disguises himself as a bear and Chingachgook as a beaver, the group is reunited at the grand council of the Delawares. Here Magua is permitted to carry off Cora, and there is a short third chase, a kind of coda to the other two, during which Cora and Uncas are killed and Magua meets his just doom.

The fable is worth retelling only because it is so clearly permeated with, and expressive of, the optimism that is the major tone of the American idea. All turns out well; even the deaths of Cora and Uncas are absorbed in the feeling of total optimism, for their fates are made inevitable by the laws of progress and Cooper's convictions of the fundamental order of the universe. Uncas, the last of the Mohicans, must give way, in sad dignity, to the civilization that has made him an anachronism. Cora must pay the price of the "taint" in her blood. In short, *The Last of the Mohicans* summarized the American official faith; and as the century of progress went on, the archetypes developed by Cooper became the stereotypes of the dime novelists and the writers of cowboy fiction and merged with the elements of the Horatio Alger myths to provide our most vivid popular public dreams.

2. Poets of Affirmation: Bryant

The optimism Cooper expressed by fusing in fiction a faith in man's natural goodness with a belief in the value and necessity of progress through civilization found expression as well in a number of influential poets. Like Cooper these writers were of a transitional literary mood—between the sober, regular neoclassicism of Church, Freneau, and Barlow and the newer impulses toward emotional fervor and toward a reliance on the intuition in place of the reason that the English romantics were making the most persuasive attitude of the day. Yet like Cooper these of whom we speak were far more at home with the mood of the Enlightenment than with the feeling of the romantics; they began by assuming the pattern of meaning by which their society was making sense of its universe, and they wrote poems that, in both their content and form, expressed the essential optimism of the American creed.

The career of William Cullen Bryant provides a good summary of both the achievements and the self-imposed limitations of these affirmative voices. He started with a verse about the way in which a life-loving man of the Enlightenment must face the bitterness of death and ended with a public address on the glories of nineteenth-century political progress. And in the course of his career, which nearly spanned the century, he wrote a series of poems— many of them of a quiet and ordered beauty—that with rare exceptions were lyric affirmations of the value of man and nature. Like Franklin, for whom he felt lifelong admiration, Bryant had a hardheaded awareness of the "guilt and misery . . . sorrows, crimes, and cares"[11] of the world; but he held to the deistic view that these evils were deviations from a natural order that was healthy and reasonable and whose lineaments were discernible in the structure of the natural world. So he could ask us to

> enter this wild wood
> And view the haunts of Nature. The calm shade
> Shall bring a kindred calm, and the sweet breeze
> That makes the green leaves dance, shall waft a balm
> To thy sick heart.[12]

He felt that the child and the savage, who is the child of the race, were both close to the natural order; the Indian was

> fresher from the hand
> That formed of earth the human face
> And to the elements did stand
> In nearer kindred than our race.[13]

As in Cooper, this feeling for the fundamental dignity of man, a feeling best symbolized by the reverence for the child and for the savage, was not a desire to reverse the process of history nor a retrospective yearning for a golden age of childhood or savagery but rather a basis for a belief in the advancement of the race. Bryant made this reconciliation between primitivism and progress the subject of his longest poem, *The Ages*. This series of Spenserian stanzas begins with a description of a longing for "the golden days" celebrated by "high-dreaming bards."[14] He gently blessed this yearning for the past: "Peace to the just man's memory; let it grow/Greener with the years."[15] This blessing, however, did not imply a corresponding despair for the fate of men in the future "who rise/To dwell upon the earth when we withdraw."[16] Quite the contrary. Nature "in her calm, majestic march"[17] provided the basis for a continuing optimism; "the beautiful world"[18] gives us still her "fair page"[19] upon which we can read the truth; and, most important, we can listen to history while she recites to us the story of the advancement of the race from the darkness of barbarism to the light of American civilization.

In one brief line Bryant summarized the meaning of Eden for the American idea. Eden was the "genial cradle of our race,"[20] the mythical summary of the belief that man was conceived by a benevolent nature. Leaving that cradle, man started up the long hard path of progress, and his first savage stages were chaotic horrors from which he gradually ascended. In prehistory

> he who felt the wrong, and had the might,
> His own avenger, girt himself to slay;
> Beside the path the unburied carcass lay;
> The shepherd, by the fountains of the glen,
> Fled, while the robber swept his flock away,
> And slew his babes. The sick, untended then,
> Languished in the deep shade, and died afar from men.[21]

In this view of human history, Greece and Rome became high points but remained low enough so that they might be transcended. Greece was respected as the birthplace of reason and of liberty, the two virtues that find greater expression in America. Yet along with the Apollonian vision of reason and the worship of freedom, Greece also was the haven of bloody oppression, from which the Christian era advanced by positing the doctrines of equality and of love.

The final stanzas of the poem were a celebration of the

present and a hope for the future: "Look now abroad—another race has filled/Those populous borders."[22] The legacy of Greece and Rome had passed to America. "Here the free spirit of mankind, at length,/Throws its last fetters off."[23] Although Europe still "writhes in shackles,"[24] she too may hope that the moment "To rescue and raise up, draws near."[25] America would undergo but one "fall" from freedom—the fall from the liberty to hate and exploit; its only fetters would be the "maternal care," and "the lavish love" of a democratic state. There was nothing to fear and everything to hope for:

who shall then declare
The date of thy deep-founded strength, or tell
How happy, in thy lap, the sons of men shall dwell?[26]

This pattern of belief, so congruent with the American idea, was expressed by the form Bryant chose, as well as by the arguments of his verse. Carefully obeying the restrictions of the intricate stanzaic pattern, with each section of eight pentameter lines followed by an alexandrine that brings it to an unhurried conclusion, Bryant unfolded the story of the race in calm, measured cadences. Carefully regular, obeying the neoclassical doctrines of moderation and restraint, his poems were written in the generalized diction of the eighteenth century, well-suited to express a general order to which all particular ideas, no matter what their diversity, ultimately conform. His metaphors displayed the similarity between man and nature, between the moral life of humanity and the moral structure of the universe. The unerring flight of the waterfowl, which shall "find a summer home, and rest,/And scream" among its fellows, was a lesson for mankind; it taught that

He who, from zone to zone,
Guides through the boundless sky thy certain flight,
In the long way that I must tread alone
Will lead my steps aright.[27]

Idea and form coalesced in a stoical humanism that enabled man to face the final mystery of death, a stoicism that was repeated throughout many of his poems but never better than in his revision of one of his earliest verses, "Thanatopsis," where, in regular, blank verse, he affirmed the deistic religion of nature's God. The poem began with a declaration of faith in the ability of nature to supply answers to the true believer, who held "communion with her visible forms." The still voice that spoke to such a communicant told him of the sepulchre that is prepared for him and for all mankind, but the two most important words of the poem are of life, not death. After seventy-one lines dealing with the common doom, the poem broke, to resume with a stanza that Bryant added to the first version. It began with the admonition to the reader: "So live." It asked the reader to turn his attention to the proper conduct of his life as the only means of meeting the bitterness of death. And the mode of conduct must be one that will insure man's dignity and his quiet acceptance of his place in the natural world: "So live," he said, that you go to your deaths like a noble Greek or Roman, not like

> the quarry-slave at night,
> Scourged to his dungeon, but, sustained and soothed
> By an unfaltering trust, approach thy grave,
> Like one who wraps the drapery of his couch
> About him, and lies down to pleasant dreams.[28]

3. Longfellow

There is even a stronger feeling of the sound of a remembered voice in the poems of Henry Wadsworth Longfellow, whose works quickly became part of the national consciousness because they were rhythmic expressions of the American idea. Like Bryant, Longfellow was deeply interested in the intuitive rather than the logical and the analytical; his cathedral, like the cathedral of the romantic movement, was a woods, whose arches were not of stones but were the vaultings of the "stately pines." The object of this worship was the ordered nature of the eighteenth-century deists, and the proper worship of this order was the wordless sympathy that is the capacity of all men: "Listen ere the sound be fled,/ And learn there may be worship without words."[29] If words be used, however, they should be the expression of a rational mind, which imitates the regularity and the structure that Longfellow believed was the fundamental law of the universe, and not the "howling dervishes of song,/Who craze the brain with their delirious dance."[30]

This conviction about the fundamental order and virtue of nature had some typical corollaries in Longfellow's poems. One was a humility about the role of art and the artist, for it was "Not Art but Nature"[31] that traced the lovely lines of his cathedral. He therefore could respect the work of the minor craftsman as well as the major artist and could give sympathetic praise to the "humbler poet,/Whose songs gushed from his heart."[32] These songs were not the actual prayer of the true believer but rather the "benediction,"[33] and they serve to affirm, rather than to formulate, the deepest verities and therefore bring the calmest peace. This is why, when we hear them,

> the night shall be filled with music,
> And the cares that infest the day
> Shall fold their tents, like the Arabs,
> And as silently steal away.[34]

Longfellow's conviction of nature's goodness was part of a genuinely sanguine faith in the value of his contemporary America. His early travels, much as they delighted him with the richness of European culture, filled him as well with a sense of the blessedness of having been born an American. His interest in the past was no antiquarian reverence for a remote time and was virtually free of romantic longing for another era. He searched through European cultures to find the universal values that America shared with them and selected and celebrated those aspects of French, Spanish, German, and Scandinavian culture most suited for an optimistic era. He loved both Italian literature and landscape for its mellow sunniness. He was passionately fond of Spain but repelled by its tragic depths; he refused to believe Calderón's bitter insistence that life was but "an empty dream." In one of his last poems, he acknowledged the tolling of the bells of San Blas, which seemed to call out warnings and complaints about the future. To their yearning to "bring us back once more/The vanished days of yore,/When the world with faith was filled," he answered that they called "in vain," that the past was "deaf" to their prayers, and that

Out of the shadows of night
The world rolls into light;
It is daybreak everywhere.[35]

To convictions about the goodness of nature and about the value of the present and future, he joined an affirmation of the goodness of natural man, and he expressed this affirmation through his profound interest in the folk song, the ballad, the saga; folk literature, he felt, expresses the truths of common humanity in forms that most directly appeal to the common listener and the reader. So he searched for material that would provide America with its own resources of confidence in man's power and virtue and in a conviction of man's involvement with the forces of the universe. He found such matter in the Indian legends reported by Henry Schoolcraft,[36] and he retold them in a meter imitative of the Icelandic sagas he so admired. Hiawatha, he said, was his "Indian Edda."[37]

At the outset he made clear the motive both of his choice of a subject and of his treatment of it. He told the legends of the Ojibways for those

whose hearts are fresh and simple,
Who have faith in God and Nature,
Who believe that in all ages
Every human heart is human.[38]

The legend that followed was a reconciliation of primitivism with progress. Hiawatha was the prophet and deliverer sent to the savages, not because they were better than the civilized men who followed them, but because

in even savage bosoms
There are longings, yearnings, strivings,
For the good they comprehend not.[39]

The Indian prophet and leader's godlike birth, his education, his hunting and fishing exploits, his marriage, his troubled times, and his death and departure are recounted in trochaic rhythms that made their doggerel way into the nation's consciousness with a sureness matched by few other poems. Together with Leatherstocking and Uncas and Chingachgook, Hiawatha became one of the vital embodiments of the belief in human nobility that was the foundation of American optimism.

Like Cooper's archetypes of the cult of primitivism, Hiawatha and his legend aroused no insoluble difficulties in reconciling a sadness over the fate of the primitives with an optimism about their significant place in the larger course of human history. The most effective part of Hiawatha's story was a parable of the necessary progress of civilization. The section is entitled "Hiawatha's Fasting" and tells of the coming of a spirit from the "Master of Life," who descends in answer to the prayers of Hiawatha. He comes, the spirit says, because the prayers are "for profit of the people,/For advantage of the nations." As the parable developed, it became an account of the birth of agriculture out of man's struggles with a powerful and threatening but ultimately benign nature, which dies, but dies into life, so that the cycle of fertility may be renewed. The spirit that appeared to Hiawatha after his fasting was Mondamin, the corn god, and he announced the mystery: he was the "friend of man," but man must wrestle with him to learn "How by struggle and by labor/You shall gain what you have prayed for." Mondamin was tall and beautiful in garments of green and yellow; he foretold the triumph of man, which would mean the god's death and his new life; he described how he must be buried and cared for "Till I wake, and start, and quicken,/Till I leap into the sunshine." Hiawatha wrestled with him and slew him, buried him and cared for his grave, and then

> at length a small green feather
> From the earth shot slowly upward,
> Then another and another,
> And before the Summer ended
> Stood the maize in all its beauty.

Whereupon Hiawatha cried in rapturous affirmation of the goodness of the god of nature, who brings life from death: "It is Mondamin! Yes, the friend of man, Mondamin!"[40]

The whole of the saga repeats this optimistic cycle of tragedy experienced and overcome. Hiawatha, a demigod of sunshine in a world filled with hate, must rule by love. After slaying the great White Pearl-Father of disease and death, he succumbs to cold, hunger, and famine; but at the end the air is again "full of freshness," the earth is "bright and joyous," and Hiawatha, wearing the exultant look of "one who in a vision/Sees what is to be, but is not," stands with his arms lifted to the sun, its brightness on his face and shoulders. He welcomes the arrival of a new prophet of love, a coming heralded by the bees, the avant-garde of the white man's progress. Hiawatha urged his people to accept the need for progress and change, to listen to the wisdom of new prophets, because they were the voice of "the Master of Life" who had "sent them/From the land of light and morning!"[41]

The most complete expression of the American idea, *Hiawatha*, in its unfortunate doggerel rhythms, its lack of specificity, its absence of understanding of the nature of the Indian actualities, is one of the least successful of Longfellow's poems. In others, however, the oft thought ideas were as well expressed as at any other time in the century. Henry Adams, describing his country's deepest commitments as the point of departure for his education, chose Longfellow's lines from "The Arsenal at Springfield" to summarize the belief in man's progress through reason:

Were half the power that fills the world with terror,
Were half the wealth bestowed on camps and courts
Given to redeem the human mind from error,
There were no need of arsenals nor forts.[42]

Adams, of course, was ironic; he quoted Longfellow as the point of departure for a rejection of "State Street" with its beliefs in progress, reason, and perfectibility. Yet a half century later in the darkest days of the Western world, when it seemed that the forces of barbarism and darkness were about to extinguish the culture's enlightenment, it was Longfellow's words that the great leader of the English-speaking peoples used to rally the forces of the democratic Western world. The fusion of style and idea was complete; the "Making of the Ship" made effective the symbols of progress and natural goodness that were America's sustaining faith and that Winston Churchill selected to summarize the idea of America.

4. Lowell

The stable, settled culture of Boston that was the product of nearly two centuries of New World history and of the families that were a result of eight generations of unions between Puritan divines and wealthy merchants produced two writers who gave the American public style urbane private expression. One of them, Oliver Wendell Holmes, gave this culture its name: he called it "Brahmin" to express the sense of intellectual aristocracy he felt to be its best feature. And there was no more complete Brahmin than Holmes's younger friend, James Russell Lowell. This gifted patrician admired the way in which "Pride, honour, country, throbbed"[43] through Bryant's poems, but he ranged farther than Bryant in both materials and manner. Basing all his work upon the same fundamental acquiescence to the articles of the American faith, he both expressed this belief and felt secure enough in it to protest, to mock the many deviations from it that were increasingly a part of the nineteenth-century scene. He was an accomplished writer of a kind of literature that can only be written by someone who believes in the basic value of the culture of which he is a part. Only someone who believes in the fundamental health of the patient and believes he can cure the diseases that impair that health can use the healing irritant of satiric, as opposed to ironic, laughter. In Lowell we hear an American version of the satire of Juvenal and Pope, which spoke, and could only speak, from the security of an agreement with the unspoken premises of their age. "I am the first poet," he proudly, although wrongly, announced, "to express the American Idea."[44]

The point of departure for Lowell's poems and essays was the eighteenth-century faith in the natural world and in nature's God. His early poems were filled with the secularized faith of the deistic, unitarian world of Franklin and Jefferson. For Lowell as for them, the world was essentially good, and nature was essentially beneficent. Although "Good never comes unmixed"[45] and although there is pain as well as joy and darkness as well as light, still "one heart lies beneath, and that is good."[46] This faith in the goodness at the heart of nature was translated immediately into a corresponding faith in the essential goodness of man. Like all other believers in this faith, he expressed respect for the child and for the untutored as symbols of this goodness. Loving the society of the cultivated, he nevertheless found it necessary to pay at least lip service to "simple souls . . . Unswerved by culture from their native bent." Their appeal to him comes, he averred, from their "being primal man/And nearer the deep bases of our lives."[47]

Directed away from otherworldly concerns, Lowell's face was turned toward the concerns of this world. As for the Augustans, for him the proper study of mankind was man. Like the men of the eighteenth century, he very early felt that "the worst intoxication man can feel/Is that which drains the burning cup of zeal."[48] And especially was he suspicious of religious fervor that turned its back upon the physical and the material universe in inspired quest for that which lies beyond. He addressed himself with moderation and decorum to the normal world of outward appearances as they are commonly observed and made this outward world the subject of his poems. His worship was the worship of humanity as the only proper way to worship God; whatever strength he had was the strength "won by love of human kind."[49] This optimistic humanism received expression again and again throughout his long creative life, which was also, quite as to be expected, the successful, secure public life of a public figure—the eloquent teacher, the wise editor, the successful diplomat.

The Vision of Sir Launfal, one of his most anthologized poems, has as its theme the unity of the religions of nature and man, and this unity provides the structure, which consists of two brief narrative passages associated with two relatively long preludes. Regarded as introductions to the story of the search for the Grail, the two preludes are awkward and overlong. Seen as what they are—two hymns to two aspects of nature, the benign and the threatening—and related to that portion of the narrative that follows them, they justify Lowell's religious optimism.

The first prelude is a hymn to spring—to warmth, growth, fertility. The second is concerned with winter—with cold, harshness, decay, death. The first narrative section deals with outgoings, with exuberant questing, with spirited and hopeful searching. The second narrative section deals with failure. Yet it is not in the first mood—in the days of June, whose precious rarity is celebrated in words dear to the popular heart—that the vision of Sir Launfal is achieved. Instead, the Grail of significance is found in the second mood—the mood of defeat and despair, of cold and snow and disease—heralded by the prelude that begins: "Down swept the chill wind from the mountain peak."[50] By mismatching the pair of opposites, by linking the exuberance of spring with the fact of failure and the grimness of winter with the fact of final triumph, Lowell projected his optimism about the natural and human condition, where even, where *especially*, out of adversity comes final goodness:

Heaven is not mounted to on wings of dreams,
Nor doth the unthankful happiness of youth
Aim thitherward . . .
'T is sorrow builds the shining ladder up,
Whose golden rounds are our calamities.[51]

This optimism about nature and man led him, not away from society to the recluse from society, but toward society and toward the importance of social man. Not that he liked "the masses." He sounded very clearly the distinction between men as a mob and men as a collection of individuals in two lines that foreshadow the thought of the modern sociologist: "Hating the crowd, where we gregarious men/ Lead lonely lives, I love society."[52] He felt that "God and Heaven's great deeps are nearer/Him to whose heart his fellow man is nigh."[53] The aspect of transcendentalism least attractive to him was the tendency, latent in Emerson and overt in Thoreau, to love nature but to hate man. This combination he called "the mark of disease" and "one more symptom of the general liver-complaint."[54] He attacked Thoreau for holding the "very shallow view that affirms trees and rocks to be healthy, and cannot see that men in communities are just as true to the laws of their organization and destiny."[55] Impatient with the hermeticism of Thoreau, Lowell was even more scornful of the "dead souls" who have "cast their hope of human kind away."[56]

His essentially Renaissance spirit placed the highest value upon the whole, social man and upon his deeds and a secondary, supporting value upon art. Social performance was the supreme human art, he felt; and those arts that celebrate the actions of men are handmaidens to the higher arts of living. His *Ode Recited at the Harvard Commemoration* is a poem to the humanism that, he said, was Harvard's greatest glory. The *Ode* began with the humility of the artist in relation to the more comprehensive beauty of human activity: "Weak-winged is song,/Nor aims at that clear-ethered height/ Whither the brave deeds climb for light."[57] The participation of the university in the greatest of all the deeds of the century—the Civil War for the Union and for human freedom—was the crowning glory of its arts and sciences. They prepared the men who could partake of "that high privilege that makes all men peers,/That leap of heart whereby a people rise/Up to a noble anger's height."[58] Actions, performances like these, he told his audience, are "the imperishable gains" that "certify to earth a new imperial race."[59]

These deeds were evidence of the advancement of the race and its slow progress toward betterment—a belief to which Lowell clung, sometimes with the desperation of a believer who finds his faith slipping away. In the *Commemoration Ode* he spoke of Lincoln as the great example of human progress, of the "vexing, forward-reaching sense/Of some more noble permanence." When she created Lincoln, he said, nature threw her "Old-World moulds aside," and, "choosing sweet clay from . . . the unexhausted West . . . shaped a hero new." This new hero was no "lonely mountain-peak of mind" but a "Broad prairie rather, genial . . . Fruitful and friendly for all human kind."[60] Lowell had earlier seen the events of Europe as partaking of this same forward movement. The visionaries of the revolutions of 1848 were part of a Western dream, and "The dreams which nations dream come true/ And shape the world anew."[61] The struggle for freedom was an outpouring of the light of liberty, which reveals the vision of human possibilities:

And down the happy future runs a flood
Of prophesying light;
It shows an Earth no longer stained with blood,

Blossom and fruit where now we see the bud
Of Brotherhood and Right.[62]

These dominant tones of rationalism, optimism, and a belief in progress were often tempered by an awareness of the power of their opposites. Although an heir of the Enlightenment, Lowell also appreciated the romantic revolt from reason and admired many of its expressions. Quite significantly, however, he sought to domesticate and moderate the romantic surge toward the unknowable. He called Coleridge's definitions of imagination, for example, the "common sense" of the unseen world, as the understanding is the "common sense" of the world of perceptions. And in his general estimate of poetry, which summarized his commitment to the rational and his suspicion of the imagination, he said that great verse should have "breadth as well as . . . depth" and that "it should meet men everywhere on the open levels of their common humanity . . . and not merely on their occasional excursions to the heights of speculation or their exploring expeditions among the crypts of metaphysics."[63]

The conflicts among rational and intuitive faiths made *The Cathedral* one of his most complex and interesting poems. Lowell's appreciation of the medieval spirit expressed in the cathedral at Chartres was as complete as that of Henry Adams: he had passed beneath the triple northern porch under the "stern faces bleared with immemorial watch"[64] and had been overwhelmed by the emotion and the mysticism of the Gothic order: he found it "graceful, grotesque . . . Heavy as nightmare, airy-light as fern,/Imagination's very self in stone."[65] Reeling under the impact of this assault upon his rational convictions, he felt the incomparable appeal of an age of faith and the corresponding coldness of "This age that blots out life with question marks,/This nineteenth century with its knife and glass."[66] In this mood he wondered if the world had improved with the coming of the "Western giant coarse,/Scorning refinements."[67] His optimism, however, chastened and strengthened by its awareness of the magnificence of an earlier faith and a lost civilization, returned at the end. The "Western giant . . . this shirt-sleeved

Cid . . . this backwoods Charlemagne,"[68] he felt, shall "Spite of himself . . . learn to know/And worship some ideal of himself."[69] Although miracles had faded out of history, there remained the testimony of nature that God is "far above,/Yet in and of me!"[70] So, walking out through the magnificent portals of the past to the homelier present, he was afraid, not of the withdrawal of God, but of the loss of man's capacity to see the truth—the truth that He was "Walking Thy garden still . . . Missed in the commonplace of miracle."[71] This is a shrewd inversion: not the "miracle of commonplace," a phrase that would express surprise that the commonplace could be miraculous, but rather the "commonplace of miracle," a locution that compels us to understand the whole of nature as a continuing revelation.

At the end of this most searching and most skeptical of his poems, he returned to the same conclusion he had advised in his earlier sonnet: "think not the Past is wise alone." The bud of time, he had said then, was always opening "fuller" and encouraging "the soul with odor of fresh hopes."[72] At both the beginning and the end of his life, Lowell expressed an acceptance, albeit with something of a sigh, of the century of "knife and glass" of which he seemed so dubious in *The Cathedral*. In an early sonnet he wrote, "I grieve not that ripe Knowledge takes away/The charm that Nature to my childhood wore," and then averred that "The real doth not clip the poet's wings,—To win the secret of a weed's plain heart/ Reveals some clue to spiritual things."[73] And much later he returned to the same theme: in "Science and Poetry" he declared that one is no foe to the other, for poetry can take the advances of science as the stuff of a new "Age of Wonder" whose magic it can identify and celebrate.

Lowell's enlightened conviction that reason and experience were the stuff of reality and that the "weed's plain heart" could provide the modern miracles that poetry might celebrate led him to a major innovation in our literature—the adoption of folk dialect as a proper medium for verse—and to the defense of the common language of the common man as the medium of literature. If it be in the use of the vernacular that Hemingway saw all American literature as originating in *Huckleberry Finn*, he should have looked back further—

to 1848 and the publication of the first series of Lowell's *Biglow Papers*. They were, Howells said later, the first American works of realism; Howells was led to so extravagant a claim by the extraordinary vitality of these dialect pieces. Lowell invented Hosea Biglow, a shrewd, commonsensical commentator on the affairs of men and nations. Using him as his mask and two other homespun characters as the foils for his beliefs, Lowell expressed the feelings of all believers in the American idea as it confronted the national crime that would be the greatest threat to its future. Imagining "such an upcountry man" as he "had often seen at antislavery gatherings, capable of district-school English, but . . . falling back into the natural stronghold of his homely dialect"[74] whenever his emotions were aroused, he created Hosea Biglow to embody the lean "common-sense" of the New England character, "vivified and heated by conscience."[75]

A language, he said, must "suck up the feeding juices secreted for it in the rich mother-earth of common folk,"[76] and he tried to invigorate American literature with just such juices. "The Courtin'," a little poem inserted in *The Biglow Papers*, is a model of the American vernacular. The voice is the voice of the country, and point of view is the vernacular perspective: a man of the people, a folk hero who can perform his technical job with competence and precision:

> six foot o' man, A 1,
> Clear grit and human natur',
> None couldn't quicker pitch a ton
> Nor dror a furrer straighter.

The range of metaphor and simile and image was within the range of the perception of this folk hero; allusions are made to both natural and social events with which he and his audience are familiar; when Zeke is with his "Huldy,"

> long o' her his veins 'ould run
> All crinkly like curled maple,
> The side she breshed felt full o' sun
> Ez a south slope in Ap'il.

And the "courtin'" itself is treated with folk dash and compression and a loving eye for folk exaggeration:

she gin her cheer a jerk
Ez though she wished him furder,
An' on her apples kep' to work
Parin' away like murder.

The climax is reached when

Says he, "I'd better call again";
Says she, "Think likely, Mister":
Thet last word pricked him like a pin,
An' . . . Wal, he up an' kist her.

Whereupon her mother comes in and finds her

pale ez ashes
All kin' o' smily round the lips
An' teary roun' the lashes.[77]

So we have the happy ending: part of the folk optimism that was the major tone of the American vernacular when it combined with the idea of America to give it the vitality and expression of the workaday language of the common man.

The little glimpse of ordinary social life of "The Courtin'" was not, however, the major motive of *The Biglow Papers*. Their main concern was to hold up to laughter the vices and foibles of man with the essentially hopeful, comic end of reform. Lowell affirmed American beliefs by ridiculing errors that endangered those beliefs. To defend the essential worth of all men, he attacked the institution of slavery; to defend the possibilities of republicanism, he attacked the divisiveness of the South; to defend the ordinary man's ability to form and support good governments, he attacked the corruptions of political self-seekers who were casting discredit on self-government. These beliefs, and these specific dangers that threatened them, would be the concern of the satiric realism of DeForest, Howells, and Mark Twain; they were the soul of *The Biglow Papers*.

The first of these dangers is the major object of Hosea Biglow's homely scorn. He rejects service in the Mexican War, which, he feels, is waged solely for the extension of slave territory. However, he reaches beyond the issue of slavery to demonstrate that black thralldom is but a general symptom of the rejection of the American idea of human equality:

Ain't it cute to see a Yankee
Take sech everlastin' pains,
All to git the Devil's thankee
Helpin' on em weld their chains?
Wy, it's jest ez clear ez figgers,
Clear ez one an' one make two,
Chaps thet make black slaves o' niggers
Want to make wite slaves o' you.[78]

The other major evil—the pusillanimity, the selfishness, the corruption of the politician—is derided through the portrait of the trimmer, Increase O'Phace, who avers, "A marciful Providence fashioned us holler/O purpose thet we might our princerples swaller,"[79] or in the caricature of a presidential candidate who asks his supporters to tell the voters that

on the Slavery question
I'm RIGHT, although to speak I'm lawth;
This gives you a safe pint to rest on,
An' leaves me frontin' South by North.[80]

In *A Fable for Critics*, Lowell's satire is more good-humored and rests even more clearly on the basis of affirmation. In *A Fable* we perceive the identification of the satirist with the objects of satire—his feeling that they are one in their common tendencies to fall from the ideal. Lowell made himself unreservedly the butt of the sharpest lines in the poem. Lowell, he says of himself, will never the top of Parnassus " 'come nigh reaching/Till he learns the distinction twixt singing and preaching.' "[81] The galloping anapestic tetrameters help to soften the bite of the satire even more; they race along with an ease and a rush that help to carry the reader past and over the individual barbs. He said of them that they were "a *jeu d'esprit* . . . rapidly written . . . for my own amusement"[82]—very much the urbane, self-deprecatory pose of the gentlemanly amateur that was part of Lowell's Augustan spirit of moderation, both the disclaimer and the pose add to the sense of tolerance. His rhyming is often ingenious. He not only uses double and triple rhymes but often treats them in unexpected fashion: for example the hidden rhyme that identifies the pronunciation of the English poet's name: "I think there are two per-/-sons fit for a parallel—Thompson and Cowper."[83] In this medium, where the style soothes the satiric sting, he wrote some shrewd and just appraisals of the contemporary American literary scene: of Poe "with his raven, like Barnaby Rudge/Three fifths of him genius and two fifths sheer fudge";[84] of Holmes's style, "In long poems 'tis painful sometimes, and invites/A thought of the way the new Telegraph writes";[85] of Thoreau treading in Emerson's footsteps "with legs painfully short";[86] of Cooper, who has drawn only one character that is new, "His Indians, with proper respect be it said,/Are just Natty Bumppo, daubed over with red."[87] Above all, his lines on Hawthorne compress a world of insight about that "genius so shrinking and rare/That you hardly at first see the strength that is there."[88] This willingness to use his art for social, utilitarian purposes, evident in *A Fable for Critics* as well as in *The Biglow Papers*, demonstrated the fundamental commitment of Lowell to the basic patterns of belief of the society of which he was a part. Believing in its literature no less than in its informing style, he could treat it to the healing irritant of satire, and the style he inevitably used to express his affirmation was the concrete and earthbound images and diction that made the symbols of his culture effective.

5. Holmes

Ten years Lowell's senior, his close friend and colleague during their long lives, and standing together with him at the center of the Brahmin culture, Oliver Wendell Holmes was the writer who carried much of the mood of Franklin and Jefferson into the nineteenth century. His world, like Lowell's world, was the world of the central faiths of his society; he was thoroughly at home in republican, middleclass America, and he expressed this sense of identity in essays and poems that, more than any other American writing, deserve to be called neoclassical. Like the Augustans, Holmes had the self-assured, secure sense of ease in his environment. Resembling Bryant and Longfellow and Lowell, he was even more representative and more influential than these other poets of affirmation in his particular emphasis upon the scientific method as the major instrument for realizing the possibilities of his world and as the principal means of moral as well as material betterment. In advocating the role of science, he created the atmosphere for the growth of the dominant philosophy of the American idea—the philosophy that would later be given the name of *pragmatism*. The philosophical formulations of William James, as well as the imaginative forms of Howells and Mark Twain, owe much to the influence of the man whom Henry James described as the "little doctor from Cambridge."

The essence of this influence was a robust commitment to life, a radical sanguinity, a hopefulness founded upon a belief in the universe as ordered and significant and upon the eighteenth-century conviction that nature embodies a divine order according to which man must organize his moral and social life. "The great end of being is to harmonize man with the order of things,"[89] he said through the character of the Professor at the Breakfast Table. And in this order, strengthened by the conviction that the worth of truth will eventually be proven and that error will eventually be corrected, man can involve himself with the material affairs of the world. The words he used echoed Bryant, whose statement he possibly found congenial because of its medical metaphor: "Truth gets well if she is run over by a locomotive, while Error dies of lockjaw if she scratches her finger."[90]

Health and sanity for Holmes were the order of the universe and a firm foundation for an optimism based upon the use of man's reason and sentiment to bring himself into equilibrium with that order. The belief in evil at the heart of a fallen world, he declared, is a belief that "all men's teeth are naturally in a state of total decay." Nonsense, he told his listeners. "There are a good many bad teeth, we all know, but a great many more good ones."[91] In just such a perspective appeared to him the inhumanities of men: these are symptoms of disease, of lack of health, or—to use the psychological term—of *insanity*. "Anything that is brutal, cruel, heathenish, that makes life hopeless for most of mankind and perhaps for entire races . . . ought to produce insanity in every well-regulated mind."[92]

The principal "heathenishness" he saw in his own culture was the doctrine of Original Sin and its promulgation by the Puritan tradition. This was the "barbaric" notion to which he alluded when he talked of a theory that "makes life hopeless for most of mankind."[93] The least violent of his attacks came during his speculation on the origins of the doctrine in Catholicism: "I have sometimes questioned," the Professor said, "whether the many libels on human nature had not been a natural consequence of the celibacy of the clergy."[94] Yet Augustinian pessimism, along with its Protestant manifestations, was one of the few concepts that made him lose his tolerance and good humor. He called Puritanism that "miserable delusion."[95] The Professor sitting at the Breakfast Table summarized Holmes's hatred of fanaticism: "If a man hangs my ancient female relatives for sorcery, as they did in this neighborhood a little while ago, or burns my instructor for not believing as he does, I care no more for his religious edicts than I should for those of any other barbarian."[96] The Puritans, he said, were "those wretched fools, reverend divines and others, who were strangling men and women for imaginary crimes a little more than a century ago."[97] Jonathan Edwards may have been a "remarkable man," but his brain was as well adjusted "for certain mechanical processes as Babbage's calculating machine," and his congregation treated him quite properly when they "turned him out by a vote of twenty to one, and passed a resolve that he should never preach for them again."[98]

Edwards's rejection by his congregation was one of the pieces of evidence Holmes offered to prove the validity of his optimistic belief in the homely sense of common men as the best means of knowing reality. The mistake of Puritanism was to leave "common sense and common humanity out of its premises."[99] "The laymen," he declared, "have to keep setting the divines right constantly."[100] As in theology, so it is in philosophy: the ultimate court of appeal lies in the common perceptions of most men. He described the philosopher as a man who unwraps a truth painfully, and at the end of the process, "we recognize it as a diminutive and familiar acquaintance whom we have known in the streets all our lives."[101] From the point of view of literary criticism, the most significant aspect of Holmes's reliance upon common sense was his belief that value in art is a function of acceptance by an informed public. Not for him was the ideal of the solitary, alienated artist: "Produce anything really good, and an intelligent editor will jump at it."[102]

Just as his view of the value of the world—its partial evil but its substantial goodness and healthfulness—started with a revulsion from Puritan pessimism, so did his view of the way in which we know the world begin with an attack upon false modes of knowledge—the superstitions, the traditional errors, the false mythologies of the past. These outmoded beliefs were, for him, "lumps of nonsense" that *"we the people*, Sir, some of us with nut-crackers, and some of us with trip-hammers, and some of us with pile-drivers, and some of us coming down with a whish! like air-stones out of a lunar volcano, will crash down on . . . till we have made powder of them like Aaron's calf!"[103] In this attitude toward the superiority of present reason over past superstition, Holmes turned naturally to an identification of the past with darkness and of the present with light. "Ancient error" was for him like the rock in whose dank shadows dwells the "old lying incubus" to which the empiricist puts "the staff of truth."[104]

This belief in the superiority of scientific empiricism to all past forms of "knowing" was the major prop of his world view—a view that, on the whole, the mythologies of the past must be carefully reconsidered and the false mythologies distinguished from the true by each generation: "Rough work, iconoclasm,—but the only way to get at truth."[105] Indeed, his scientific prejudice even suspected the value of man's symbol-making and myth-making faculties. There is a sense of grudging in his admission that "man is an idolator or symbol-worshipper by nature," for he then adds, "which, of course, is no fault of his." He tried to be fair, however, and said that his opposition was only to the "local and temporary symbols," which must be "ground to powder."[106]

Yet Holmes was no traducer of the emotional life of man— far from it. His belief in science and the scientific method as the principal weapon in man's arsenal of cognition was not a belief that man should live by reason alone; rather it was the conviction that man should live in a way of which reason would approve. Instincts are given to us to be regulated; any system that assumes the need for exterminating them is sheer insanity, he wrote. Like William James, whose views on science and religion would be much like his, he declared: "Science . . . in other words knowledge,—is not the enemy of religion; for if so, then religion would mean ignorance. But it is often the antagonist of school-divinity."[107] Holmes was aware that the emotional commitments of men are their supreme commitments, the most important aspects of their humanity; indeed, he recognized that it constituted the essence of their being. Illusions, he suggested, are necessary. He asked only that illusions be subjected to the check of empirical reason and, if they be shown to be at variance with the truths of experience, that they be renamed "delusions" and be discarded. As illusions, however, they must be cherished: "When one . . . has lost *all* his illusions, his feathers will soon soak through, and he will fly no more."[108] The "good and true and intelligent men whom we see all around us, laborious, self-denying, hopeful, helpful," and—most important—the women, whom Holmes worshipped as the embodiment of the best tendencies of the species, carry in their hearts, he felt, the sentiment of love. Together with the sentiment of creation and the sentiment of tenderness toward the weak and helpless, the affective sentiment, he declared, is the true religion for which America must make its new symbols.[109]

The ways of knowing the world, then, are twofold—a way of knowing natural things that may be measured quantitatively and a way of knowing those things that cannot be measured nor analyzed. And the latter mode of knowledge is intuitive, immediate, and total. "What should you think of a lover who should describe the idol of his heart," he asked, "in the language of science, thus: Class, Mammalia; Order, Primates; Genus, Homo; Species, Europeus; Variety, Brown; Individual, Ann Eliza; Dental formula,

$$i \frac{2-2}{2-2} \; c \frac{1-1}{1-1} \; p \frac{2-2}{2-2} \; m \frac{3-3}{3-3} ?"^{110}$$

For love, for the perception of beauty, the sentiments are the proper faculty, and "poetry," the only proper language. In talking of trees, for example, the Autocrat of the Breakfast Table urged his companions to speak of them "as we see them, love them, adore them in the fields, where they are alive."[111] Not a philosopher, Holmes made no attempt to reconcile these two areas of knowledge—knowledge of physical facts, which could be described in the language of science, and knowledge of universal ideals. This duality is everywhere apparent in his essays and poems and foretells the same duality in William James and the American pragmatists.

One of the outmoded beliefs to which Holmes put the staff of scientific analysis, one of the false myths he tried to exorcise, was that of the superiority of the savage to the civilized, of the ignorant to the cultivated. While he believed in the common sense of common man, he meant by *common* the consensus of mature opinion and by *sense* the achievements of civilized minds that had learned their lessons from experience. He was the first of the "party of hope" to reject one of the myths that had been used to foster a part of the American idea: the idea of natural goodness had received its imaginative mythological expression in the parables of the noble savage and the superior child; translated into the second half of the nineteenth century, these parables became an antiintellectual defense of the primitive and an attack upon the civilized. Instead of bolstering the idea of progress with an affirmation of the capabilities of man, they became a weapon for the attack upon progress; in other words, to use Holmes's terms, "natural goodness" became, not an illusion, but a delusion. And as such it was the object of his attack. Children, he said, with a cheerfulness that took away the sting, "are little wretches . . . as superstitious as naked savages."[112] All other things being equal, he admitted, he preferred the man of family to the man with none, for "the man who inherits family traditions and the cumulative humanities of at least four or five generations"[113] is more likely to possess the qualities of reason, tolerance, and decency that, to Holmes, meant civilization.

Part of the reason for his rejecting the myth of the noble

savage and the divine child was his awareness of the importance of heredity in determining behavior; but this awareness
led him, not in the direction of deterministic despair, but to
a defense of the idea of progress based upon an awareness
of the inevitability of certain moral and physical evils. The
disposition to these evils, Holmes knew, is as inevitable, as
"determined," as are other processes of nature: but they *are*
processes of nature and hence are open to man's understanding and his social control. They are not the products of
a supernature about which man has no knowledge and over
which he has no domain. Moral evils, therefore, like disease,
have their causes; these causes can be understood; they can
also be the object of sympathy rather than of fear. "We . . .
have nothing but compassion for a large class of persons
condemned as sinners by theologians, but considered by us
as invalids," said the doctor to the minister in *Elsie Venner*.
And then he went on to say that "our notions of bodily and
moral disease, or sin, are apt to go together."[114] The motive
behind Holmes's two "medicated novels" was to demonstrate the operation of natural causality in the formation of
aberrations of character and behavior. On another, less serious occasion Holmes declared: "It is such a sad thing to be
born a sneaking fellow"; if one happens to be born with
"such congenital incapacity that nothing can make a gentleman of him," he is entitled "not to our wrath, but to our
profoundest sympathy."[115] The transfer of evil from the realm
of mystery and the supernatural absolute to the realm of the
definable, the knowable, and, hence, the controllable was a
source of chastened hope rather than of despair. It was
chastened because it included the acceptance of the reality of
evil; there was no feeling that evil, as Emerson put it, was
"merely privative"; for Holmes it was not simply absence of
good; it was very real, but it was subject to the sovereignty of
man's reason: it had natural causes; it could be confronted; it
could be understood and perhaps meliorated.

The myth of the noble savage, then, was no longer needed
and, indeed, could be a temptation to a false and blind view
of reality. Instead, the moderate, reasonable assumption that
man and nature were mixtures of good and evil, with the
evidence pointing to a supremacy of the good—this belief

was a sufficient prop for his acquiescence in the idea of progress. His attitude toward the relation between English and American civilization is instructive in this connection. Holmes felt himself and his society a normal development from English eighteenth-century culture; he argued that "the American is the Englishman reinforced."[116] The feeling here is of progression, advancement, improvement over the past; at the same time there is a due acknowledgement of the values of the past upon which the present can build. This double attitude is even more apparent in *The Professor at the Breakfast-Table*, where he contrasts the Old World with the New and declares, in a startling reversal of the usual attitude toward the comparative youth and maturity of the two civilizations, "They are children to us in certain points of view. They are playing with toys we have done with for whole generations." The superiority was based upon the widening of the democratic spirit: "We do think more of a man, as such . . . than any people that ever lived did think of him. Our reverence is a great deal wider, if it is less intense."[117] An increase in the range of humanism, he felt, was the basis for the new literature and the new religion of America: "Democratic America has a different humanity from feudal Europe, and so must have a new divinity."[118]

The literary forms in which this humanistic, enlightened world view was presented were variations of the forms that eighteenth-century England had used for its literature of cultural affirmation. The *Spectator* papers of Steele and Addison were the precedents for Holmes's charming, informal essays on society, science, literature, history, religion, philosophy, which were published in *The Autocrat*, *The Professor*, and *The Poet at the Breakfast-Table*. The setting of the essays is significant: to use a boarding house as the place for the conversations, to describe the interplay between a group of thoroughly commonplace and middle-class participants and their social "autocrat"—surely this tells us much about the commitments of the author. The Autocrat and the Professor and the Poet are the author's various disguises, and, like the Autocrat, Holmes could say to this undistinguished group of listeners: "I hope you all love me none the less for anything I have told you."[119] Early in the volume bearing his name, the

Professor describes himself, and the description is familiar; it is of Oliver Wendell Holmes: optimistic, believing in the significance of the world of common experience, proud of his breadth of interest, skeptical of narrowness, and intolerant only of fanaticism: "Here am I . . . a man who has lived long enough to have plucked the flowers of life and come to the berries,—which are not always sad-coloured, but sometimes golden-hued as the crocus of April . . . contented enough with daily realities, but twirling on his finger the key of a private Bedlam of ideals . . . loving better the breadth of a fertilizing inundation than the depth of a narrow artesian well."[120] The Autocrat-Professor-Poet reigns over an oval table about which were collected the other boarders; with one exception they are fairly dull people; but "what a comfort a dull but kindly person is, to be sure, at times": they comprise the Landlady, her son, christened "Benjamin Franklin," the "Kohinoor" (a business man who sports a diamond), the Venerable Gentleman, the Divinity Student, A Young Fellow, the Landlady's Poor Relation; and then the most completely defined of the characters, the "Little Gentleman"—so ugly he is called The Sculpin. A small, gallant, generous, high-minded man, he embodies the poor homely commonplace of moderate American life in which Holmes believed so deeply.

The treatment of The Sculpin is consistent with Holmes's affectionately satirical mode. Holmes put in his mouth statements of many of the extreme positions to which Holmes himself was often attracted and about which he could engage in gentle self-mockery—the superiority of America to Europe, the heady sense of a new revelation for a new world, the infinite preference for Boston over any other place in the universe. "Boston sunsets," cried the ugly and endearing little enthusiast, "perhaps they're as good in some other places, but I know 'em best here. . . . American skies are different from anything they see in the Old World . . . A new nursery, Sir, with Lake Superior and Huron and all the rest of 'em for wash-basins! A new race, and a whole new world for the new-born human soul to work in!"[121] This device of projecting his opinions through a comic character, looking at him objectively, and laughing at him satirically and fondly—this was but an overstatement of the self-satire that was the central device of all his essays. For the Autocrat, the Professor, and the Poet, too, are fictional characters; and while Holmes, in the preface to *The Autocrat*, indirectly assumed responsibility for their views (an earlier "Autocrat," he said, was his immature "son"), still the assumption of the mask, no matter how transparent, afforded him an opportunity to detach himself, to step back, to achieve a distance, and to mock his own pretensions as well as those of his fellow man. The posture, in other words, is suitable to the true satiric mode as we have seen it in Lowell as well. The very method seems to say to us: "these are but my opinions; these views are no more infallible than those of other fallible men." And so, in the technique of these essays, we have a reinforcement of Holmes's belief in neoclassical moderation and tolerance.

The same gentle self-deprecation pervades most of his poetry. Indeed, it determines his stance as a semiprofessional, rather than a professional, maker of verse. He disliked the excessiveness, the immoderation of the claim that the art of poetry is a supreme and unconditioned human activity. "There are times," the Autocrat told his listeners, "in which every active mind feels itself above any and all human books." There are physiological sensations that are "entirely beyond the reach of symbols!" he exclaimed. "Think of human passions as compared with all phrases. Did you ever hear of a man's growing lean by the reading of 'Romeo and Juliet,' or blowing his brains out because Desdemona was maligned?" His hierarchy of values gave a contingent and subordinate place to art. "I have always believed in life rather than in books," he wrote. "I suppose every day of earth, with its hundred thousand deaths and something more of births,—with its loves and hates, its triumphs and defeats, its pangs and its blisses, has more of humanity in it than all the books that were ever written, put together."[122]

The bulk of his poetry, therefore, was occasional verse, celebrating many of the minor, and some of the major, social events that he believed to be the fabric of civilized reality. Sometimes these "events," or experiences, were centered upon individuals; Holmes treated them generally with an affectionate satire, so gentle that it bordered on reverence:

My aunt! My dear unmarried aunt!
Long years have o'er her flown;
Yet still she strains the aching clasp
That binds her virgin zone. [123]

And the rest of the poem told of the mistaken caution of her father, whose excessive care resulted in the pathos of "one sad, ungathered rose/On my ancestral tree."[124] His poem written for the *Atlantic* dinner combined the same sense of poetry-as-an-occasion with an optimism about the possibilities of progress; there was the tone of sustained gentle mockery, a mockery directed at himself and his hopes, which were identical to the hopes of all those gathered about him. He proclaimed the truth of his society's belief in progress but then stepped away from it and objectively observed the self-contradictions built into the belief. To the great experiment in spreading culture through the medium of the *Atlantic Monthly*, he addressed this toast: that it shall prosper "till all we are groping for/Has reached the fulfilment we're all of us hoping for."[125] When it came to describing the consummation devoutly to be wished, Holmes gently pointed out the inadequacy of all utopian ideals based upon imposing the dreamer's standards of goodness upon the world: he will hope for the spread of education

Till the roughs, as we call them, grown loving and dutiful,
Shall worship the true and the pure and the beautiful,
And, preying no longer as tiger and vulture do,
All read the 'Atlantic' as persons of culture do![126]

The self-deprecation of the occasional poems is one aspect of the satiric vision—the satire directed against one's own pretensions. Although the satire he directed at others was usually tempered by this self-mockery, there was no moderation in several of his poems that dealt with the immoderate. The portrait of the "whey-faced" preacher in "The Moral Bully" was a devastating one: it lacked the usual softening touch of sympathy for a common human failing. The history of Puritan intolerance, and of the Enlightenment's rage against it, was summarized in Holmes's description of the pastor as one "whom small disturbance whitens round the lips." There was a picture of life-denying fanaticism in "the lean phantom, whose extended glove/Points to the text of universal love"; the portrait was filled out with a summary of his sermons, which "with grim logic" proved "that all we love is worthiest of our hate." The poem reached a real anger at the conclusion and asked bitterly if "every scarecrow, whose cachectic soul/Seems fresh from Bedlam" has "The right to stick us with his cutthroat terms,/And bait his homilies with his brother worms?"[127]

However, this tone is as unusual in his religious poems as it is in his secular verse; and the most famous of his attacks on Puritanism, "The Deacon's Masterpiece; or, The Wonderful One-Horse Shay," is in his major mood. This is one of the poems that tests most severely the critical faculty, and indeed the whole nature, of literary criticism. Its simplicity, its ease, its accessibility, its unpretentiousness appear to make comment unnecessary and explication an affectation. It seems to lie there—cheerful, impudent, open to the inspection of any and the enjoyment of all. Its very qualities, in other words, seem to deny its seriousness; and yet, they do not deny its value, a value that is bound up with its lack of pretension.

Its subject is the opposition between absolute systems that enslave the minds of theologians and philosophers and the supreme value in Holmes's vision of the world: the common sense of the common man. Holmes gave us the prose argument for the poem a year later in *The Professor at the Breakfast-Table*, when, during a running attack on Jonathan Edwards, the Professor declared: "A man's logical and analytical adjustments are of little consequence, compared to his primary relations with Nature and truth; and people have sense enough to find it out in the long run; they know what 'logic' is worth."[128] So the perspective of the poem is the perspective of the folk: the world is seen through this "sense" of the people, which reduces pretentiousness, no matter how sanctioned by intellectual tradition, to dust.

The voice of this people's sense is in the doggerel rhythms of the poem—the ballad voice of the folk. The concerns of the poem are folk concerns: the attention to details of building, making good use of proper materials, traditions of craftsmanship for utilitarian purposes—in short the "vernacular perspective." The description of the construction of the shay is the longest of the poem, and it dwells with loving attention on the details of its construction and on the utility— and, therefore, the beauty—of the materials with which its parts were made:

The crossbars were ash, from the straightest trees,
The panels of white-wood, that cuts like cheese,
But lasts like iron for things like these.

The folk perspective, the vernacular, is maintained to the end; the conclusion is the perennial joke of the people—the "pratfall"—the surest way to humble pride: the actual descent of the proud to the hard earth, the ending of pretentiousness on the painful fact of the buttocks black and blue. The "pratfall" of comedy is the counterpart of the fall of man in tragedy—the counterpart and the radical opposite. It reduces a cosmic and final descent to a temporary worldly mishap and uses the occasion as a warning, a chastening lesson that will improve the future. "The Deacon's Masterpiece" is a general "pratfall" for Western man. It is not a tragedy that man's systems are imperfect, the poem tells us; it is not a tragedy that nature's systems are involved with decay and with radical, even cataclysmic, change; it is rather an affirmation of the truth that the universe is an open universe, in which the only absolute is change. Anything man constructs, whether it be carriages or systems of belief, must be part of this truth; and any absolute system—whether it be of theology, government, or technology—is subject to the common sense of the open-ended universe. This was the attitude that received its expression in "The Wonderful One-Hoss Shay."

Seen in this light, certain elements of the poem assume an added resonance. Why, for example, did Holmes choose to identify the year of the shay's construction with certain historical events? One event is significantly omitted: the publication of Jonathan Edwards's last tracts, which with relentless logic destroyed the possibilities of belief in freedom of the will and therefore attacked the basis of enlightened optimism. Since this was the event to be allegorized in the poem, since this IS the shay itself, the event was not mentioned. Instead, three other facts of human historical experience were described. One was the fact of human despotism, the particular despotism that America triumphantly, and hence comically, had ended. The transitoriness of this aspect of the world's evils was made apparent by the casual dismissal implied in the lines describing George II of England: "Snuffy old drone from the German hive." A second identification of the shay is with the royal system of warfare. Americans had been skeptical of the rigid battle formations of Braddock's army; both Franklin and Washington warned the English that they were ill-suited to the New World's conditions. When Braddock's army, then, was "left without a scalp to its crown," there was a large admixture of the comic sense of satisfaction at humbled pride in the reaction of the American colonists. The third, and most significant, event of the year was the Lisbon earthquake—a cataclysm that religious zealots had used to postulate the essential evil of the world and had insisted upon viewing as a retribution for man's wickedness. However, the galloping cadences of the rhymed couplets made the horror one event, like many others, in the mutability of the world and removed it from any sense of tragic significance: "That was the year when Lisbon-town/Saw the earth open and gulp her down." At the end, precisely a hundred years later, the instantaneous dissolution of the chaise provided a minor, a very minor, echo of the instant destruction of a far-off European city; this juxtaposition tells us that the systems of men and the constructions of men are ridiculously small when compared to the "Earthquake shock."[129] Yet at the same time these same shocks are domesticated to the scale of man; they in turn have no more effect on the world's history than the thrill that the earth felt when it received the parson's rump; thus are both natural events and human institutions absorbed in a comic perspective, for both have a comic objective: the humbling of pride and the implication of a happy ending, either cosmic or historical, both for nature and for suitably chastened man.

The occasional poems and "The Deacon's Masterpiece"

are meant as light verse, but Holmes also addressed himself with high seriousness to the major question of his century—the relation between knowledge and belief, religion and science—and he wrote two impressive poems on this subject. The less successful of the two was the more pretentious: "Wind-Clouds and Star-Drifts"; yet it is not without its beauty, and it is a dignified statement of the man-centered optimistic creed of the nineteenth-century scientist. It was a poem in twelve parts, which began with the musings of a young astronomer as he waits for the sky to clear. While he waits, he thinks of the history of human aspirations and inevitably compares them to the vastness of the universe. Such comparisons make him feel the gloom of those for whom space has become the new monster, elbowing man out of the cosmos, and he does not

> marvel at him who scorns his kind
> And thinks not sadly of the time foretold
> When the old hulk we tread shall be a wreck,
> A slag, a cinder drifting through the sky
> Without its crew of fools![130]

Leaping ahead in his imagination to the end of the earth and speculating whether it will perish in ice or in fire, he chooses fire as his preference, for it may be that then the earth will become "a new sun for earths that shall be born."[131] Such visions make him feel the oneness of men who have always searched for knowledge: "I am as old as Egypt to myself." Yet they bring him back to the neoclassical longing to limit himself to "one's poor patch/Of this dull spheroid and a little breath/To shape in word or deed to serve my kind."[132]

His heart, he knows, "is simply human; all my care/For them whose dust is fashioned like mine own."[133] He will express himself in verse, one of the "veils of language" beneath which he dares to be himself; he knows that his will be no great talent: only "a slender-margined, unillumined page"; but he will trust his fellows to read it "in the gracious light of love."[134] So conclude the first three sections—they have posed the problems; the next sections discuss his growth as a scientist—as one who has learned from a master as the neophyte learns from the priest; and there is the strong sense of science as the new religion in these lines. He had been trained to

> find the glimmering specks of light
> Beyond the unaided sense, and on my chart
> To string them one by one, in order due,
> As on a rosary a saint his beads.[135]

And in this religion of scientific quest, he had "learned to search" that he may "know/The whence and why of all beneath the stars."[136] His life, therefore, had been "a challenge, not a truce." And he could not believe that the Father who had given him the urge to quest would deny his right to ask his questions.

Then the astronomer deals with the kind of God in whom the scientist is able to believe. It is not the God of the barbarians, nor of Greece and Rome, nor the vengeful God of Israel. It must be a God worthy of the dignity of enlightened and emancipated man.

> This is the new world's gospel: Be ye men!
> Try well the legends of the children's time . . .
> Ye are as gods! Nay, makers of your gods,—
> Each day ye break an image in your shrine
> And plant a fairer image where it stood.[137]

The images that men would make in a new world and a new age are the subject of the last sections of the poem. It is part of "our subtle selves"[138] to long to have images and idols. However, these new images, worthy of the dignity of scientific man, will be in the image of the best of men and, more especially, will present the face of woman's unselfish love. Holmes a decade earlier had said, with the self-mockery of his guise as the Autocrat of the Breakfast Table, "I have been ready to believe that we have even now a new revelation, and the name of its Messiah is WOMAN!"[139] Yet he was deadly serious when, in "Wind-Clouds and Star-Drifts," he wrote that

> Love must be still our Master; till we learn
> What he can teach us of a woman's heart,
> We know not Him whose love embraces all.[140]

This was Holmes's unabashedly sentimental belief, which demonstrated the way in which his scientific awareness, his knowledge that "God has made/This world a strife of atoms and of spheres,"[141] is part of a general faith in the essential beneficence of nature and of man.

A less pretentious, and more successful, fusing of science and religion was his little poem "The Chambered Nautilus." It bears informative comparison with Poe's sonnet "Science," which attacked the vulturous, peering eye of scientific analysis. Homes's imagination was inspired precisely by the kind of scientific analysis that Poe found intolerable; quite literally, the dissection of a beautiful organic object by an empirical scientist was the stimulus for "The Chambered Nautilus." Instead of drawing from the spectacle a moral of despair, Holmes drew from it a counsel of cosmic hope and affirmation.[142]

The sketch of the nautilus in a scientific encyclopedia had removed the shell from the realm of mystery, mythology, and romance and had seen it with the kind of "peering eye" that Poe deplored; this wrench from the world of myth to the world of empirical reality is the subject of the first two stanzas of Holmes's poem. The first stanza deals with the shell as it had been when it was perceived by the romantic imagination and was believed to be sailing

In gulfs enchanted, where the Siren sings,
And coral reefs lie bare,
Where the cold sea-maids rise to sun their streaming hair.

The second stanza introduces a world in which realities have replaced the romantic dream: the myth of the shell as a ship is "wrecked"; the innermost secrets of its structure can no longer excite the mythical imagination, for the secret lies stripped and bared: "Its irised ceiling rent, its sunless crypt unsealed!" At this point the poem apparently reaches the usual romantic agony—the pain at the sight of beauty violated by the prying cold prurience of the scientist's dissection. However, Holmes prepared us for something quite different when he described the inner reality of the shell as a "crypt"— with the sense of primitive concealment and gloomy decay of the word—and when he called it "sunless." In contrast, the following stanza, which gives in detail the actuality of the shell's physical construction as seen by the empirical investigator, is filled with light: "lustrous" and "shining" are the two adjectives that dominate the atmosphere of the lines. We trace the progress of the organism, from its small center outward around the spiral of growth; each of the cells becomes larger and more beautiful, while the body of the creature stretches "in its last-found home" and knows "the old no more."

The next stanza points out the direction we can expect the poem to take. From a dead object comes a new life; from the inert mysteries are born truths clearer than any proposed by mythology or romance. The truth is of both the possibilities and the significance of moral and spiritual progress. The possibilities are that man can build his larger mansions and that each temple can be nobler than the last. The significance of these successive enlargements of rational concepts is that each of them is a growth that apparently cuts man off from heaven at the same moment that it shelters him (each temple shuts him from heaven with a "dome more vast");[143] yet, by a logical continuation of the process, each successive expansion of the rational is the means by which the ineffable is finally accomplished. The scientist's empirical curiosity is no bar to this achievement; on the contrary, it is the means by which the ceilings of man's aspirations were lifted from the low vault of the past to the infinitely receding horizons of knowledge.

IV~Romantic Defense of the Idea

1. Emerson

Although by the 1830s the enlightened, rational doctrines of
  Jefferson and Franklin had generally become the commonplaces of both political and religious thought in America, in
New England in particular a growing religious liberalism had
  fed the American official faith in the goodness of man and in
   his worldly betterment. In turn, religious liberalism had
   been nourished by the faith in worldly progress and had
  emerged as Unitarianism, which was the creed of writers
  such as Bryant, Lowell, Holmes; of the most persuasive
   theologians; and of the center of intellectual strength,
Harvard College. The faith that Ralph Waldo Emerson heard
      preached during his years at Harvard (1817–21) was
  thoroughly cleansed of the "diseases" of emotionalism and
  fervor and of the feeling of immediate revelation that was
central to the tradition of the Reformation. Men like Francis
Bowen, Alexander Everett, and Andrews Norton preached a
  thoroughly secularized creed, in which a wrestling with God
      had given way to a struggle for social betterment and in
which intuition and revelation had been replaced by reason
and common sense. Alexander Everett told his followers, "It
    is the glory of Newton and Locke, to have directed their
    labors . . . to the most important subjects in physical and
         intellectual science; and the splendor of the results
corresponded with, or even surpassed, all that might have
been expected . . . of the new method."[1] In this he echoed

Charles Chauncy, minister of the First Church of Boston, who had deplored the stress upon emotion of older religious ways and had declared that when passions are emphasized above reason, "it can't be put People should run into Disorders." Religion, Chauncy went on, approves itself "to the Understanding and Conscience . . . and is in the best manner calculated to promote the Good of Mankind." As Perry Miller has observed about this sermon: "The transformation of this segment of Puritanism from a piety to an ethic, from a religious faith to a social code, was here completed."[2]

There had earlier been strong reactions to similar kinds of rationalism in England. Inveighing against Voltaire and Rousseau, proclaiming the supremacy of a higher reason over the understanding, describing the transports of ecstatic delight that brought them to the center of the meaning of things, Coleridge and Wordsworth had revived the sense of wonder and mystery in an increasingly secularized world. Strongly influenced by these romantics, Ralph Waldo Emerson's was the American voice that cried that his country's official faith must keep and extend its strong basis in religious fervor or succumb to crass materialism and the selfish sacrifice of means to ends, which are the constant dangers of a secular creed. It was Emerson's vision that took American faith in the values of the common man and his world of experience and charged it with the vibrancy of a religious devotion; in so doing, he restated and dramatized the value upon which the good society must rest—the sanctity and inviolability of the free individual. The means he used to embody this vision were a highly original poetry and a poeticized prose, and the principal mode he employed for both was a use of symbols that at first glance seems to have something in common with the emblematic mode of the Puritans, for Emerson's images were involved with spiritual reality. Although the Puritans considered the physical facts "shadows" and "delusions," Emerson saw "every natural fact" as a symbol of a "spiritual fact"; he meant by *symbol* a new kind of identity, undreamed of in the religion of the Puritans or in the philosophies of the Enlightenment. The image of art, properly chosen, became for Emerson a "bodying forth" of the physical reality it names; the physical reality it names is a bodying forth of a spiritual reality; and each one is not separate from but identical with its counterpart. When he trumpeted that "natural facts are symbols of physical facts. . . . Words are signs of natural facts,"[3] he gave American literature one of its most creative doctrines and made possible the art of Thoreau and Whitman, both of whom were vitalized by the belief that their symbols could be made one with the reality of the physical and spiritual universe.

Thoreau and Whitman—the one with his expansion of the individual into nature, the other with his expansion of the body into the civilized as well as the natural world—were the heirs of Emerson's vision of the symbolic nature of the private man. For it was this private man who became Emerson's supreme symbol; all his philosophy and religion proclaimed the infinitude of the private soul.[4] Whereas Edwards struggled to refine out of his nature all pride in individuality and yearned to be destroyed, to be "swallowed up" in God, Emerson envisioned the private soul's expanding to encompass the infinite. He could feel the "perfect exhilaration" and gladness "to the brink of fear" as he became a "transparent eyeball" and "part or parcel of God."[5] And shortly after this mystical experience he confided frequently in his journals that the individual is no partial being in the universe but is the whole: he is the world.

These were the mystical terms in which Emerson expressed his faith in the essential goodness of man, his joy in this life, his faith in the future. He gave the American idea of progress the vitality of an essentially religious fervor. His words aroused a sense of eager expectancy: the world is young, he told Americans; they could write their own epics and their own Bibles. The conservative, the man of fear and doubt, the worshiper of the past, is, Emerson declared, a necessary part of the universal pairing of opposites, but he is the negative part, like cold or evil. The innovator, the man of hope, he who looks forward—this man Emerson took to his heart.

The basis of Emerson's hope for the future was a radical optimism that saw a completely beneficent universe; for Emerson life, joy, resurrection, comedy were positive; evil, terror, agony, tragedy were negative. Tragedy could not be a viable form for modern America, he felt, for it depended on the notion of "an immense whim; and this is the only ground of terror and despair in the rational mind, and of tragedy in literature."[6] Since for him the world is not whim but order and plan and since the nineteenth-century mind must perceive it as such, there could be no basis for the tragic form.

And this was no myopic view of reality. As Emerson's sympathetic critics have frequently pointed out, he was not blind to evil and pain; he acknowledged them and then surmounted them with a sense of their place in a cosmic order. In prose this doctrine sounded cold and even heartless: "In the death of my son, now more than two years ago, I seem to have lost a beautiful estate,—no more. I cannot get it nearer to me."[7] In the poem written immediately after the event, however, we have the dramatic record of the struggle of a soul with the agony of loss:

On that shaded day,
Dark with more clouds than tempests are,
When thou didst yield thy innocent breath
In birdlike heavings unto death,
Night came, and Nature had not thee;
I said, "We are mates in misery."

Then came the sober triumph of his intuitive knowledge of the fitness of all things—a knowledge "beyond the reach/Of ritual, bible, or of speech" as it led him "past the blasphemy of grief."[8]

In this account of his deepest pain, we have the summary of his faith: the universe is totally double, but its ambiguity is not the doubleness that would later torment Melville; it is the doubleness of perfectly complementary halves, of opposites that were reconciled in the unity of total goodness: the opposites of death and life, joy and grief. He saw the truth of both complementary parts; he knew the reality of both hemispheres of the moral world; but "past utterance and past belief" he knew the transcendence of a unity of joy, life, hope; his vision was of cosmic comedy. For him, then, as for the writers of the Enlightenment, the answer to the question of *value* is that experience is valuable; whatever exists is good. Franklin's robust optimism was one of the grounds of

Emerson's admiration for the Philadelphia sage. He would take issue with the philosophy of Swedenborg more often than with that of Franklin,[9] for Swedenborg was too much concerned with a vision of evil. The doctrine of the Enlightenment that "all partial evil" is "universal good" was rephrased in Emerson's theory of "Compensation." In his journals and later in his essay on the Swedish mystic, Emerson defended the existence of evil as a necessary part of total goodness: "The carrion in the sun will convert itself to grass and flowers; and man, though in brothels, or jails, or on gibbets, is on his way to all that is good and true."[10] Emerson not only agreed, then, with the artists and image makers of the American creed that the physical world and our perceptions of it are good and true but stated his conviction in more extravagant terms than had yet been heard. "The misery of man," he wrote, "appears like childish petulance when we explore the steady and prodigal provision that has been made for his support and delight on this green ball which floats him through the heavens."[11]

Emerson's essays and poems, then, reaffirmed the official American faith in the value of the world of appearances. Art is not only a statement about what life is worth; it is also a statement about what it means. And to this fundamental question of the meaning of things, Franklin, Jefferson, and Holmes had all given the "commonsense" answer: the world is *there*; it is real; it was framed by "Powerful Goodness," and therefore it has meaning as well as value. The image of Dr. Johnson answering Berkeley's argument by kicking a stone lies behind the acceptations of the Enlightenment. Emerson believed that the acceptance of the reality of things as they appear might become a materialism that values comforts and conveniences as ends in themselves and that treats the tools and techniques that are made to extend man's power—and hence to free his energies for creative roles—as the purposes of life and not as the means to higher levels of spiritual being. It was in this sense of a shallow view of the meaning of material things, rather than in a rejection of their significance, that Emerson wrote his famous rejection of materialism: "Things are in the saddle/And ride mankind."

To the fundamental question of the meaning of the universe, Emerson gave a different answer—one that resulted in the same reverence for the world of fact; but he based this reverence upon a new conception: the world, Emerson announced, was a representation, a bodying forth of the spirit. Instead of postulating a dualism, with the physical world but a paltry shadow of divine things, Emerson proposed an absolute unity, in which the physical world is identical and coextensive with the spiritual world. "Things," then, are not inanimate; flesh is not a falling away from spirit; rather things and flesh ARE the spiritual facts. This was what Emerson meant by *symbol* when he said that "natural facts are symbols of spiritual facts." This insight, close to Wordsworth's views and much indebted to Coleridge's terminology, was Emerson's answer to the basic question of the meaning of the world outside of mind. It was an answer that kept the ideal, which was threatening to drift away from America's deep involvement with physical reality, closely and indissolubly interlocked with it.

Viewed logically, the symbolic nature of the world is a fundamental paradox. It says that *a* is different from and yet identical with *b*—that the physical exists and yet is completely one with the ideal. It therefore demanded a quite different answer to the question of the way we can know and perceive the truths of the universe. For the men of the Enlightenment, the answer sufficed that the reason, operating upon the perceptions of the physical universe, produced our knowledge. This process, however, is incapable of dealing with a reality that is at once material and spiritual, where all is true as well as beautiful—where God appears in every cobweb and where good inevitably streams through evil agents. So, for a form of knowing, Emerson insisted upon the supremacy of that instantaneous apprehension of the fitness of things for which the usual term is insight, or intuition, or inspiration. He often used a term that Coleridge and Carlyle (interpreting, and sometimes misinterpreting, Kant) called the higher Reason. By the time this conception of the supreme intuition had filtered through the English romantic mind, all of Kant's limitations upon the function of the intuition had been lost, and the Reason—which, in capitalized form, was the name for the creative faculty that perceived the truth of the noumenal world—was regarded as the supreme mode of knowing all the truths of the universe: "There is no doctrine of the Reason which will bear to be taught by the Understanding,"[12] Emerson told the graduating class of the divinity school. The latter term is what the Enlightenment meant by *reason*. The former term is the transcendental name for the intuition—for that part of the creative power of God that is in every man and therefore does not only perceive the higher truths but makes new forms and new truths.

Only by the use of this faculty of higher Reason can the basic "movement" of Emerson's universe—the vibration between opposites that constitutes truth—be apprehended. The "swinging," as Robert Frost puts it in our time, between poles is itself the ultimate truth. The understanding is incapable of perceiving the oneness of two substances bound into a dynamic unity by the oscillation between them: good and evil, solitude and society, contemplation and activity, ideal and real, physical and spiritual. Only the Reason can fix this flux long enough for us to know it:

Flow, flow the waves hated,
Accursed, adored,
The waves of mutation . . .
And, out of endeavor
To change and to flow
The gas becomes solid,
And phantoms and nothings
Return to be things.[13]

This was the Emersonian faith: to the question of the value of the world, he replied that it was totally good; to the question of its meaning, he replied it was a symbol; to the question of the way we shall know it, he answered through the higher Reason. When Emerson applied his principles of intuitive knowledge of a symbolic universe to the individual and to art in American society, it had an electrifying effect. For both the American individual in general and the American artist in particular, his words were a call to intellectual freedom and to self-reliance. Emerson's Phi Beta Kappa address, said Holmes, was our declaration of intellectual independence. "Emerson awakened us," wrote Lowell, by sounding "the trumpet that the young soul longs for."[14] It was a trumpet call of independence, not only from the trammels of the past, or tradition, but also from fears of the future. Calling upon the American in general and the American scholar in particular to worship the world of a Franklin with the rapture of a Jonathan Edwards, Emerson provided the American idea with a religious sanction. Like Franklin and Jefferson he concentrated our attention on the immediate and present and on the future. Jefferson's words to Madison—"the earth belongs . . . to the living; the dead have neither the power nor rights over it"—were echoed in Emerson's "the dead sleep in their moonless night; my business is with the living."[15] Franklin's dual dedications at the beginning of his autobiography—to the value of his own life and to the hope that its examples would improve the lives of others—Emerson reinforced by an appeal, not to the common sense of the analytic understanding, but to the uncommon sense of the intuition. He paid due respect to the past, to memory, to tradition; to these, he declared, we cannot overstate our debt. He added, however, that the present has the supreme claim: we must embrace the past only as subordinate to the present.

Emerson not only gave emotional vigor to the American faith in its belief in its present; he also provided it with an idealistic sanction for its concerns with the tools and techniques that were the product of man's application of his understanding to the world about him. "We can help ourselves to the *modus* of mental processes," he wrote in his essay on memory, "only by coarse material experiences. A knife with a good spring, a forceps whose lips accurately meet and match, a steel-trap, a loom, a watch, the teeth or jaws of which fit and play perfectly, as compared with the same tools when badly put together." These tools, he said, give us the only terms by which we can describe "the difference between a person like Franklin or Swift or Webster or Richard Owen, and a heavy man who witnesses the same facts or shares experiences like theirs."[16] His range of metaphor therefore included the machine as an illustration of positive attributes: "The way in which . . . any orator surprises us is by his always having a sharp tool that fits the present use." Toward the end of his career, his sense of humanistic acceptance of the progress of civilization prompted him to make his most dramatic and persuasive statement of the possibilities of applying human knowledge to the control of the physical universe. His famous call to "hitch" your "wagon to a star" was an admonition to harness the forces of nature to increase the power of man: "Now that is the wisdom of a man," he said, "in every instance of his labor, to hitch his wagon to a star, and see the chore done by the gods themselves. That is the way we are strong, by borrowing the might of the elements. The forces of steam, gravity, galvanism, light, magnets, wind, fire, serve us day by day and cost us nothing."[17]

The tool, the machine, all the apparatus of a civilized and commercial society are as real and as significant aspects of the world as the grain of sand, the ocean drop, the flower, and the bee; and all of these common objects of ordinary life should be the concern of all men—preachers, artists, scholars as well as farmers, merchants, and laborers. For Emerson the significance of common things was an evidence of the influence of democracy in all spheres. One of the signs of the coming of a better future, he said, is the fact that along with the growth in political democracy there had grown as well the tendency in the arts to explore and poeticize "the near, the low, the common." And he followed this with his famous expression of faith in the meaning and value of the world of social, political, and commercial—as well as natural—reality:

I ask not for the great, the remote, the romantic; what is doing in Italy or Arabia; what is Greek art, or Provencal minstrelsy; I embrace the common, I explore and sit at the feet of the familiar, the low. Give me insight into to-day, and you may have the antique and future worlds. What would we really know the meaning of? The meal in the firkin; the milk in the pan; the ballad in the street; the news of the boat; the glance of the eye; the form and gait of the body;—show me the ultimate reason of these matters; show me the sublime presence of the highest spiritual cause lurking, as always it does lurk, in these suburbs and extremities of nature; let me see every trifle bristling with the polarity that ranges it instantly on an eternal law; and the shop, the plough, and the ledger referred to the like cause by which light undulates and poets sing;—and the world lies no longer a dull miscellany and lumber-room, but has form and order; there is no trifle, there is no puzzle, but one design unites and animates the farthest pinnacle and the lowest trench.[18]

The application of this set of beliefs to the questions of the source, form, and function of art led to a coherent and influential doctrine of aesthetics, one that provided the basis for an American romanticism of the commonplace. Owing much to Plato and more to Coleridge, it yet had an originality of expression that made it persuasive to native ears. It became the doctrine that helped to make Thoreau and Whitman and that has continued to have its effect long after its source has been discredited by changing moods in American intellectual fashion. His identification of functionalism as the test of beauty, together with underlying safeguards against a too rigidly utilitarian and mechanistic interpretation of this doctrine, has provided the basis for the practice of Frank Lloyd Wright and the theories of Lewis Mumford. His insistence upon art as the free expression of subliminal energies has meant much to a generation tutored in an awareness of the primal forces of id and instinct in the Freudian image of man. His insistence upon the symbol as the primary unit of the poetic imagination, his redefinitions and reevaluations of the power of myth and fable as supreme, if indirect, truth—these definitions and emphases helped to form the art of Thoreau and Whitman and Emily Dickinson and to provide a tradition in America for modern poetic theory. In every case, these aesthetic doctrines helped to reinforce the basic American idea: the doctrine of spontaneity emphasized the value of the individual American's perceptions; the emphasis upon symbolic form demonstrated a new basis for the value of the physical and the immediate; the reverence for mythology demonstrated the democratic nature of a process common to all men and impelled American writers to attempt an American mythology, rather than to despair over the loss of a myth-making faculty.

Like Coleridge, Emerson revered the creative imagination as the true artistic impulse. The forms that the artist builds through the use of this power, he declared, become organisms with life and vitality of their own; like the creative power of God, the creative powers of men make new and vital forms: "the maker of a sentence like the other artist launches out into the infinite and builds a road into Chaos and old Night."[19] Yet this creation of the artist, it must be emphasized, is a paying back into the universe of energies and forms that are *there*; the poet, the artist, is no maker of meaning in an otherwise meaningless universe (that will be Henry Adams's despairing view: "chaos is the law of nature, order the dream of man").[20] Quite the reverse: "When I watch that flowing river," Emerson said, "where, out of regions I see not, pours for a season its streams into me, I see that I am a pensioner, not a cause." And he concluded that all his visions come from "some alien energy." What was true for him was true for the artist in general: "poetry was all written before time was, and whenever we are so finely organized that we can penetrate into that region where the air is music, we hear those primal warblings and attempt to write them down."[21] There is an infinite reservoir of form that is tapped by the imagination, for the world is a total poem: "The sea, the mountain ridge, Niagara, and every flower-bed, pre-exist, or super-exist in pre-cantations,"[22] Emerson told us and went on to say that the poet is he who "with an ear sufficiently fine" overhears the "pre-cantations" and tries to write them down.

This emphasis upon the intuitive source of art led quite naturally to an insistence upon the importance of the original inspiration and upon the willingness of the artist to allow its free expression. Here once again we have a theory calculated to give a dramatic reinforcement to an optimistic view of modern man and his place in the world. In effect, the theory preached that the cosmos is an orderly one and that art is an "overhearing" of that order. Further, it reinforces a preoccupation with the present and the future, for it suggests that the imitation of old traditions and forms can be impediments to the recapturing of beauty by placing it at one remove from its original source. This theory provided American literary history with the radical opposite of Poe's emphasis upon the calculated and careful arrangement of parts in an attempt to capture a beauty that is not part of man but that, on the contrary, is a realm from which man has been alienated.

Emerson proposed an emphasis, not on metres, but on the "metre making argument"[23] that makes the form inevitable; the beginning of every poem is "a thought so passionate and alive that like the spirit of a plant or animal it has an architecture of its own, and adorns nature with a new thing." Like many of Emerson's statements, this was hyperbole, an exaggeration of one of the two poles that together constitute the truth; he would himself employ conventional metres, rhythms, stanzaic patterns; but the emphasis upon passivity demonstrates the way in which an aesthetic doctrine is entangled with a thinker's basic convictions about what the universe means and what it is worth: Emerson's vision was that man is not a defiant giver of form; he is a participant in the form-giving proclivities of the cosmos; by putting himself in harmony with these powers, he makes himself capable of the harmonies of art.

One of the consequences of Emerson's beliefs, then, was that originality was stressed heavily. It follows from his doctrine that each age must have its own expression of primal energies. Another consequence was a conception of form that insisted that all beautiful and significant structure results not from the imposition of order from without but from a growth out of "inner necessities." The content of a poem, the functions of a building, the intuition of a painting will each determine and demand a form peculiar to its nature. The term latterly given to this view is *functionalism*; Emerson did not use the word; his contemporary, Horatio Greenough, came close to it when he wrote that beauty in architecture is the "promise of function."[24] Like Greenough, Emerson stressed the development of outward form from inner need; since the inner needs of every age are unique, it followed that there was a unique American art. Through his accent upon this uniqueness, Emerson pointed the artist's eye toward the present and the future: "Why need we copy the Doric or the Gothic model? Beauty, convenience, grandeur of thought and quaint expression are as near to us as any." In the same passage he indicated the kinds of "inner necessities" that compel the growth of outward form: "the climate, the soil, the length of the day, the wants of the people, the habit and form of the government." Studying these, "the American artist . . . will create a house in which all these will find themselves fitted, and taste and sentiment will be satisfied also."[25] "House" and "architecture" are used here as a metaphor representing the forms of art and art itself. In his essay on beauty, however, he turned to architecture specifically and said that "artistic embellishment is deformity" and "any real increase of fitness to its end is an increase of beauty."[26]

The doctrine of functionalism would prove appealing to the rational mind of the nineteenth century and would support its enthusiastic involvement with contemporary American developments in society and technology. Not so attractive would be the extent to which Emerson rescued the conception of mythology and fable from the low status to which Oliver Wendell Holmes and Mark Twain would relegate it. The rationalism of the Enlightenment threatened to impoverish mankind's rich emotional resource of the symbolic formulations of myth by regarding them simply as primitive superstition. For the "Fall of Man," Holmes's Autocrat of the Breakfast Table told his listeners, science substitutes the "Rise of Man"; for the myth of tragedy, man substitutes the reality of the triumph of science. A quite opposite attitude was the one that Emerson both practiced and preached, and by his example and doctrine he helped to keep the myth-making faculty alive. Myth, for Emerson, was not primitive lie but eternal and timeless truth. Yet his view of mythology was neither a retrospective nor a pessimistic, backward-looking devotion but a forward-looking one, completely consistent with, indeed supportive of, the American idea. While paying due respect to the fables of the past, using them for the source of his arguments in the essays and for the vital allusory force of many of his poems, Emerson also insisted that the capability of making myths was equally strong in the contemporary American artist and that the materials for these fables could be found as readily in American society.

His essays constantly displayed his indebtedness to mythology as insight into the truth of the value of the contemporary world. His conception of the need for the American scholar to be a whole, not a partial, man he derived from "one of those fables which out of an unknown antiquity convey an un-looked for wisdom."[27] The message of Christ, that he was God and could perform miracles, he told the listeners at the divinity school, had the truth of myth—that "God incarnates himself in man, and evermore goes forth anew to take possession of his World."[28] In describing the oneness of the good, the true, and the beautiful and the mystery of the total involvement of each with the others, he summarized the fundamental assertion of all mythologies: "the Universe has three children, born at one time, which reappear under different names in every system of thought." When he named his three mythologies, one of the three was the belief that constitutes the vital "myth" of the modern world: the scientific fable; science, he implied, has the same power and truth as the Christian and the Graeco-Roman myth: they are all concerned with the same unity in three-ness, whether the individual components be called "cause, operation and effect; or...Jove, Pluto, Neptune; or...the Father, the Spirit and the Son."[29]

Just as he fused ancient and modern philosophies through myth, so did Emerson show the unity of the poetry of all times by demonstrating its origin in religious ecstasies. Intoxication was what he sought: the divine inebriation of inspiration that created the individual symbols called poetry and the cultural symbols called myth. "Bring me wine," he cried, "but wine which never grew/In the belly of the grape." Wine, rather, that came from

> a nocturnal root,
> Which feels the acrid juice
> Of Styx and Erebus;
> And turns the woe of Night
> By its own craft, to a more rich delight.

Then with dramatic suddenness he fused the pagan with the Christian mythologies, telescoped the intervening centuries, and made past time one with the present with the quick, bitter statement: "We buy ashes for bread;/We buy diluted wine."

The wine, the poetry he called for, must be "Blood of the world,/Form of forms, and mould of statures." With the startling synthesis of sense perceptions that laced his prose, he flooded the world with the light of wine and then made it an infinity by allowing it to defy the ordinary laws of finite nature: "Wine that is shed/Like the torrents of the sun/Up the horizon walls." And then he returned to a fusion of pagan and Christian imagery by proclaiming the endlessly creative powers of poetry, which becomes the bread and wine of a new sacrament:

Water and bread,
Food which needs no transmuting,
Rainbow-flowering, wisdom-fruiting
Wine which is already man,
Food which teach and reason can.[30]

The Germanic mythologies in "Merlin," the Oriental mythologies in "Brahma," "Days," "Hamatreya" became materials for his art; by using them, he announced the possibilities of myth-making in America; and in his essay on "The Poet," he called for the "genius . . . with tyrannous eye" who would see the "value of our incomparable materials, and [see] in the barbarism and materialism of the times, another carnival of the same gods whose picture he so much admires in Homer." Commonplace, commercial, industrial America, he declared, rested "on the same foundations of wonder as the town of Troy and the temple of Delphi." With these germinal words, the American idea received its definitive expression of a romantic style suitable to the significance of the material world—a poetry that would use the things and forms of common perceptions to announce and celebrate the immanent meaning of our "stumps and their politics, our fisheries, our Negroes and Indians, our boasts and our repudiations, the wrath of rogues and the pusillanimity of honest men, the northern trade, the southern planting, the western clearing."[31] America was a poem in Emerson's eyes, and its idea was the structure of his reality. His symbolic style was a style to make effective the dominant symbols of his culture and not to create private symbols that would replace them.

2. Thoreau

The message that Emerson spoke to America was heard by Henry David Thoreau, and the emphasis that it placed upon the private individual was the feature of the Emersonian vision that Thoreau dramatized in his life and work. Several decades of revisionist criticism have attempted to cut Thoreau loose from Emerson and to demonstrate his independence, or even his revolt, from his master. Yet the attempt is futile, for Thoreau lived in Emerson's spiritual house as well as in his actual manse, and the book he made at Walden Pond stood on Emerson's ground just as surely as did the hut that he built there. Emerson's comments about his young friend in 1841 were just: "I told H.[enry] T.[horeau] that his freedom is in the form, but he does not disclose new matter. I am very familiar with all his thoughts,—they are my own quite originally drest."[32] The vigor and the inspiration, the fusion of the material world with the ideal, the merger of the practical and the visionary, the sense of confidence in man and his possibilities—these had been the legacy of Emerson to the American idea; the belief in a supralogical source of art, the functional relation of form to content, the use of natural images as symbols that are one with their spiritual meanings, and the conviction that the fable is a supremely powerful form of knowledge—these had been the aesthetic corollaries of Emerson's creed; both the creed and its corollaries formed the basis for the beliefs and the art of Thoreau.

Affirmation is the dominant tone of the books that form his principal legacy: *A Week on the Concord and Merrimack Rivers* and *Walden*. They are both, as he said of *Walden* in particular, "brags": not odes to dejection, but morning crows of a chanticleer. Their essential matter is the sounding of an everlasting "yea" to the meaning and value of man and nature. Thoreau's eye was on this world, not on the next; his gaze was the gaze of the visionary, even the mystic; but it was Emerson's peculiar brand of mysticism, not Plato's and certainly not Jonathan Edwards's. "One world at a time," he murmured on his deathbed, when he was asked to prepare himself for the next. He found fault with the New Testament for its otherworldliness: "There are various tough problems yet to solve, and we must make shift to live, betwixt spirit and matter, such a human life as we can."[33] With this conviction about the essential value of physical experience, Thoreau quite naturally found a literary mode that used the natural image in the same way that Emerson depicted the embodiment of spiritual reality. Indeed, his mission in art and in life was to press as close as possible to physical reality—to wedge his feet downward through the effluvia to the hard bedrock of the physical fact and to report this experience in the perception of the real with loving and reverent detail, so that others would be persuaded to join him in similar confrontations with reality.

For Thoreau as for Emerson, the important physical facts were those of nature—that part of the universe that is not changed or added to by man. For the physical fact of man himself and for all his works—his family, his agriculture, his politics, his society—Emerson had a theoretically equal reverence, for they could be symbolic of spiritual transcendence: the railway, he observed, is as significant for poetry as the spider's web. In theory, Thoreau agreed. "There is more religion in men's science than there is science in their religion," he wrote and added: "Let us make haste to the report of the committee on swine."[34] Yet Thoreau possessed a deep strain of asceticism that made him recoil with physical revulsion from the flesh—his own and others—and caused him, often against his conscious will, to reject not only the institutions of men but their physical presence as well. In this area of the physical world, he was purely Platonic; in his treatment of human love and friendship, he therefore looked beyond the physical and saw the body and its involvements, not as symbols, but as emblems of a higher spiritual reality. He regarded sex not as an Emersonian symbol—as real and as valuable as the spiritual—but as an Edwardian emblem: that is, as an inferior and debased lust, a paltry shadow of a far greater spiritual reality. Even friendship, his ideal of human relations, was always that—an ideal. The universal that he sought in other men and women was the soul, not their fleshly selves. Sometimes his rejections were violent; he could not spare his moonlight and his mountains for the best of men he was likely to get in exchange. "Often," he said, "I would rather undertake to shoulder a barrel of pork and carry it a mile than take into my company a man";[35] or "wherever a man goes, men will pursue and paw him with their dirty institutions."[36] He disliked his own body and called it "sickly and sluggish."[37] He wondered if "chivalry and knight errantry" did not "suggest or point to another relation to woman other than leads to marriage."[38] In describing the inferiority of agriculture to hunting, he said of the hunter and the gardener, "There is something vulgar and foul in the latter's closeness to his mistress, something noble and cleanly in the former's distance."[39]

Feeling this ascetic revulsion from the body of man, Thoreau recoiled from bodies of men—from the familial and the social group. The domestic scene of poor John Field and his "brave wife" with her "round greasy face and bare breast"[40] caused him to flee across the meadow, where he received his mystical vision of the need for untrammeled and irresponsible wildness: as he "ran down the hill toward the reddening west," he heard his Good Genius tell him with "faint tinkling sounds" to "fish and hunt far and wide day by day."[41] Repelled by the family, he was even more repulsed by the social organization: for him the village was organized principally to abuse the individual, for its houses were "so arranged as to make the most of mankind, in lanes and fronting one another, so that every traveller had to run the gauntlet, and every man, woman, and child might get a lick at him."[42] The political state, he felt, "can hardly be said to have any existence whatever. It is unreal, incredible and insignificant."[43]

This ascetic reaction away from society accounted for his restriction to the wild and the natural and his solitary involvement with it. He could not become the lover of all things, of all physical facts, that Whitman would be. Although he would occasionally pay lip service to the value of the mechanical, he hated the machine, and he could not take the railroad and the printing press into his range of admiration as potential embodiments of spiritual truth. He did, however, perform a series of symbolic acts of self-reliance for all mankind and described these acts in a prose so spare and lean, and yet so full of implication, that his acts, and the two books that best described them, would become testaments to the meaning and value of the individual, to the significance of the immediate physical world, and to the possibilities of man if he will accept the rhythms of nature as the rhythms of his life. While he was skeptical of material progress, he wrote a persuasive work on man's ability to find a way of life that would realize his capacities. He gave eloquent support to one-half of the basic premise of the American idea while redirecting the other half—the belief in progress—away from a concern with progress in the technological control of nature and toward a concern with progress in the spiritual realization of the individual.

He went to Walden to make himself into a transcendental symbol, not by expanding outward to all humanity—his asceticism would not allow such a democracy of physical contact—but by contracting the universe down to Walden Pond, by following his own exhortation to "simplify, simplify."[44] He created in his description of his stay at Walden a transcendental New World epic, with himself as the hero and with the scene a small pond an hour's walk from Concord. For if Emerson were right—and Thoreau was sure he was—as a solitary single man he was as important and as significant as a race, and his pond was spiritually the size of any ocean or any sea that had spawned the peoples whose exploits were sung in the ancient lays. The daily life he led, his "economy," was as significant as the complex civilizations that grew up by those other bodies of water. His founding of his society of "one" was as important an event as the inception of "Rome or Greece, Etruria or Carthage, or Egypt or Babylon."[45]

These had been the scenes of other, earlier epics to which Walden or A Week on the Concord and Merrimack Rivers, he said, should not be considered qualitatively different or inferior. What if we cannot read these ancient names on our cliffs? he asked; "are our cliffs bare? . . . What though the traveler tell us of the ruins of Egypt, are we so sick or idle that we must sacrifice our America and to-day to some man's ill-remembered and indolent story? Carnac and Luxor are but names . . . Carnac! Carnac! here is Carnac for me."[46] Walden Pond, he wrote, was perhaps already in existence "on that spring morning when Adam and Eve were driven out of Eden." He wondered "in how many . . . literatures" it "has been the Castilian Fountain."[47] Its water, he suggested, "is mingled with the sacred water of the Ganges," its vapors are "wafted past the site of the fabulous islands of Atlantis and the Hesperides," and its ice "melts in the tropic gales of the Indian seas, and is landed in ports of which Alexander only heard the names."[48]

At this site the transcendental hero, a man simple enough to be universal, set up his civilization, not by rejecting society, but by selecting from its institutions only those that he found vital. The ruling metaphor is economic: the pond's shore, he said, is "a good place for business, not solely on account of the railroad and the ice trade . . . ; it is a good port and a good foundation. No Neva marshes to be filled."[49] He erected his capitol there, with neighbor Seeley, an Irishman, looking on. "He was there to represent spectatordom, and help make this seemingly insignificant event one with the removal of the gods of Troy."[50] There by the banks of Walden, the new civilization faced the problems of all cultures. First the meeting of physical necessities: food, clothing, shelter; and then the problems of economics: the costs of labor—the relation between what a thing costs to produce and what it can be marketed for. After these had been provided, they in turn gave the occasion for discussions of the principles upon which their healthful and efficient state might be established, principles summarized by his call for radical simplicity and the functional adaptation of forms to inner purpose. Then the higher and more abstract concerns of cultures were discussed: its philanthropies, in which Thoreau, as an individualist, was totally uninterested; its philosophies; its art; then its amusements; and finally its social life, which, for him, consisted in making one more place around his fire. "I had three chairs in my house; one for solitude, two for friendship, three for society."[51]

This account of his founding of a civilization takes up the first six sections of Walden. As with most epics, there would be twelve parts; so Thoreau devoted eleven sections more, from "The Bean-Field" to "Spring," to a recapitulation of the first year of his stay by the pond; by reducing his actual sojourn to this yearly cycle, from spring to spring, he elevated the time into the cycle of the optimistic transcendantalist—of life dying to be reborn into new life. He started with the planting and cultivation of the beans in June ("The Bean-

Field"), went on through their months of summer growth and their later summer harvesting ("The Village"), and then through the autumnal period of fising and hunting; September and October merge imperceptibly into late fall ("The Ponds," "Baker Farm," "Higher Laws," "Brute Neighbors"), when Thoreau, our demigod, is happiest, for, as he reported earlier, his genius stems from an earlier prehistory of man than that of his agrarian life. He feels freest when he can roam, hunt, fish, and observe the birds, the woodchuck, and the ants at his ease. The cold of late autumn makes it necessary for him to concern himself with the building of his chimney ("House-Warming"), and then the snows of winter hold the earth in suspense ("Former Inhabitants," "Winter Visitors," "Winter Animals," and "The Pond in Winter"); finally the spring, coming after its first rivulets have eaten into the sandy bank of a railway cut and have created a pulpy mass of convolutions, demonstrates the way the universe is rooted in the ugly horror of a gestation that is the necessary prelude to the glories of bodily and spiritual resurrection. "The grass flames up on the hillsides like a spring fire . . . as if the earth sent forth an inward heat to greet the returning sun." The mention of grass looks forward to another transcendentalist's use of this particular humble object as the great physical representation of the spiritual: "the symbol of perpetual youth, the grass-blade, like a long green ribbon, streams from the sod into the summer . . . lifting its spear of last-year's hay with the fresh life below."[52]

To summarize the narrative is deceptive, for the movement of the work is not a flow but an imperceptible merging of one season with the next. At any time, as is true in the passage of the year and of life, we are never quite aware of the exact moment, the point when spring becomes summer, summer becomes fall, autumn becomes winter; we are never certain when the past becomes the present, the present becomes future; there is an enlarged sense of leisure, of time treated as an object in space, around which the observer may and should loaf and loiter. The sense of large leisure helps to give the work a feeling of timeless existence—the eternity of mythology. Thoreau was like the artist of Kouroo, whose parable is told in the last section of *Walden*: "As he made no compromise with Time," Thoreau wrote of the Hindu craftsman, "Time kept out of his way."[53] Like the artisans of India, Thoreau fashioned a timeless symbol; the Indian artist's medium was wood, his was words; but both had worked carefully and therefore had constructed a symbol of a natural fact; it was therefore a symbol of a spiritual fact; by transcendental algebra the result equalled eternity.

Walden was Thoreau's principal contribution to the romantic invigoration of the American idea. Its force lay in its affirmation of the near, the immediate, the native. At the feet of modern man lay the world—ready to be explored and to be used for his spiritual evolution. The world is no show, no delusion, no web of ambiguities. At its root is simple reality: the reality of rocks, waters, woods, seasons—yes—and the fundamental tools of civilization. Man's mission is to engage this reality; there is always the awareness that the world's value lies in its spiritual life, that the universe is fundamentally "the outward and visible type" of the world of the spirit. Unlike Edwards's types and emblems—physical realities—life itself, as ordinary men may live it, is the *only* embodiment of the spirit. To confront this spirit in its only possible form, Thoreau went to the woods: "to front only the essential facts of life" and not "to practice resignation . . . to live deep and suck out all the marrow of life, to live so sturdily and Spartan-like as to put to rout all that was not life."[54] He wished to teach his fellow countrymen to savor and cherish the reality that was their common existence. "Why should we live with such a hurry and waste of life?"[55] He wanted men to face facts, not to look through them or beyond them. There is, he implied, in the outer world a hard basis of truth that is the foundation of all living, and he called upon us to take our positions with him and "work and wedge our feet downward through the mud and slush of opinion, and prejudice, and tradition, and delusion, and appearance . . . through poetry and philosophy and religion, till we come to a hard bottom and rocks in place, which we can call *reality*."[56]

Walden provided the basis for a radical optimism—a conviction of the meaning and value of the physical world. Despite Thoreau's misanthropy, his words contained the second necessary ingredient of the idea of progress: a belief in the possibilities of man. He rested this belief upon a variation of the romantic conviction of the essential value of the natural being—for "goodness," read "power"; Thoreau believed in the ordinary man's power of improvement through his own efforts. Not for him was the determinism and sense of original sin of the Puritans nor the sense of futility of Poe and Melville. Instead he had the conviction, the optimistic romantic conviction, that ordinary man was fundamentally capable of reaching the goal of a rich life.

The typically American confidence in youth, and belief in the child and the childlike, is a product of belief in the essential power of nature, for the child is nearer to the divine origins; his instincts have the touch of this divinity; we can trust them and cultivate them. Thoreau reinforced his culture's belief in youth. "It is because the old and the weak feel their mortality," he wrote, "and think they have measured the strength of man" that they cling to outworn patriotisms and religions. "The prospect of the young," on the other hand, "is forward and unbounded, mingling the future with the present."[57] His favorite visitor to Walden was a simple, Homeric woodchopper whom nature made with "a strong body and contentment for his portion . . . that he might live out his threescore years and ten a child."[58] Of all the participants in his adventure at Walden, "girls and boys and young women" were the most successful lovers of the wilderness; the failures were "young men who had ceased to be young" and the "old and infirm and the timid."[59] In an Emersonian approval of originality and a rejection of tradition and convention, he called originality "the divinest thing," labelled tradition and received opinions the "old clothes" of God with which adults made scarecrows for children, and asked, "When will they come nearer to God than in these very children?"[60] Convinced of the value of the individual and of the goodness of natural man, Thoreau wrote his masterwork to prove the ability of common men to master their fates. His self-reliance was offered as testimony to the truth that "it is very rare that you meet with obstacles in this world which the humblest man has not faculties to surmount."[61] His experience at Walden is offered as a "brag," not only for his own accomplishments, but as a crow of triumphant possibilities for all men. "I learned this, at least, by my experiment; that if one advances confidently in the direction of his dreams, and endeavors to live the life which he has imagined, he will meet with a success unexpected in common hours."[62]

"The life" that man could and should imagine is not a life of return to savagery and actual primitive innocence. It is a return to the primal sanities that can be found in any mode of existence. *Walden*, as we have seen, was not a book about the barbaric but a book about civilization—the civilization of one man by the shores of his waterway, the Tigris-Euphrates or the Nile of transcendental America. It was a civilization complete with economy, commerce, agriculture, the arts. An actual return to primitive existence might be possible but undesirable: "it is certainly better to accept the advantages, though so dearly bought, which the invention and industry of mankind offer."[63] While he might long for wildness and yearn for a "New Hampshire everlasting and unfallen," Thoreau knew that for mankind in general, and even for himself, this longing was not a prescription for action but rather an emotion that every man-made civilization must account for. His purpose was to make a symbolic gesture for all men, a gesture that says to all Americans: this is what you are capable of; you can apply this lesson to your own life; you can make a success of your own existence. *Walden*, like Franklin's *Autobiography*, was a success story—the story of a profitable and successful venture in living, offered, like Franklin's story of his career, to show how other men might profit from one man's experiment in the confrontation with life.

The symbolic, rather than the literal, nature of his experiment was confirmed by a telling passage at the beginning of *Walden*, where Thoreau indicated that the method he had used to plumb the depths of reality was not to be taken as a universal mode: "I do not mean to prescribe rules to strong and valiant natures . . . nor to those who find their encouragement and inspiration in precisely the present conditions of things, and cherish it with the fondness and enthusiasm of lovers." Then he added a phrase that demonstrates his fundamental affirmation of life and defines his quarrel with the world as a lover's quarrel: "To some extent," he said, "I reckon myself in this number."[64]

This basic affirmation found its expression in Thoreau's style. Quick to point out spiritual and psychological meanings of physical objects—the owl as representative of our dark thoughts, the pond as evidence of infinity, the leaf of grass as the resurrection—he nevertheless treated these meanings as *extensions* of the intrinsic significance of natural things, not as substitutes for the things themselves. He demonstrated his reverence for objective reality by describing every vein of a leaf, every marking of a bird, every motion of a woodchuck. The physical universe was for him, as for Emerson, symbol and not emblem.

The most famous of his naturalist's passages—the battle of the ants—illustrated this affirmatively symbolic view of the physical world. The method of description Thoreau used in this instance was the metaphorical interplay between the world of man and the world of insect. We might pause for a moment to remember the smallness of the amount of existence granted the insect by Jonathan Edwards and how at a crucial juncture he humiliated man by comparing him to this low object on the scale of being. The movement of Thoreau's metaphor was precisely in the opposite direction. The ants were elevated to the status of men—men of epic greatness. He called them "legions" or "myrmidons"; a single ant who came into the fray was sent there by his Spartan mother who bade him "return with his shield or upon it"; or, perhaps, Thoreau mused, "he was some Achilles, who had nourished his wrath apart, and had now come to avenge or to rescue his Patroclus." There was not a fight in the history of Concord, Thoreau suggested whimsically, "that will bear a moment's comparison with this, whether for numbers engaged in it, or for the patriotism and heroism employed," and "the results of this battle will be as important and memorable to those whom it concerns as those of the battle of Bunker hill, at least." He never learned the outcome of the struggle but was as one whose feelings had been "excited and harrowed by witnessing the struggle, the ferocity and carnage, of a human battle before my door."[65]

Much of this had the tone of the mock-heroic, of course,

and its exaggeration suggested a satire of human pretensions. Yet its major tone was good-humored respect and reverence, a comic affirmation of the transcendentalist's conviction that the common is as important as the rare, that the small is as significant as the immense, that the grain of sand contains the universe, and that a mouse is a miracle. Instead of belittling man by showing him to be the same stuff as meaningless insects, Thoreau elevated the insects by showing them to be the same stuff as man; through this comparison, and the direction in which it moves, he demonstrated the significance of the entire range of organic existence. Just as the ant is equal to the man, so is the man equal to the universe; thus one man's residence by a pond for one of the earthly cycles can be the equivalent of the eternal cosmic drama of birth, death, and resurrection.

Ants, woodchucks, flowers—these were areas of imagery generally congenial to the Emersonian poet; but in the transcendental vision railroads, banks, and tariffs have equal spiritual resonance. Thoreau's use of imagery derived from the world of business and industry is evidence of his divided commitments to the progress of civilization. Emotionally attracted to the wilderness and to man's prehistoric savage nature on the one hand, he was committed, on a more conscious and rational level, to every simple, healthy environment that man has made and to the instruments that he invented to make that environment better.

The reconciliation of these two attitudes provided a basis for the philosophy of *Walden*—a civilization must be constructed that will use and promote, not suppress and deny, the instincts of man. This doubleness permeated Thoreau's style, in which metaphors drawn from the technical advances of nineteenth-century civilization are a principal source of imagery. The machine as an end in itself is hateful; the machine subordinated to man and his nature is acceptable. Obsession with getting and spending is an abomination, but useful commerce is a blessing. Thoreau reported how he once read some scraps of newspaper in an abandoned mountain cabin; it seemed to him "that the advertisements, or what is called the business part of a paper, were greatly the best, the most useful, natural, and respectable." In contrast to the editorial columns, the commercial sections were "more closely allied to nature, and were respectable in some measure as tide and meteorological tables are . . . commerce is really as interesting as nature."[66]

This hardheaded approach of the Yankee peddler was continually made evident in his style. Walden was "a good place for business." He determined "to go into business at once, and not wait to acquire the usual capital." He wished to transact "some private business with the fewest obstacles." He could succeed, he knew, with "a little enterprise and business talent." He had always tried to acquire "strict business habits; they are indispensable to every man." He did not wish to live what was not life, for "living is so dear."[67] He would keep a ledger book of income and outgo and would think it proper that this careful accounting be given its due place in his art.

The mechanical was the source of more ambivalent feelings than the commercial; and this ambivalence found its expression in quite opposite modes of metaphor. On the one hand Thoreau often evoked the machine as the image of heartless, regimented, constricted society: "I am not responsible for the machinery of society," he said in his essay on "Civil Disobedience." In calling for passive resistance, he asked that our lives be "counter friction to stop the machine."[68] In general, his images tended to spring out of his underlying discomfort with technology: "Every machine . . . seems a slight outrage against universal laws." Although there was no possibility that Thoreau would express much of Emerson's conviction that the machines of men could range instantly on the same eternal laws that govern the spider's web, there was, nevertheless, in the disciple no outright rejection of the mechanical but rather an emphasis on the deep need to subordinate it to other and greater considerations. "Even a greater than this physical power [of the machine] must be brought to bear upon that moral power." In its rightful place the machine could serve; it could not only serve humanity in general, it could also serve the artist by supplying a comparison that would bring home to the reader the sense of the sturdiness, reliability, and strength of the natural universe. When he wished to describe the precision and dedication that should accompany man's every act, he first used a comparison drawn from handicraft: "Drive a nail home and clinch it so faithfully that you can wake up in the night and think of your work with satisfaction." And then he extended the metaphor from craft to industry by finishing his paragraph with a reference to the machine as a representation of strength and endurance: "Every nail driven should be as another rivet in the machine of the universe."[69]

His treatment of the railroad in *Walden* was a summary of this ambivalence toward the machine—an underlying feeling of antipathy combined with a conscious acceptance of its significance and value. In the midst of a passage describing the circling hawk, the "tantivy" of wild pigeons, the mink, the bending sedge, he introduced the sound of the train: "for the last half-hour I have heard the rattle of railroad cars"; then followed a telling comparison that implied an acceptance of this symbol of modern technology into the continuum of significant physical facts: "now dying away and then reviving like the beat of a partridge." The sound of the engine was the soothing call "concord." Then the attitude changed; the whistle of the locomotive penetrated his woods "like the scream of a hawk." A feeling of breathless discomfort accompanied the series of descriptions of the despoiling of the country for the needs of the city and the return of commodities from the city to the farm.

Then another change in attitude: this unpleasantness was succeeded by an Emersonian description of the engine as a magnificent addition to the imaginative, as well as the physical, life of man; it became a "travelling demigod," a "cloud-compeller," who would "ere long take the sunset sky for the livery of his train." When he heard the "iron horse with his snort like thunder," it seemed "as if the earth had got a race now worthy to inhabit it." The key word here was "seems," and he repeated it ironically; if only all were as it seems, if only man used the machine for noble ends, if only "the cloud that hangs over the engine were the perspiration of heroic deeds . . . if the enterprise were as heroic and commanding as it is protracted and unwearied!"

After this negative assessment, however, a positive attitude returned: "Have not men improved somewhat in punctuality

since the railroad was invented? . . . We live steadier for it."
He was impressed by the "enterprise and bravery" of the
men who worked on the road; he found that "commerce is
unexpectedly confident and serene, alert, adventurous, and
unwearied. It is very natural in its methods withal, far more
so than many fantastic enterprises and sentimental experiments." When he saw the cattle train, however, and observed
"a carload of drovers, too, in the midst, on a level with their
droves now," he felt that the "pastoral life is whirled past
and away," and he crossed the tracks "like a cart-path in the
woods." He would not have his "eyes put out and . . . ears
spoiled by its smoke and steam and hissing."[70]

The railroad reappeared at the end of *Walden* in a quite
different circumstance; but in this changed capacity it also
demonstrated Thoreau's combination of distaste and acceptance: emotional rejection and intellectual acceptance of its
place in the total organic scheme of things. Its treatment here
demonstrates, too, the extent of Thoreau's optimism. Before
the coming of true spring, he observed the action of the thaw
upon the sides of a deep cut made by the railroad. Instead of
a sentimental moan over the despoliation of nature by the
machine, he made the startling admission: "Few phenomena
gave me more delight than to observe the forms which
thawing sand and clay" assume on the sides of the railroad
embankment. Then he wrote a description of the slow ooze
of the colored sands through the snow and frost, "making
heaps of pulpy sprays" that remind the observer of human
and animal organs, "of brains or lungs or bowels," and of
"excrements of all kinds." The grotesque sight, the "heaps
of liver, lights, and bowels" was a "phenomenon more ex-
hilarating" to him than the fertility of vineyards. They were
final proofs that there is nothing inorganic in nature, that
man and the things made by man are absorbed into one
continuum of being. The final metaphor of the passage was a
triumphant affirmation of the place, the subordinate but
secure place, of the mechanical and the man-made in relation
to nature. Nature is compared to a giant furnace. The "folia-
ceous heaps" along the bank are likened to the slag of the
smelter, evidence that "Nature is 'in full blast' within." The
works of man are small and inferior but not inconsequential.

"You may melt your metals and cast them in the most beautiful moulds you can; they will never excite me like the forms which this molten earth flows out into." Then he concluded with an affirmation of the capacity of man to shape his environment just as the natural world is shaped by a superior power: not only the forms of earth "but the institutions upon it are plastic like clay in the hands of the potter."[71]

He had taken a scar on the face of his beloved land and had converted it into a symbol of the unbroken continuity between the organic and the inorganic, the man-made and the natural. He similarly used the grotesque forms of the first thaw—the apparent ugliness of the excremental—as an illustration of the stuff from which comes the true spring, sending its green glories—"its symbol of perpetual youth, the grass blade"—streaming into the summer. Death—the death of winter, the apparent decay of pulpy waste—he converted into life and beauty, and his prose poem became an epic hymn to the triumph of man and the human spirit: "So our human life but dies down to its root, and still puts forth its green blade to eternity."[72] His experiment in living had been a success. Having proven by the experiment that man can confidently move in the direction of his dreams, he left his story at the end of the first year's cycle—at the moment of the conquest of death by life, of the winter by the spring. He constantly reminded us in taking his leave that his experiment must not be seen as a prescription and a call to literal action but as a symbol of the possibilities open in quite different ways to every man: "If you are chosen town clerk, forsooth, you cannot go to Tierra del Fuego this summer; but you may go to the land of infernal fire nevertheless."[73] He continues in this same grimly humorous but deeply earnest vein: "How long . . . would a man hunt giraffes if he could? Snipes and woodcocks also may offer rare sport; but I trust it would be nobler game to shoot one's self." The Walden of everyman is within as well as without; each man can order his life so that he confronts the realities of the world about him and knows his own inner largeness; each can be "a Columbus to whole new continents and worlds"[74] within himself. In this confrontation with reality, the external world is no shadow or delusion but a reality both in its own right and as the means by which inner realities can be objectified and perceived. The epic hero of *Walden* discovered this truth through the adventures of his year; his experiment in knowing reality and in understanding the place of man in nature was a success; but his crow of triumphant affirmation, his book called *Walden*, is not one of egotism but a symbol of the potential triumph of all men: "I brag for humanity rather than for myself."[75]

3. Whitman

Magnificent as it was, Thoreau's brag was almost reticent compared to that of a poet from Long Island who sent Emerson copies of his privately printed first volume of poems in 1855. Walt Whitman's *Leaves of Grass* seemed to Thoreau, as it seemed to Emerson, "very brave and American";[76] Thoreau quite naturally was "not disturbed by any brag or egotism in his book." Emerson went further and saluted Whitman at the beginning of a great career that, he predicted, would lead to the writing of great American poetry. Whitman became, and has remained, the poet of American affirmation, a veritable prophet for men like William James who would come to regard him as the supreme contemporary example of "healthy-mindedness." Whitman, like Emerson, took the American idea and gave it the vitality of a religious faith; like Emerson, whose dictates he followed with a faithfulness that was his only deviation from the Emersonian creed, he contributed to the intuitive and emotional supports that any conviction about the significance and value of the material world must have if it is to endure. Furthermore, he gave the American idea what Emerson and Thoreau were constitutionally unable to provide: the foundation in a spirit of democratic love whose most convincing symbol is the physical union between human bodies. The life-giving power of sex was introduced into American literature by this monumental maker of monumental verse, and it was introduced in an artwork that, like Thoreau's, would attempt to create a transcendental symbol of one man who would represent all Americans and all mankind. Thoreau, however, had created his symbol by a process of narrowing and simplifying—of reducing all human experience to the experience of one man as he worked his feet down to the bedrock of reality at Walden Pond. Whitman moved in the opposite direction; he created a man out of words, a demigod who would expand outward in endless complexity and complication to include his nation, his world, and his cosmos.

The necessary ingredients for this kind of aspiration were already there in Walt Whitman before he heard Emerson. From his devoutly Quaker mother and from her favorite preacher, Elias Hicks, he derived his deep sense of the inner spirit and of the essentially spiritual nature of the universe; from his father and from the atmosphere of his newspaper office, he received the influence of Paine and Jefferson with their insistence upon the salvation of man's spirit through democracy, reason, and progress. This same combination had also formed the mind of Emerson, who had blended the two streams of thought with German and Oriental idealism into a religion for Americans in general and into an aesthetic for the American artist in particular. In 1842 Whitman heard Emerson lecture on poetry and called it "one of the richest and most beautiful compositions, both for its matter and style, we have heard anywhere."[77] This was undoubtedly the lecture that was published soon after as "The Poet," an essay that provided the key to almost everything Whitman became and to almost everything he wrote.

It gave a sketch of the total personality Whitman presented to the world in the second half of the century. The dress and manner he assumed may well have been adapted from the picture of the Christ-like vagabond portrayed in a contemporary French novel,[78] but the character was drawn from Emerson's description of the kind of man the poet should be. The essay was the reason for Whitman's withdrawal from the getting and spending of commercial society: "Thou shalt leave the world," Emerson told the poet—Whitman was sure he was speaking to him—"and know the muse only . . . God wills also that thou abdicate a manifold and duplex life."[79] Emerson described the attitude the American poet should strike: "Doubt not, O poet, but persist. Say 'It is in me, and shall out.'"[80] Whitman obediently said, *"Walt you contain enough, why don't you let it out then?"*[81] For he knew he must "permit to speak out at every hazard,/Nature without check with original energy."[82] Emerson asked for the advent of a "genius . . . with tyrannous eye,"[83] and Whitman took all of the universe into his compendious vision: "I skirt sierras, my palms cover continents."[84] This genius, said Emerson, must not conform to ordinary custom or bow to popular approval: "Thou must pass for a fool and a churl for a long season";[85] Whitman agreed and reemphasized: "I wear my hat as I please indoors or out."[86]

Even more important than the definition of the American poet's pose was Emerson's articulation of his religion; and in the formulations of the sage of Concord, Whitman found the summary of that fusion between the Enlightenment and Quaker mysticism that had been his dual heritage. The fusion lay in Emerson's conception of the material world as a symbol of the spiritual and therefore as the primary object of the poet's attention—the sole embodiment of the spirituality that is his ultimate goal and the ultimate object of his aspiration. With this statement in his ears, Whitman could write:

I will make the poems of materials, for I think they
     are to be the most spiritual poems,
And I will make the poems of my body and of mortality,
For I think I shall then supply myself with the poems
     of my soul and of immortality.[87]

Emerson had declared that the poet knew the world only through his intuition, which spoke freely and somewhat wildly. Whitman took all things of the world as "hints"; he took them and accepted them but always was leaping swiftly "beyond" them in order to "nearer bring."[88] "No shutter'd room . . . can commune with me," he wrote. "But roughs and little children better than they."[89] When Whitman "heard the learn'd astronomer" and saw the "proofs" and "the figures" and heard the attempts to know the mystery of the stars through rational analysis, he reported:

How soon unaccountable I became tired and sick,
Till rising and gliding out I wander'd
     off by myself,
In the mystical moist night-air, and from
     time to time,
Look'd up in perfect silence at the stars.[90]

This was Whitman's acquiescence both to the Emersonian belief in the symbolic nature of the material universe and to Emerson's conviction that it could be known only through a transcendent intuition. Furthermore, Whitman agreed with Emerson that this is a totally good universe in which all evil can be understood as part of total beneficence. He ended his summary of his postures and beliefs, *Song of Myself*, with a halting recollection of what he had learned in his mystical transports: "It is not chaos or death—it is form, union, plan—it is eternal life—it is Happiness."[91] This view of the universe as totally good led him quite inevitably to a tone of triumphant optimism: "Of Life immense in passion, pulse, and power,/Cheerful, for freest action form'd under the laws divine,/The Modern Man I sing."[92]

The world of Whitman, it is evident, was an Emersonian world, and Whitman's mission was to convert Emerson's theories into poetic practice. The differences between the two imaginations were all of degree rather than of kind, but the differences were large nevertheless; in a variety of ways they constitute a substantial enlargement of the range and power of American imaginative optimism. Emerson asked that the American poet take account of both the natural and man-made aspects of his world and that he see the possibilities of "the barbarism and materialism" of the times as well as "the incomparable materials" of social and civic developments. "America is a poem in our eyes; its ample geography dazzles the imagination, and it will not wait long for metres," [93] he told America from the platform and through the pages of his essays. "We do not," he admitted in honest self-appraisal, "with sufficient plainness or profoundness address ourselves to life, nor dare we chaunt our own times and social circumstance."[94] His own poetry and prose, almost empty of attention to the urban aspects of American life, preferred the more usual romantic themes of the natural and the unspoiled.

Not so Whitman. Worshipping the prairies and the rivers and the ocean rolling in on Long Island's shores, he also affirmed the reality and significance of the city streets. In "Give Me the Splendid Silent Sun" he summarized the inclusiveness of his vision. Divided into two parts, it states the doubleness of the modern world: a world of nature and a world of civilization, a world of solitude and a world of society. "Give me the splendid silent sun," he began, "with all his beams full-dazzling,/Give me juicy autumnal fruit ripe and red from the orchard . . . /Give me solitude, give me Nature, give me again O Nature your primal sanities!" Although he asked for these untouched gifts of God, he still loved his city, and he therefore began his second series of demands with "Keep your splendid silent sun,/Keep your woods O Nature, and the quiet plains by the woods." The overstatement is calculated to redress the romantic imbalance. Whitman was far from rejecting the beauties and the healing powers of nature; rather, in his turning away, in his admonition that seems almost a rejection, he tends to exaggerate to make his point that the social facts that he will celebrate are no less important than the natural facts that had been, for a generation, almost the sole concern of poetry. He then called the roll of the urban realities that he must have and must celebrate:

Give me faces and streets—give me these phantoms
    incessant and endless along the trottoirs!
Give me interminable eyes—give me women—give me
    comrades and lovers by the thousand!

The "shores and wharves," the "theatre, bar-room, huge hotel," the "torchlight procession," the "dense brigade bound for the war"—he called for all of them so that he might make them part of himself through poetry, and he ended the poem with "Manhattan faces and eyes forever for me."[95]

Whitman extended Emerson's theory into practice, not only through his involvement with social facts, but through his willingness to follow one of Emerson's suggestions to its inevitable conclusion—to the use of the natural fact of sex as the supremely poetic symbol. If, as Emerson proclaimed, the natural facts are symbolic of spiritual facts, then the more commonplace, the more usual, facts are the most meaningful. If, as Emerson said and Whitman agreed, the concept of union—of the reconciliation of opposites by the transcendent One—is the supreme spiritual fact, then it surely and inevitably follows that the complete embodiment of the idea of spiritual union is the physical act that unites the sexes and gives us earthly evidence that the two become one, that death becomes life. Emerson hinted at this possibility. "The soul makes the body," he wrote and added, later in the essay, "All the facts of the animal economy, sex, nutriment, gestation, birth, growth, are symbols of the passage of the world into the soul of man."[96] The meanings of the universe, he said, will be revealed only to "a lover, a poet."[97] However, he and Thoreau were incapable of capturing the power of the sexual symbol for poetry.

Whitman was not only capable of capturing it—he made it one of the basic concerns of his verse. He not only specifically sang of "The Body Electric" and, in "Children of Adam" and the "Calamus" poems, of the "pent-up aching rivers" that merge in men and in women, but he used sex as a metaphor to describe every other kind of natural and human relation and experience. From the "leaves stiff or drooping in the fields"[98] to the ocean that "madly . . . pushes upon the land, /With love, with love"[99] the whole of nature is involved, in Whitman's vision, in a sexual union:

Smile O Voluptuous cool-breathed earth . . .
Far swooping elbow'd earth—rich apple-blossomed
    earth!
Smile, for your lover comes.[100]

The merging of the night sky, the "bare-bosom'd . . . mad naked summer night," with the "elbow'd earth" was seen as a consummated marriage; so was the coming of the daylight, perceived as the issue of the cosmic coupling of night and dawn:

Bridegroom night of love working surely and softly
    into the prostrate dawn,
Undulating into the willing and yielding day,
Lost in the cleave of the clasping and sweet-flesh'd
    day.[101]

And in *Song of Myself,* the poem that summarizes everything Whitman was or would try to do, when he described his passing into the mystical trance in which he would be enlarged successively to the dimensions of America, the universe, and God, the transport inevitably and rightly took the form of a sexual congress, of the body ravished by the soul:

I mind how once we lay such a transparent summer morning,
How you settled your head athwart my hips and gently
      turn'd over upon me,
And parted the shirt from my bosom-bone, and plunged
      your tongue to my bare-stript heart,
And reach'd till you felt my beard, and reach'd till
      you held my feet.[102]

The power of Eros was Whitman's contribution to the style of the American idea.

The rest of *Song of Myself* was a description of the successive stages of Whitman's expansion through the spatial and temporal universe until it became one with God. "Who touches this touches a man,"[103] Whitman wrote at the end of his *Leaves of Grass,* and by this transcendental formula he meant that whoever touched his book would also touch a Titan. For words, Emerson said, are one with things, things are one with the spirit that they body forth, and the individual soul is identical with God. To create, through words properly articulated, a human being who would therefore also be America and who would also be Man and therefore God—this was Whitman's conscious aim. He quite deliberately set out to do the impossible, to create for Americans their great mythological figure—"Walt Whitman, a kosmos, of Manhattan the son,"[104] taking "the exact dimensions of Jehovah."[105] He would try to do what had theretofore been the power of the folk mind alone—to create an American Christ, a John Henry or a Paul Bunyan, an entity that might, like all true myths, gather into itself all the aspirations of a race and give each individual of that aggregate a sense of the power he shares with the "liberating god." Such has always been the task of mythologies, and Whitman from the outset tried to make this his program: in his preface to the 1855 edition, he declared his desire to be "the age transfigured."[106] His was the frank ambition "to articulate and faithfully express in literary or poetic form, and uncompromisingly" his own "physical, emotional, moral, intellectual, and aesthetic Personality, in the midst of, and tallying, the momentous spirit and facts of its immediate days, and of current America —and to exploit that Personality."[107]

The whole of the *Leaves of Grass*—the more than six hundred poems that appeared in the nine editions that grew between 1855 and 1891—was the creation, in words, of a man who would "tally," or correspond to, "the momentous spirit and facts . . . of current America." Like Thoreau's man by the pond, this man was the triumphant summary of the possibilities of all men. He sang of himself, "a simple, separate person," and, according to the transcendental formula, by singing of himself he at the same moment uttered "the word Democratic, the word En-Masse." He chanted of "physiology from top to toe," but at the same time that he celebrated the limbs, the heart, the genitals, the bowels, he celebrated the soul, which is identical with these physical counterparts. His song of the "Modern Man" would be, therefore, a cheerful song, a song of "life immense in passion, pulse, and power."[108] Its cheerfulness would be not only an affirmation of the possibilities of his contemporary civilization, it would be as well an affirmation of the possibilities of an art for that society. When the phantom of the past pointed its finger at him and scornfully declared that only the battles of history are worth recording, he answered that he was the "Changer of Personality, outlining what is yet to be," projecting "history of the future."[109] In all things, then, Whitman was the poet of optimism and affirmation for whom Emerson had looked in vain in 1842 and whom he found embodied in all his robust substance in the pages of the slim volume sent to him in 1855.

The poems in that volume, and all the poems that Whitman would methodically add to that first core, were descriptions of the stages in his own spiritual and physical development transformed, as was Thoreau's work, into the description of the stages in the life of a god. *Song of Myself* was the summary poem, containing the germs of all the future developments of the American god, outlining everything this American hero would feel, would be, would become. Although it was untitled in the first edition that Emerson read, it was given the name "A Poem of Walt Whitman, An American" in the second version (1856) and in 1860, simply "Walt Whitman."

When it finally received its present title in 1881, it had received several internal additions calculated to make it entirely clear that the creation of one man's life would try to be the creation of all men's lives. In this edition, which gave the poem its permanent name, he added at the very beginning the phrases:

Born here of parents born here from parents the
     same, and their parents the same,
I, now thirty-seven years old in perfect health begin,
Hoping to cease not till death.[110]

And, in a similar attempt to make the poem's identification with the One who becomes All, he added, in the first edition to appear after the Civil War, allusions to the "fratricidal strife" of which, of course, he could not have been aware in 1855.

To construct through words, and the images aroused by words, a being who, when properly seen, encompasses the reader, all men, and the physical and spiritual universe—no less than this is the astounding pretension of this germinal poem. Its theme is "The All," that Platonic plenitude that stretches from the lowest to the highest. The difference between Plato and Emerson lay in the latter's insistence upon the physical world as the sole symbol of the spiritual accessible to man; so Whitman's "All" stopped at the edge of the physical and the knowable; having captured this half of the "All" ("With the twist of my tongue I encompass worlds and volumes of worlds"), he would at that very moment capture the spiritual dimension as well; at every step of his expansion throughout the commonplace world of sensual experience, he reminded his audience that every physical fact he so lovingly described was "A scented gift and remembrancer designedly dropt,/Bearing the owner's name someway in the corners."[111] This immense program would not be fulfilled by any operation of the rational, analytical understanding; only the higher Reason, only the intuition as it freed itself from the confines and inhibitions of logical analysis, was capable of such a task. Emerson's moments of supreme knowledge arose from an experience in nature—from the ecstatic moment of complete vision at twilight on a winter's evening in

Boston Commons. Whitman's moment of vision—one that William James quoted as the best available description of the mystical moment—came through sexual ecstasy. As the soul ravished his body on a summer morning, the poet had his instantaneous apprehension of the eternal fitness of things and then proceeded to the expansion outward into the universe in what has been called an "inverted mystical experience." It was inverted because it is a successive assimilation and accretion of the flesh, the body, and the physical world in place of the traditional stages of mystical purification of spirit from the "dross" of the material.

What could be the "organic form" to contain such an argument? What could possibly be the structure that might embody the sense of, quite simply, everything? In terms of words, diction, image, Whitman tried to contain the conception of plenitude by using an amazing range and variety. The rhythms of the poem vibrate between the two extremes of English verse rhythms. They are sometimes prosaic with a general iambic movement but with such variation that they can be identified as poetry only because the lines do not come out to the margins:

The President holding a cabinet council is
    surrounded by the great Secretaries

or

The crew of the fish-smack pack repeated layers of halibut
    in the hold.[112]

Yet they are sometimes as highly artful as the dactyllic lines at the conclusion:

Failing to find me at first keep encouraged,
Missing me one place search another,
I stop somewhere waiting for you.[113]

In these bardic rhythms the succession of dactyls and trochees, with their insistent falling cadence, are varied in the last lines by substitution of two iambic feet—one at the beginning, the other at the end—so that the "you" is dramatically emphasized; the conclusion of the song thus emphasizes the universality with which the poem began. The "Song of

Myself"—rhythm as well as sense insists—is a poem of all men; at the end it fulfills the promise of the first lines: "what I assume you shall assume/For every atom belonging to me as good belongs to you."[114]

The language had similar variety; it ranged from "blab" and "dung" and "bowels" and flat descriptions like the "Yankee girl works with her sewing-machine or in the factory or mill"[115] to "vitreous pour of the full moon"[116] or to the imaginative and lovely image that summarizes Whitman's belief in the oneness of life and death—the description of the leaves of grass as "the beautiful uncut hair of graves."[117] The poem included in its characters the range of American people, from the prostitute with the bonnet bobbing "on her tipsy and pimpled neck"[118] to the president's lady; from the murderer, the Negro laborer, and the "venerealee" to the president. The plenitude of space was in it—from the "brown ants" and the "mossy scabs of the worm fence" to the galaxies; all time was there too—the moment of now and the depths of the past in which all the gods of men become telescoped and assimilated into the American god: he can "skirt sierras"; his "palms cover continents"; [119] he speeds through space; he takes upon himself the "exact dimensions of Jehovah,/Lithographing Kronos, Zeus his son, and Hercules his grandson."[120]

All of this was poured into the form that has been called a precise, although inverted, recapitulation of the seven stages of the classical mystical experience:[121] "Entry into the Mystical State, Awakening of Self, Purification of Self, Illumination and Dark Night of the Soul, Union in Faith and Love, Union in Perception, and Emergence." The poem's strict conformity to these formal stages is doubtful, and an attempt to fit the various stanzas into each stage comes up against the unyielding fact that many of the sections refuse to be so confined. Certainly, however, the first five stanzas constituted an entry into a trance, and the last three (50, 51, and 52) comprised an emergence: "Wrench'd and sweaty—calm and cool then my body becomes,/I sleep—I sleep long."[122] What intervened between these two sections was a rough, and not altogether consistent, description of the successive stages of the enlargement of the "I" of the poem through the physical and material universe (sections 8–32), then through the reaches of space and the depths of time (sections 33–40), and finally into the Oversoul when he becomes identical with God (40–49).

The poem began with the identification of the poet and the reader and in eleven more lines summarized the transcendental poise of the American artist who is qualified to ask fellows to accompany him on his cosmic journey. This artist starts with his own experience ("I, now thirty-seven years old in perfect health begin"),[123] for he has the conviction that the immediate, the near, the familiar, is the most universal. He is a thoroughly original personality ("Creeds and schools in abeyance"); his art will be a product of his passive acceptance of the primal impulses of nature ("I loafe and invite my soul. . . . I permit to speak at every hazard/Nature without check with original energy.") The next three sections provide the necessary preliminary preparations for the voyage that will soon take place. There is first the firm assertion of the importance of the senses, for only by the acceptance and the celebration of the body can knowledge be achieved. He describes his delight with the smells of the world ("Houses and rooms are full of perfumes"); with the ineffable feel of atmosphere, which is without palpable scent and yet which can intoxicate; with tactile sensations—tickling, respiration and inspiration; with sounds; with kinesthetic sensation ("a few embraces, a reaching round of arms"). This is the kind of man with whom we will "stop this day and night" and with whom we will "possess the good of the earth and sun." Then comes the declaration of other important attributes of this companion of ours—he is not only "gross" and "nude," as he will describe himself in a later section, but he is "hankering" as well; he is one who proclaims the fundamental importance of sex as the affirmation of the significance of the universe, which proves that "there was never any more inception than there is now," for there is "always the procreant urge of the world."

The greatest obstacle to the poet-seer of America will be the enervation of doubt and despair—the paralyzing fear, in the face of the realities of vice, disease, and death, that the universe may be either evil or meaningless; there first must be a confrontation of evil and tragedy before the poem that will be Man can be made. "Trippers and askers" surround the poet; sickness, battles, "the fever of doubtful news, the fitful events" must be acknowledged and then placed in their proper perspective: "These come to me days and nights . . . /But they are not the Me myself." He stands "apart from the pulling and hauling"; he will "witness and wait."

Then, purified, he is ready to receive his lover; his senses await the ravishment of his soul, a ravishment described in a literal act of physical union. At the moment of release, there is a surge of cosmic perception: "Swiftly arose and spread around me the peace and knowledge that pass all the argument of the earth." It begins with the enormous pulse of knowing "that the hand of God is the promise of my own" and subsides through a brief catalogue of the significant commonplace:

And limitless are leaves stiff or drooping in the
        fields,
And brown ants in the little wells beneath them,
And mossy scabs of the worm fence, heap'd stones,
        elder, mullein, and poke-weed.

After this experience of mystical union, the potential man-god can arise from the summer morning to start his progress through the world. The start is quiet but intensely significant, for it is with a child bearing the leaves of grass in its hands: the child, for Whitman as for Emerson and Thoreau, the vessel of goodness, and the leaves of grass, the humble, ubiquitous, and therefore inclusive symbol. Whitman turns the idea of the meaning of the grass over and over, until his attempts at discovering its meaning become a summary and explanation of the transcendental aesthetic mode. When the child fetches it to him and asks, *"What is the grass?"* he answers first that he does not know; he cannot "know" in the logical, analytical sense of cognition. He can only suggest its possible meanings, all of which it not only represents but is identical with. By the time he is finished, we have been made to feel the truth upon which his theory of art, as well as life, is based: in the physical fact we come as close to eternal truth as we can get. He gives a series of possible

"meanings" for the leaf of grass. It is an image of his optimism, "the flag of my disposition, out of hopeful green stuff
woven"; it is a symbol of God's presence, "the Handkerchief
of the Lord"; it is a symbol of rebirth and resurrection and of
eternal life, "the produced babe of the vegetation"; it is a
symbol of democracy, "a uniform hieroglyphic" that grows
"among black folks as among white." It is a symbol, finally,
of the reconciliation of death with life, "the beautiful uncut
hair of graves."

After this analysis of the method of symbolism, a method
for creating life out of words, for demonstrating the oneness
of the word with the thing, there is a reassertion of Whitman's identity with all he sees (section 7) and then a sequence of visions to depict the absorption into the poet of the
physical world of the immediate and the familiar. Although
the subsequent sections of the poem are a narrative of the
poet's journey into the cosmos, the method of development
within each section is often the presentation of a succession
of apparently unrelated images; the result is a total form that
can exist independently in space and that convinces the
reader that its parts do not follow each other in consecutive
fashion, with each part coming either before or after the
parts adjacent to it, but rather that all the parts exist together
and form an entity that he must perceive simultaneously,
totally, and completely. The term *spatial* has been used for
this kind of poetic form, and it has been claimed that it is
typical of modern art. Whitman used it as the organic form
for his vision of plenitude. It is an attempt to create out of an
essentially temporal medium (words) a form that then denies
its temporality and exists in space as a complete unity rather
than in time as a succession of parts. The series of images,
many of them widely separated in space and widely variant
in meaning, has none of the usual transitions between parts.
The result is a sequence of pictures flashing before the mind's
eye; accustomed as we are to literary images that are related
to each other by some logical device, we perceive these unrelated pictures as existing simultaneously, just as the multitu-
dinous events and facts of actuality exist simultaneously, and
we take these unrelated pictures as together making up a
world.

The technique is that of a twentieth-century art—the motion picture—and there goes under the name of *montage*. In the motion picture a series of images, flashed on the screen without the usual transitions of "fade in" and "fade out," is accepted as occurring at precisely the same time, as having a concurrent existence. A historian of the motion picture has suggested that this fidelity to the surface of reality, and to the apparently unconnected events of actuality, is the same kind of expression of faith that lay behind Whitman's earlier use of the technique of montage in poetry. After describing how the true film "clings to the surface of things," Siegfried Kracauer observes: "Perhaps our condition is such that we cannot gain access to the elusive essentials of life unless we assimilate the seemingly non-essential? Perhaps the way today leads from, and through, the corporeal to the spiritual? And perhaps the cinema helps us to move from 'below' to 'above'?"[124] In poetry this cinematic technique of montage is not sufficient by itself to compel a belief in the value of the world of perception. Linked to an imagery of weirdness or surrealism or to a style in which images of the tawdry commonplace are joined to images of a richer past, as in *The Waste Land*, the technique of montage can be an effective evocation of despair. However, used with images drawn from common life and treating these images with warmth and reverence, the technique is a marvelously effective means of communicating both the actuality of the immediate human experience and its meaning and value.

So in section 8 Whitman begins his montage. Sometimes the images are fragments of vision: "The little one sleeps in its cradle,/I lift the gauze and look a long time, and silently brush away flies with my hand." Sometimes they comprise a series of fragmentary sounds: "The blab of the pave, tires of carts, sluff of boot-soles, talk of the promenaders." Sometimes the images are of more detailed experiences: the joys of having the talk around the trapper's fire, sailing with the crew of a clipper ship, attending a frontier marriage, caring for a runaway slave; the prurient yearnings of a woman as she watches the nude bathing of twenty-eight young men in the sea. So starts the first part of the expansion of the poet into the immediate world about him—by the accretion of quickly changing images whose only unity is that they are commonplace, familiar, and American. At this point, in section 17, he can therefore assert the attainment of his status as the representative man:

These are really the thoughts of all men in all ages
    and lands, they are not original with me.
If they are not yours as much as mine they are
    nothing, or next to nothing.

The next stanzas comprise a sketch of the personality that has been formed. The man arrives "with music strong"; he has set his table equally for the wicked and the righteous, the "heavy-lipped slave" and "the venerealee." He is a natural fact, like the daylight or the "early redstart twittering through the woods," and is quite as astonishing as they. He is "hankering, gross, mystical, nude"; he is original and independent, the "poet of the Body" and the "poet of the Soul." He observes the coupling of the bare-bosomed night and apple-blossomed earth. He incorporates within himself wickedness as well as goodness, for he knows that wickedness is but part of the balance of compensation in a good universe. He walks with positive assurance: "My gait is no fault-finder's or rejecter's gait." He accepts time as the dimension that "rounds and completes all." He is a mystic and knows that "baffling wonder alone completes all"; but he is a mystic of materialism, for he accepts reality and shouts, "Hurrah for positive science! long live exact demonstration!" This is the man who becomes a man-god with the pronouncement that he is "Walt Whitman, a kosmos, of Manhattan the son," who would be slain by the "dazzling and tremendous" sunrise if he "could not now and always send sun-rise" out to his fellow men. Ecstatic with sound and touch, he states his faith in the significance of the commonplace:

I believe a leaf of grass is no less than the journey-work
    of the stars,
And the pismire is equally perfect, and a grain of sand
    and the egg of the wren,
And the tree-toad is chef-d'oeuvre for the highest,
And the running blackberry would adorn the parlors of
    heaven,

And the narrowest hinge in my hand puts to scorn all
    machinery,
And the cow crunching with depress'd head surpasses any
    statue,
And a mouse is miracle enough to stagger sextillions
    of infidels.

This part of the poem ends with the vision of a man-god and of the animals with whom he easily and frankly identifies himself: "They bring me tokens of myself," he says and with that mounts a "gigantic beauty of a stallion," uses him a moment, and then relinquishes him. He has no need of the beast; he is himself a centaur: "Why do I need your paces when I myself out-gallop them?"

With the announcement at the opening of section 33, he begins the second stage of his expansion: "Space and Time! Now I see it is true, what I guess'd at." Up to this point his enlargement has been to the physical, the immediate, the contemporary, the familiar. Now his "ties and ballasts" leave him; he can "skirt sierras"; his palms can "cover continents." His new dimension includes contemporary life and society in a catalogue of events that stretches over twenty centuries and takes in "the city's quadrangular houses," "the white and brown buckwheat," the falls of Niagara whose cataracts he playfully uses as a veil for his godlike countenance, bee-hives, and "the sweating Methodist preacher." He breaks the bonds of time and begins his expansion into the past: "Walking the old hills of Judea with the beautiful gentle God by my side"; he breaks, as well, the bonds that tie him to the earth and begins "speeding through heaven and the stars" as he incorporates the moon in his own body: "Carrying the crescent child that carries its own full mother in its belly."

His voyage in time and space, however, leads him inevitably to the confrontation of horror: the torment of history, the emptiness of space, the reality of immense waste places and deserts both of the universe and of the human spirit. The vast ice fields that for Poe and Melville were evidences of the overwhelming truth of the senselessness of history and of nature—Whitman incorporated these, too, in his vision; he saw them and accepted them as "some vast ruined city,/The blocks and fallen architecture more than all the living cities of the globe." For Melville the polar wastes symbolized the leprous atheism from which we shrink; for Poe they symbolized the emptiness at the core of the world; for Whitman, too, they are a vision of terror, but for him the terror will be accepted, absorbed, and then surmounted.

Not immediately, however. First there must be a sterner test for the man-god to face before he can become god-man. First he will be so appalled by the facts of history that they will seem too much for him to assimilate. He tries to say that he will contain them:

All this I swallow, it tastes good, I like it well, it
     becomes mine,
I am the man, I suffer'd, I was there.

Yet the scenes he witnesses, the agonies of the hounded slave, the massacres of the Mexican-American War, the old-time sea struggle, the cholera patient—these overcome him. It is as if the sum of the world's evil were more than the sum of its good. So in an extreme, though momentary, despair he finds that the awareness of evil has forced him into a posture of pessimism: "Askers embody themselves in me and I am embodied in them." Quite uncharacteristically he finds himself transformed into a supplicant: "I project my hat, sit shame-faced, and beg."

This despair, however, is but the final stage of his spiritual growth, the necessary last ingredient of plenitude. Having lost himself in the depths, he is then qualified to ascend the heights: "Enough! Enough! Enough!/Somehow I have been stunn'd. Stand back!" He had made "the usual mistake" and had thought that he could be on the outside of the terrible truths—that he had been deceived into thinking that he "could look with separate look" on his "own crucifixion and bloody crowning!" The important word is "separate." So long as he had not been overcome, overwhelmed by evil, he had been apart from it. Having abandoned himself to evil, having allowed "the trippers and askers," the doubters, to embody themselves in him, he becomes not an onlooker at the crucifixion but the crucified one, capable therefore of assuming his final role—the role of a redeeming God:

Magnifying and applying come I,
Outbidding at the start the old cautious hucksters,
Taking myself the exact dimensions of Jehovah,
Lithographing Kronos, Zeus his son, and Hercules his
        grandson,
Buying drafts of Osiris, Isis, Belus, Brahma, Buddha.

As a god-man, an American god, he moves among his people and provides them with the icons of a new mythology: "By the mechanic's wife with the babe at her nipple interceding for every person born." He does not despise other creeds; he simply assimilates them:

Making a fetish of the first rock or stump, powowing
        with sticks in the circle of obis,
Helping the llama or brahmin as he trims the lamps
        of the idols,
Dancing yet through the streets in a phallic procession,
        rapt and austere in the woods a gymnosophist . . .
Accepting the Gospels, accepting him that was crucified,
        knowing assuredly that he is divine.

Along with the believers and their beliefs, he absorbs the skeptics and their questions. Emerson, in a similar vein, had written the words of the transcendent One: "I am the doubter and the doubt/And I the hymn the Brahmin sings."[125] Whitman, like Emerson, absorbed the "down-hearted doubters dull and excluded" and "the sea of torment, doubt, despair and unbelief." Could he have had Melville in mind? Possibly. He described the spasms of existential despair as the splashing of the flukes of a stricken whale, contracting "rapid as lightning, with spasms and spouts of blood"; the god-man can say to the Melvilles and the Poes: "Be at peace bloody flukes of doubters and sullen mopers,/I take my place among you as much as among any."

Although he is a worshipper of the present and future, Whitman knows that "the past is the push of you, me, all, precisely the same." Yet he knows, too, that the future, "what is untried and afterward," "will in its turn prove sufficient, and cannot fail." The expansion is now complete; he is now God who is Man, and he can say: "It is time to explain myself—let us stand up." The next six stanzas (44–49) are concerned with the kind of explanations that can be given by one man to another. He is once again the Whitman of the earlier sections of the poem, but we must, with the experience of the bulk of the vision behind us, see him, and therefore ourselves, as "an acme of things accomplish'd" and "an encloser of things to be." He stands on this spot "with . . . robust soul." Once more he appears as lover, loafer, and tramp. However, we know the dimensions of this being and the meaning of his "perpetual journey." We stand with his left arm around our waists and his right "pointing to landscapes of continents and the public road." We have in our ears his words: "Not I, not any one else can travel that road for you/You must travel it for yourself." He wills us to be bold swimmers, "to jump off in the midst of the sea, rise again, nod to me, shout, and laughingly dash with your hair." With his experience behind us, we know that the "soul is not more than the body . . . that the body is not more than the soul" and that "nothing, not God, is greater to one than one's self is." Death is known to us, and we are unafraid; life is known to us as "the leavings of many deaths." We watch the god-man that is Whitman, that is ourselves, "ascend from the moon . . . ascend from the night."

And so the amazing experience is near its end. The god awakens and, once more a man, no longer ravished by his ecstasy, he incoherently stammers,

There is that in me—I do not know what it is—but
      I know it is in me
Wrench'd and sweaty—calm and cool then my body becomes
I sleep—I sleep long.

What has been learned can be stated only in the cry that summarizes transcendental optimism:

Do you see O my brothers and sisters?
It is not chaos or death—it is form, union, plan—
      it is eternal life—it is Happiness.

We do not leave him in these generalizations; we leave him in a final vision that recaptures fleetingly the dimensions of the god we have seen created in words, a god who is of the stars and of the mud:

I depart as air, I shake my white locks at the runaway sun,
I effuse my flesh in eddies, and drift it in lacy jags.
I bequeath myself to the dirt to grow from the grass I love,
If you want me again look for me under your boot-soles.
You will hardly know who I am or what I mean,
But I shall be good health to you nevertheless,
And filter and fibre your blood.
Failing to find me at first keep encouraged,
Missing me one place search another,
I stop somewhere waiting for you.

The rest of Whitman's life and work were devoted to filling in the details of *Song of Myself*; and not once did he abandon its program. He lived on through the Gilded Age, through the industrialization of America, through the growth of rapacious commercial individualism, and he was blind to none of it; in prose he would say that "society, in these States, is canker'd, crude, superstitious, and rotten . . . the depravity of the business classes of our country is not less than has been supposed, but infinitely greater."[126] Yet these, like the doubts in *Song of Myself*, were surmounted by an optimism that took these evils as part of a triumphant progress.

Whitman's style was a projection of his culture's dominant idea. The natural facts of its civilization became his symbols. And the most revealing aspect of his technique is his use of the machine as stuff of poetry. For the true believers of the American faith, the machine was the sign of hope and of the future; for the disbelievers it was an emblem of despair. And of all the machines the one that was most deeply interwoven with the American hopes of the nineteenth century was the railroad. Although Thoreau had treated this major symbol with reservation and ambivalence and Emerson had suggested that it was the proper stuff of poetry, Whitman demonstrated in this, as in almost everything else, the way in which he was the supreme spokesman of transcendental affirmation. He wrote his praise of this instrument of advancement in "To a Locomotive in Winter." For him the railroad was the "type of the Modern—emblem of motion and power—pulse of the continent." He regarded its mechanical details with a reverence that other poets had reserved for organic nature:

Thy black cylindric body, golden brass and silvery steel,
Thy ponderous side-bars, parallel and connecting rods,
    gyrating, shuttling at thy sides.

He described each part of the engine: springs and valves, the "tremulous twinkle" of its wheels, the smoke like "pennants" above the stacks, and then "the train of cars behind, obedient, merrily following." He took the engine into the world of the organic and made them one. For Whitman the machine was just as sure and telling a fact as the prairies or oceans, which he had celebrated elsewhere and which he had used for the same purpose of knowing spiritual reality. Its sounds are the music of independence, triumph, conquest:

Fierce throated beauty!
Roll through my chant with all thy lawless music, thy
    swinging lamps at night,
Thy madly-whistled laughter, echoing, rumbling like
    an earthquake, rousing all . . .
Thy trills of shrieks by rocks and hills return'd,
Launch'd o'er the prairies wide, across the lakes,
To the free skies unpent and glad and strong.[127]

The railroad's conquest of space was one of the two major images of another of Whitman's postwar poems—a poem that was a direct response to the most dramatic event of American industrial history, the meeting of the Union Pacific and Central Pacific Railroads in 1869. This same year had witnessed the joining of the Mediterranean (and hence the Atlantic) to the Red Sea (and hence the Pacific) by the opening of the Suez Canal. Out of these two triumphs of the mechanical, Whitman made his most impressive later poem, "Passage to India," which celebrated the technical, scientific, industrial advances of the age by using them as symbols of the evolution of the spirit. In his treatment of these landmarks of material progress, Whitman demonstrated the way in which the transcendental poet achieved the necessary fusion (one of Whitman's favorite words) of the physical and the spiritual. He showed how, by his attention to the present, the poet might incorporate the present and the future and how, by his concern with the events of human history, the poet at the same moment depicts the transcendental truths.

The opening of "Passage to India" showed Whitman in a typical posture: "Singing my days,/Singing the great achievements of the present." He had begun his career by shouting, "Hurrah for positive science! long live exact demonstration!" To the lexicographer, the chemist, the geologist, the surgeon, the mathematician, he had exclaimed, "Gentlemen, to you the first honors always!"[128] And then in the "Passage to India," he continued to sing "the strong light works of engineers,/Our modern wonders." After naming three of these miracles—the Suez Canal, the transcontinental railroad, and the transoceanic cable—he established the ruling metaphor of the poem—a description of all progress as a line that stretches out in a westward "forward" direction, only to turn again upon itself in a perfect circle and define, in the only way possible for finite man, the truth of progressive change, which is at the same time a return to the beginning, a reconciliation of the tormenting paradox of a belief in eternal perfection with a belief in eternal change. The first attempt to express this paradox was the comparison of the present to a "projectile," its direction and force "utterly formed, impell'd by the past" and, by inference, destined, if the push be strong enough, to return to the source of its power. The poem would later develop additional lines of force, seemingly extending in one direction but bending back upon themselves: the lines of the westward explorers and of the railroad. More immediately, however, came the task of defining the source of modern power—the "myths and fables of Eld, Asia's, Africa's fables, the far-darting beams of the spirit, the unloos'd dreams." It was a passage back to these that the human race had been striving to achieve. This line of movement, bending back upon itself, is "God's purpose"; therefore in singing of the "worship new" of science and technology, of "captains, voyagers, explorers . . . engineers . . . architects, machinists," Whitman was singing "in God's name" and for the sake of the soul.

Two of these symbols, the canal and the railroad, had to be made accessible through words. They could not be left to generality; they had to be realized; so in twenty-two lines they were evoked by saying the words that are the things. First the Suez:

The strange landscape, the pure sky, the level sand
  in the distance,
I pass swiftly the picturesque groups, the workmen
  gather'd,
The gigantic dredging machines.

And then the railroad, different "yet thine, all thine, O Soul, the same":

Marking through these and after all, in duplicate slender
  lines,
Bridging the three or four thousand years of land travel
Tying the Eastern to the Western sea,
The road between Europe and Asia.

The recent expression of the scientific, inquisitive mind was the fulfillment of the same exploratory surge that moved the travelers of the Renaissance: America verified the dream of Columbus; the "rondure" of the world was accomplished. This rounding, and the place of poetry in it, was the subject of the fifth stanza, one that had been written earlier but then slipped into the place waiting for it in a later poem. Restating what Whitman had said again and again, it repeated Emerson's conviction that the right words were symbols of the transcendent spirit. In "Out of the Cradle Endlessly Rocking," he had described the awakening in the boy's heart of his mission as a poet and had described the ocean, the child, and the bird as members of a trinity whose threeness was made into imperishable One by the "word." In "When Lilacs Last in the Dooryard Bloom'd," he had demonstrated how death could be understood and assimilated—even the death, especially the death, of the beloved comrade, Lincoln—by the fusion of lilac and star with the song of the thrush. Now in "Passage to India," Whitman made the most explicit statement of this new meaning of the Trinity: nature and man shall be fused by the poet—"The Trinitas divine shall be gloriously accomplish'd and compacted by the true son of

God, the poet." By the poet shall this seemingly "cold, impassive, voiceless earth . . . be completely justified." If the "things" that represent the materialism of the times were to be seen only as "things," they would ride mankind; if properly understood as symbols of the spiritual, they would be the way to knowing the achievements of the human spirit. This foretold the concluding sections of the poem, which blend the physical and the spiritual by making the material progress of humanity identical with the progress of the soul. However, first Whitman returned to the meaning of the historical passage to India and found it summarized in a "sad shade . . . Gigantic, visionary." This was Columbus, and his dejection, poverty, and death provided a "type" for the truth of the coming of all things to justice in "God's due occasion."

The next short stanza expanded the physical progress involved in history into an intellectual progress—not "lands and seas alone" must be rounded, but ideas must come back to their eastern origins as well; together with the voyage of men's bodies, the minds of men return to "innocent intuitions" in the "realms of budding bibles." Whitman invited the soul to accompany him on this voyage and asked it to know that its search for God is precisely identical with the search of men for the westward route to Orient. Like these physical expeditions, the quests of the spirit for transcendent knowledge moved in one direction, only to return to their point of departure. Like geographical progress, spiritual progress rounded back upon itself.

And so the opening of the physical routes to India, the completing of the mechanical means of union, was a completion of spiritual union as well—a "Passage to more than India." The canal and the railroad were symbols of the "passage to you, your shores, ye aged fierce enigmas," symbols of the "secret of the earth and sky." The launching of technological progress was the image of the launching of the soul toward the infinite; the spiritual voyage could be taken with the same sense of optimistic fervor: man's material progress is the symbol of the successful quest for God. The American idea of progress, based upon a conviction of man's natural goodness, here received its most eloquent statement in poetry.

V ~ Varieties of Rejection

1. Hawthorne

The romantic encounter with the American idea produced
not only its reinforcement by religious fervors; it also
impelled equally fervent rejections of the faith in reason and
progress and attempts to replace the idea with alternate
private patterns of belief and feeling. The same age and the
same New England nurtured Nathaniel Hawthorne as well
as Ralph Waldo Emerson, and these two imaginations
provide our culture with two quite opposed romantic
traditions—a tradition of radical pessimism as well as radical
optimism, a tradition of darkness as well as a tradition of
light. Like Emerson, Hawthorne denied the supremacy of
the analytic reason; knowledge, he felt, came from the
mystical emanation of the fragment of red cloth as he held it
in his hand at the Custom House or in the reflections of the
stream beside the Old Manse or in the fleeting apprehensions
of meaning caught in the surface of a mirror; for Hawthorne,
as for Emerson, the primary method of knowing was a
faculty different from, and superior to, logical analysis.
There were other sympathies and connections between the
two seminal imaginations as well. Hawthorne lived in
Emerson's house in Concord; he sat in Emerson's chair,
wrote at his desk, saw the same apparent view from the
window out over the field and trees to the river beyond. It
was the same view but a different perception. Hawthorne

looked at this world—this world of appearances and of the American social and political facts of the nineteenth century —and where Emerson saw a world that clothed the spirit and took its outlines from radiant goodness, Hawthorne saw a fallen universe of ruins and poisonous flowers lit with occasional gleams of sunshine. When Emerson followed Hawthorne's coffin to its grave, he walked in "a pomp of sunshine and verdure, and gentle winds"[1] and regretted that Hawthorne should have ignored these in his stories in favor of the darkness and the chill, for where Emerson saw the face of the world wearing a smile, Hawthorne had seen it wearing a frown.

A frown but not "a sneer."[2] Hawthorne would not, as would Poe and Melville, posit for long the possibilities of a meaningless or chaotic universe. The world for Hawthorne was dominated by both spiritual and moral order, but it was not a world in which nature was the perfect embodiment of eternal goodness and in which natural man—firm in the conviction that he could partake of the world's constant improvement, which, paradoxically but truthfully, was a part of its perfect rightness—took his assured place. For Hawthorne the physical and moral universe of man was instead a world of necessary imperfection, of mud as well as marble; the truth of this world was not comic, as it was for Emerson, but tragic; and the truths of its relation to the world of God lay in the shadows, not in the sunlight. Whereas Whitman would become Henry James's "supreme contemporary example"[3] of healthy-mindedness, Hawthorne was probably one of the imaginations this observant and predominantly healthy-minded philosopher had in mind when he described the other mentality: the "sick-souls, the morbid minded." These, James wrote, had not simply the "conception or intellectual perception of evil" but the "grisly blood-freezing, heart-palsying sensation of it close upon one." And James, whose robust vitality would lead him to a definitive philosophical justification for the American idea, declared "that we are bound to say that morbid-mindedness ranges over the wider scale of experience . . . because . . . evil facts . . . may after all be the best key to life's significance, and possibly the only openers of our eyes to the deepest levels of truth."[4]

These deepest levels were Hawthorne's goal, as well as Emerson's and Whitman's. However, the individual human soul and the patterns of the visible world of nature and the organizations of social institutions and communal beliefs did not for Hawthorne, as they did for the transcendentalists, symbolically body forth these deepest truths. Instead, Hawthorne looked into his heart and found it, not good, but foul and looked at the outer world and saw there a reflection of man's inner corruption. With this vision of evil, he rejected what he felt to be the easy optimisms of the American idea as it applied to man and his institutions and to nature. Having rejected the dominant structure of feeling of his contemporary society, he created a fictional world whose patterns constituted an alternative pattern of perception to that of his culture; to do this, he went back a century and more to rescue the basic outlines of the Puritan world view, and in constructing this different world, he employed fictional techniques that embodied both his rejection of his culture's dominant beliefs and his perception of fallen man.

When Hawthorne turned his back upon both the beliefs of the Enlightenment and the transcendental invigoration of those beliefs, he quite typically converted the age's two principal symbols of progress—the steamboat and the railroad—into allegories of the falsity of the American idea and of the damnation that attends a confidence in either the secularized Unitarianism of Franklin and Jefferson or the optimistic mysticism of Emerson. Although these rejections were implicit in most that he wrote, "The Celestial Railroad," an American version of *The Pilgrim's Progress*, was his most pointed criticism of the basic pattern of beliefs of his age. Starting with Bunyan's parable as model, Hawthorne demonstrated what happens when the old hard ways to salvation are smoothed over by modern conceptions of the essential goodness of man and nature and by commitments to the material comforts of this world as substitutes for the blessings of the next. The criticism assumed the form of a dream vision of a new modern road to the Celestial City, a railroad that overcame all the pain and hardship of our earthly pilgrimage. The City of Destruction was the name he gave to this world (he would call it a ruined garden, tumbled in decay, rank with the poisonous flowers of science, in other tales). It was the starting place of the journey, and his companion was a charming, glib optimist, Mr. Smooth-It-Away, who explained each modern improvement along the way. The Slough of Despond had been bridged by "volumes of French philosophy and German rationalism; tracts, sermons, and essays of modern clergymen; extracts from Plato, Confucius, and various Hindoo sages."[5] The burden of mankind, its Original Sin, was "snugly deposited in the baggage car."[6] Old guides had been pensioned off, for they had grown "preposterously stiff and narrow" in their old age. In a belief that all evil can be used for good purposes, Apollyon, the old enemy of Pilgrim, was engaged as the engineer; this demonstrated that "all musty prejudices are in a fair way to be obliterated."[7] The Hill Difficulty had been tunnelled, and the excavated debris had been used to fill up the Valley of Humiliation; the Valley of the Shadow of Death was lit by gaslight; the castle of the Giant Despair had been taken over by Mr. Flimsy-Faith, who had rebuilt it into a roadhouse "in a modern and airy style of architecture."[8] In this new version of the old story, even the monsters lost their outline and vitality. Pope and Pagan were replaced by a strange new ogre, "Giant Transcendentalist," with features so like "a heap of fog and duskiness" that "neither he for himself, nor anybody for him, has ever been able to describe them."[9]

Franklin's and Jefferson's America was the Vanity Fair of Hawthorne's satire. "Still at the height of prosperity,"[10] it was an agreeable place to stay, a place where everything, including religion and learning, had been made easy and palatable: the first, by men like "the Rev. Mr. Shallow-deep" and the second, by a system of lectures, a "sort of machinery, by which thought and study are done to every person's hand without his putting himself to the slightest inconvenience in the matter."[11] In Vanity Fair, in America, men were selling the possibilities of heavenly life for the promise of delight in this world; messes of hot pottage were in constant demand as currency, and the general transaction was the exchange of the pursuit of holiness for the pursuit of happiness. At the end, of course, the train stopped on this side of a river on the other bank of which stood the still unattained Celestial City.

The infernal machine disembarked its duped passengers into "a steam-ferry boat, the last improvement on this important route."[12] And while they saw across the river the entry into the city of two wary pilgrims who, hooted and derided, had stayed on the thorny, rocky road of old faith, they watched Mr. Smooth-It-Away turn into the fiend he had always been as he bore them off on the chill tides of the River Dis.

"The Celestial Railroad" was a thorough rejection of religious optimism; another dream vision, "Earth's Holocaust," was Hawthorne's analysis of the idea of secular progress as a gigantic bonfire into whose purging flames men throw the traditions, the forms, the customs, the beliefs of the past. Immolated was not only what was evil in the past but what was good as well. "The Titan of innovation" was described as "angel or fiend, double in his nature, and capable of deeds befitting both characters."[13] In a compulsive frenzy modern man throws one after another of old beliefs on the bonfire of the Enlightenment, only to find it sheds not more light but deeper darkness. At the end a sinister figure standing near, watching men do his work, satanically proclaims the futility of outward reforms while the cavern of man's heart remains foul.

All of Hawthorne's major works, and almost all of his shorter stories and sketches, were more or less overt criticisms of American optimism. They frequently attacked it at its root of belief in the fundamental goodness of natural man and the particular emphasis that this belief gave to the value of youth. The merchant, the politician, the aged rake, and the prurient widow of Dr. Heidegger's experiment were some of the less attractive worshippers in the cult of juvenescence: "We are young! We are young!" they cried exultingly and felt themselves "new-created beings in a new-created universe";[14] but the tall mirror told the truth, for it was said to have "reflected the figures of the three old, grey, withered grandsires, ridiculously contending for the skinny ugliness of a shrivelled grandam."[15] Not satisfied with the lesson taught by Dr. Heidegger's experiment, the oldsters resolved to make a pilgrimage to Florida and "quaff at morning, noon, and night from the Fountain of Youth."[16] When Miles Coverdale indicated to old Moodie, at the beginning of *The*

Blithedale Romance, that he was loathe to do a kindness that involved trouble to himself, Moodie, equating selfishness with youth and kindness with the lessons learned from age, thought he had better "apply to some older gentleman."[17] Pearl in *The Scarlet Letter* was one of the less fiendish child-imps that inhabit Hawthorne's tales; the worst are the group of Puritan children in "The Gentle Boy." Adults, as they wandered near them and heard "the glee of a score of un-tainted bosoms," wondered why life should "proceed in gloom" when it begins in the apparent goodness of child-hood and imagined that "the bliss of childhood gushes forth from its innocence."[18] They soon found otherwise. When little Ilbrahim drew near, "the devil of their fathers entered into the unbreeched fanatics, and sending up a fierce, shrill cry, they rushed upon the poor Quaker child. In an instant he was the centre of a brood of baby-fiends." The climax of this little scene of infant depravity was reached when Ilbra-him's crippled friend called upon him to take his hand; when Ilbrahim did, "the foul-hearted little villain lifted his staff" and struck him on the mouth "so forceably that the blood issued in a stream."[19]

No, the conviction of the essential goodness of youth was not one of Hawthorne's acceptations. Neither was its corol-lary—the essential beneficence of nature and of the natural impulses of man. *The Scarlet Letter* has many meanings; but one of them is surely that there are mortal dangers in trusting nature. The forms and limits of the town, the settlement of man, with the devices that men have made to restrain and confine men's impulses—the prison, the scaffold, and the church—were threatened on one side by the sea and on the other side by the forest. From the sea came the wild sailors who paraded in a veritable devil's masque on the day that Dimmesdale and Hester thought they might escape toward the east. In the forest Hester had proclaimed the possibilities of happiness, if only Dimmesdale would break from the constrictions of the town and its moral code to flee with her into the wilderness. "There thou art free! So brief a journey would bring thee from a world where thou hast been most wretched, to one where thou mayest still be happy!"[20] The freedom of nature corresponded to the freedom of man's natural impulses: "'What we did had a consecration of its own,'"[21] said Hester, and so deeply was this belief in the goodness of man and nature imbedded in the country's structure of feeling that at least one critic at the time took this to be the message and moral of the story: the justification of the natural sexual urges of men and women and a corresponding attack upon the outworn Puritan code.[22] Exactly the reverse was true. Hawthorne described the false happiness that followed Dimmesdale's agreement to Hester's assertion of freedom and portrayed the deceptive sunshine that burst upon the forest at that moment and brightened its solemn shades: "the objects that had made a shadow hitherto, embodied the brightness now." And then, so that we do not mistake the delusion of this brightness, Hawthorne told us: "Such was the sympathy of Nature—that wild heathen Nature of the forest, never subjugated by human law, nor illumined by higher truth."[23]

Doubting the radical goodness of man, convinced that nature was involved with evil at its deepest level of reality, Hawthorne could not but question his society's dismissal of the past and its commitment to a better future to be built by man's application of his reason to the physical world. The attitude that history could be ignored or evaded or forgotten was not only unrealistic; it was morally dangerous, he felt, for it ran counter to the facts of human experience and encouraged pride, which was the deadliest of sins. Guilt, once incurred, leaves a stain that cannot be eradicated; the past is therefore the part of man that makes him human; a rejection of the past or an attempt to escape it is doomed. "The past was not dead,"[24] he wrote in his Custom House Sketch, introducing *The Scarlet Letter*; the romance itself was concerned with American tradition and legend and took as its theme the inescapability of the results of imperfect human action. Each of his subsequent romances similarly incorporated this conservative view of the past in plots whose main motives are dark deeds that have occurred before the story begins—in the "past" of the fictional world that Hawthorne created: the cheating of Maule by Colonel Pyncheon before the opening of *The House of the Seven Gables*; the secret marriage of Zenobia to Westervelt, anterior to the first pages of

The Blithedale Romance; the mysterious involvement of Miriam with the sinister monk, which preceded the opening of *The Marble Faun*.

Although all of his work employed this motif, *The House of the Seven Gables* constituted Hawthorne's most dramatic statement of the permanence of the past and of the futility of the American attempt to ignore it. Written at the happiest time of Hawthorne's life—immediately after the success of his earlier work, the birth of his daughter, and his removal to the pleasant hills of western Massachusetts—this successor to *The Scarlet Letter* contained an apparently happy ending; Phoebe and Holgrave, uniting the feuding families of Maule and Pyncheon, take Clifford and Hepzibah from the old house and leave for the West. Indeed, "wise Uncle Venner, passing slowly from the ruinous porch, seemed to hear a strain of music, and fancied that sweet Alice Pyncheon—after witnessing these deeds, this bygone woe and this present happiness, of her kindred mortals—had given one farewell touch of a spirit's joy upon her harpsichord."[25] Yet this overly sweet ending had hidden, tarter undertones. For one thing, Uncle Venner, the home-baked philosopher who thought he heard the shade of sweet Alice sounding her happy melody to give the tale its optimistic ending, earlier had been described as a combination of Franklin and Emerson, both of whom Hawthorne found either shallow or myopic. When Hepzibah set up her pathetic little penny shop, Uncle Venner gave her "hard little pellets" of wisdom straight from the tradition of Poor Richard: "Give no credit! . . . Never take paper-money! Look well to your change! . . . Brew your own yeast, and make your own ginger-beer." While Hepzibah tried to digest these practical admonitions from the tradition of Franklin, Uncle Venner added to it the optimism associated with the American faith: "Put on a bright face for your customers, and smile pleasantly as you hand them what they ask for!"[26] And Holgrave, who bore Phoebe off, had just admitted to her, "In this long drama of wrong and retribution, I represent the old wizard, and am probably as much a wizard as ever he was."[27] He had also hinted that he would build another house, more lasting than the wooden House of the Seven Gables; in doing so, he laughingly had identified himself, not only with Maule, but with Colonel Pyncheon, the inheritor of so much misfortune.

Holgrave's proclamation that he would build a more permanent house recalled ironically his earlier rebellious cry of hope that "we shall live to see the day . . . when no man shall build his house for posterity." He had insisted that houses are symbols of all of men's institutions and that if "each generation were allowed and expected to build its own houses, that single change . . . would imply almost every reform which society is suffering for." Then he clinched the symbolic identification of the House with human history. The House of the Seven Gables, he said, "is expressive of that odious and abominable Past . . . against which I have just been declaiming."[28] Holgrave's speech was a summary of the transcendentalist's denigration of the past and an only slightly exaggerated restatement of Emerson's question: "Why drag about this corpse of your memory?" Holgrave used the same metaphor: "Shall we never, never get rid of the Past? . . . It lies upon the Present like a giant's dead body! In fact, the case is just as if a young giant were compelled to waste all his strength in carrying about the corpse of the old giant, his grandfather."[29]

Displaying all of the potential dangers of a belief in progress that Hawthorne was so quick to describe and deplore, Holgrave obeyed no law but a law of his own, according to Hepzibah. He was spurred on by the pursuit of cold objectivity in his art of photography; the incipient unpardonable sin of the cold violation of the human heart was in him as he courted Phoebe. These were hints that the future of the new Pyncheon-Maule line might not be so happy as the ghost of sweet Alice thought. The happy ending was a tainted one; the presumed leaving of the house at the end might be the beginning of another reenactment of the age-old truths of the inescapable persistence of human guilt; and the dramatic scene at the center of the plot—the attempted flight of the "two owls," Hepzibah and Clifford—was Hawthorne's view of what happens when man tries to flee from his house of history.

Although Phoebe embodied the sunshine that Sophia Peabody brought into Hawthorne's life and although the rose that she bore to Clifford suggested the new girl-child "Rose" with which Sophia had presented him while he was writing the romance, Hepzibah and Clifford, the central characters of the tale, represented much of what Hawthorne felt of himself as he inhabited the haunted house of his ancestral memories. Their involvement with the House of the Seven Gables, their reaction to the past, therefore takes on a deeper resonance. Clifford, an artist who has devoted himself to beauty, was pictured blowing bubbles from his arched window and was described as "a failure, as almost everybody is";[30] Hawthorne, in "The Custom House" sketch that prefaced *The Scarlet Letter*, had described his art as a "soap-bubble," whose impalpable beauty threatened at every moment to be broken "by the rude contact of some actual circumstance."[31] After frightening Judge Pyncheon, the tyrannical master of the family, into a fatal stroke, Clifford felt a momentary rapturous joy, the same false joy experienced by Dimmesdale after he had acquiesced to Hester's plan for escape. Clifford cried to Hepzibah (the croak in her voice is as "ineradicable as sin"), "The weight is gone, Hepzibah! it is gone off this weary old world."[32] He took her by the hand and together these "time-stricken" children started on a flight that Hawthorne transformed into a parable of America's futile attempt to escape from the past of human history. They moved as in a dream; Hepzibah repeatedly asked herself: "Am I awake?—Am I awake?" They found themselves in a railway station and then aboard a train, which, like the Celestial Railroad, became a symbol of the American idea of progress. Once aboard it, they were in a time machine that had unfixed everything "from its age-long rest." They found a complex life within: "Sleep; sport; business; graver or lighter study; and the common and inevitable movement onward! It was life itself!" It was a microcosm of the modern world. Clifford, in a delirium of excitement, described the railroad as the great liberating force in mankind's upward spiral, which freed him from his roots, from the "heaps of bricks and stones," from the memories that are "the greatest possible stumbling blocks in the path of human happiness and improvement." With feverish energy he listed all the other advances of the age: "Mesmerism . . . electricity,—the demon, the angel, the mighty physical power." Yet while he propounded his delusion of progress, Hepzibah took a different view: "With miles and miles of varied scenery between, there was no scene for her, save the seven old gable-peaks. . . . This one old house was everywhere! It transported its great, lumbering bulk with more than railroad speed, and set itself phlegmatically down on whatever spot she glanced at." When they alighted, the train, "the world" as Hawthorne called it, dwindled to a "rapidly lessening . . . point" in the distance and then vanished. The scene Hawthorne then described was the solitary way station, the end of their road and the end of the dream of progress in the nightmare vision of reality: a decayed church and an old house, both black with age. The wooden church was "in a dismal state of ruin and decay, with broken windows, a great rift through the main body of the edifice, and a rafter dangling from the top of the square tower." Clifford subsided; his hectic fantasy over, he murmured to Hepzibah: "You must take the lead now." And Hepzibah, falling to her knees, ejaculated: "O God,—our Father,—are we not thy children? Have mercy on us!"[33]

This was Hawthorne's most brilliant description of the pervasive powers of the past. He joined to this statement of the strength of history a natural corollary, the rejection of faith in material progress toward a better future, and he made his criticism of the secular religion of meliorism and reform through the character of Holgrave. "Altogether," he said of him, to emphasize the way Holgrave symbolized the posture of our society, "in his culture and want of culture,— in his crude, wild, and misty philosophy, and the practical experience that counteracted some of its tendencies; in his magnanimous zeal for man's welfare, and his recklessness of whatever the ages had established in man's behalf; in his faith, and in his infidelity; in what he had and what he lacked,—the artist might fitly enough stand forth as the representative of many compeers in his native land."[34] Holgrave was anxious that the "moss-grown and rotten Past" be destroyed and that Americans begin anew. Hawthorne stepped out of his narrative to judge this view and to find it wanting; he observed that Holgrave's belief in secular improvement was a "haughty faith"; it would be, Hawthorne felt, well exchanged for "a far humbler one," a faith based upon the truth that man's efforts are but "a kind of dream, while God is the sole worker of realities."[35]

The emptiness of the American idea was argued in Hawthorne's next romance, one that was specifically concerned with a significant contemporary attempt to put the American faith into immediate action. Hawthorne had been part of the Brook Farm experiment, upon which he patterned *The Blithedale Romance*. Hoping by his participation to make a secure place for himself and his prospective bride, he joined the community. Looking back upon it, he found its participants guilty of the same error, tainted by the same sin of intellectual pride, maintaining the same "haughty faith" that he criticized in Holgrave. The argument became more complex in *The Blithedale Romance* than in *The House of the Seven Gables*, because the views expressed in the later work were all those of the narrator, Miles Coverdale, and were colored by the character's particular prejudices and weaknesses: his pride, his lack of emotional commitment, his failure of feeling. Nevertheless, Coverdale's views correlated precisely with the comments Hawthorne had made as an omniscient narrator in his earlier stories and romances. Coverdale described the experiment as an "exploded scheme for beginning the life of Paradise anew."[36] He told of the inevitable taint at the heart of all such ventures in perfection: when they try to isolate themselves from the "greedy, struggling, self-seeking world," their first step is to investigate the ways of beating that world at its own competitive game. "I very soon became sensible," Coverdale mused, "that, as regarded society at large, we stood in a position of new hostility, rather than new brotherhood."[37] The community, he said ironically, looked forward hopefully, as if the soil beneath it "had not been fathom-deep with the dust of deluded generations, on every one of which, as on ourselves, the world had imposed itself as a hitherto unwedded bride."

This rejection of the idea of progress was not, in Hawthorne, combined with a romantic agony of rebellious hatred —quite the contrary. Hawthorne's attitude was one of calm understanding of the motives and aspirations of American progressivism combined with a quiet denial of its truth. Miles Coverdale's attitudes had the ring of Hawthorne's personal conviction in them when he mused upon the reformers' dream "of earthly happiness, for themselves and mankind, as an object to be hopefully striven for." He said of this dream: "Let us take to ourselves no shame. In my own behalf, I rejoice that I could once think better of the world's improvability than it deserved."[38] Speaking in his own person, Hawthorne had made a similar observation about Holgrave in *The House of the Seven Gables*. Holgrave's liberalism, Hawthorne wrote, and its sense of hope, was something "a young man had better never been born than not to have."[39]

Not only this sympathy with the aspirations of liberalism—however wrong—took the sting out of Hawthorne's criticism. More important in creating his balance and temperance were his deep convictions that if the world of man were permeated by evil and doomed to failure, the world of God was a world of meaning, order, value. Man's error consisted not in belief but in believing that his own "little life span" was the measure of progress and that his will could affect either his destiny or the destiny of the universe. There was a "great end" in view, but the end was God's, not man's: Hilda in *The Marble Faun* would never look for assistance from an "earthly king."[40] The universe wears an "unmitigable frown" but does not reduce our lives to meaninglessness by insulting us with a sneer of contempt. "A wider scope of view and a deeper insight" may understand that all human strivings are illusory "and yet not feel as if the universe were thereby tumbled head-long into chaos."[41]

Hawthorne was capable of facing the deepest darkness, the darkness of utter futility, and of surmounting it with a belief in light. His harrowing description of Judge Pyncheon in his death chair was one of the most frightening confrontations of absolute despair in our literature: "The features are all gone: there is only the paleness of them left. And how looks it now? There is no window! There is no face! An infinite, inscrutable blackness has annihilated sight! Where is our universe? All crumbled away from us; and we, adrift in chaos, may hearken to the gusts of homeless wind, that go sighing and murmuring about, in quest of what was once a world!"[42] However, the light came back into the scene—the pale light of stars and moonshine, to be sure, and not the bright rays of the sun, but it was light nevertheless, and it restored the world to its truthfulness, a truth of shadow and shade, with the shadows cast by the light of cosmic significance to supply the meaning. In Hawthorne's world evil, disaster, tragedy, and death were human realities, but it was a world steeled by the conviction that these sombre truths of man are part of the higher truths of a just, if inscrutable, God. Man's reality was what Miriam calls her "dark dream";[43] beneath every human foot there is a "pit of blackness" upon which "human happiness is but a thin crust."[44] Yet all of this is part of a higher reality that is ordered and significant. All might not be right with the world, but God was in his heaven.

So Hawthorne made a world of fiction that was not a world of gloom but of quiet acquiescence; it was not, however, the affirmation of the world of the American idea. Another idea, another structure of feeling, dominated Hawthorne's fiction. With surprising uniformity all his little worlds of fiction followed the same pattern. In each the motivations of his characters were shrouded in a mystery, the clues to which involved some crime or misadventure in the past; in each case this anterior misadventure had distinctly sexual or sensual overtones. The past disaster then impels a series of present mistakes, all of which have to do with human pride —usually with pride of knowledge or intellect. The various characters react to their guilt either by shunning it, by concealing it, or by acknowledging it; and with it, their complicity with all of sinful mankind. Depending upon their reactions, either they are damned or they achieve a modicum of peace.

In brief, Hawthorne took as his pattern an essentially orthodox Christian view of the world; it is close to that adopted by the Puritans of America—closer still, perhaps, to that of John Milton; but it also has convincing similarities to the fount from which Calvin and Milton drew—the doctrines of Saint Augustine. Hawthorne acknowledged both these affinities, to orthodox Puritanism and to Catholicism. In the preface to *The Scarlet Letter*, he described his Puritan ancestors, admitted their distaste for his calling, and then added:

"Scorn me as they will, strong traits of their nature have intertwined themselves with mine."[45] Although Hawthorne in his last completed romance, *The Marble Faun*, was swift to identify Hilda as a "faithful Protestant and a daughter of the Puritans," he established her in Rome in full view of the statue of St. Paul, provided her with a Virgin for her shrine, allowed an Italian matron to say of her that she was "worthy to be a Catholic," and strongly hinted of her conversion. Had it not been for "one or two disturbing recollections" and the fact that she was a "daughter of the Puritans,"[46] he said, she might have dwelt in the Convent of the Sacré Coeur forever.

This perspective, this *structure of feeling*, was embodied in Hawthorne's fictional technique; his method was part of his world view; or, to put it more precisely, his method *was* his world view. Like Edwards and Taylor his art was an art of emblem rather than symbol: he used objects of the physical world as representations of a higher reality that they but imperfectly shadowed forth; it was an art of allegory: it moved these objects through happenings that emulated not the world of ordinary events but a pattern of order beyond that world; it was an art of romance rather than of the novel; it owed its allegiance, not to the commonsense world of probability, but only to its own inner consistency. And in all these features—emblem, allegory, and romance—Hawthorne fashioned a technique made inevitable by his own dominant idea, which was at war with the major idea of his culture. He complained of his choice of romance as a structure and of allegory as a method and speculated that it would have been better to have taken the commonplace world of experience as his subject and to have sought "the true and indestructible value that lay hidden in . . . petty and wearisome incidents, and ordinary characters."[47] This was in 1850, and he then blamed himself for his inability to follow such a course. In 1859 he blamed his country for failing to provide even the materials for good romance: "No author . . . can conceive of the difficulty of writing a romance about a country where there is no shadow, no antiquity, no mystery, no picturesque and gloomy wrong."[48] In both years and in both instances he was wrong. Neither he nor his society bore any blame for his technique, nor was there any blame to be borne. Finding the basic beliefs of his society inadequate to support his need, the need of every man and every artist, to make meaning and order of his universe, he turned to a technique of fiction that could construct a different illusion: he turned to a method that used objects as emblems of an order beyond that of the orders of his society and that embodied those objects in a pattern of events that proclaimed mystery rather than clarity, darkness rather than light, and tragedy rather than comedy to be the true tones of reality.

Romance was his structure and *allegory*, his method. The first term Hawthorne defined explicitly—it was a form different from the novel, he painstakingly explained in his prefaces, in that the novel owed its audience an attempt at fidelity to normal and commonplace experience. The romance, on the other hand, owed no such allegiance but was concerned only with its inner consistency. The correspondence between the artist's world view and his medium—or, to put it more precisely, the integrity of feeling and technique—is at once apparent. A structure that follows the outer logic and pattern of its society, that is faithful to its external appearances, and that portrays the workings of its social organization pays allegiance, direct or indirect, to the dominant values of that society. The artist who makes these structures is a member of, rather than a rebel from, his society. A pattern of fiction, on the other hand, that is frankly a created world of the author's imagination is often the result of a commitment to other informing values, other ordering visions than the social and cultural context of which it is a part.

These distinctions are those that Erich Auerbach has made between the mimetic form, the novel, and the nonmimetic, or nonrepresentational, form that corresponds to Hawthorne's use of the term *romance*. Auerbach pointed out that the two opposed methods are as old as Western literature and have been from the very first allied with worldly, as opposed to otherworldly, orientations on the part of the artist. The mimetic has been concerned with the surface of observed reality; the nonmimetic, with the depths that lie beneath the surface or above it. The mimetic presents an objective world, whose reality lies "out there" for the common sense to perceive and to know; the nonmimetic is concerned with the unreality of the apparent world and with the reality of the subjective world of the imagination and perception of the artist. The mimetic clearly defines the past from the present, the present from the future and assumes that these divisions are actual and significant; the nonrepresentational observes few or no distinctions of time and attempts to telescope and blend the past and future with the "now." The mimetic deals with clearly defined causes for understandable effects; the nonrepresentational concerns itself frequently with irrational motives and with strange effects whose causes are shrouded in mystery.[49]

Hawthorne's fiction conformed to the nonmimetic, or nonrepresentational, structure, and he was forthright in defining his genre as the romance. He was not so clear about the technique of using admittedly improbable people, places, and things to represent a higher reality: the technique of allegory. Hawthorne made no attempt to distinguish *allegory* from *symbol*, or from *symbolism*; and yet a distinction must be insisted upon, for there is a world of difference between his use of physical objects in his art and the use of objects by Emerson, Thoreau, and Whitman. It may be objected that these latter three worked in different genres and that therefore a valid comparison may not be made. However, every writer chooses his world of discourse, selects and arranges his material. The world of discourse Hawthorne chose was radically different from poets like Emerson and Frost; it would be radically different from the techniques of the prose fiction of Howells, Twain, Sinclair Lewis, and Saul Bellow. Whereas Emerson and his fellow transcendentalists insisted upon the realities and value of the commonplace world of ordinary experience, Hawthorne looked through that world to some reality beyond it or beneath it. When Emerson saw the Rhodora, the "rival of the rose," he knew that it was "its own excuse for being."[50] Hawthorne plucked a rose "on the threshold of our narrative" at the beginning of *The Scarlet Letter* and hoped that it would serve to "symbolize some sweet moral blossom."[51] And this example illustrates the radical difference between Emerson's symbolic perception and Hawthorne's essentially allegorical, emblematic vision. For Emerson a rose or a man or a railroad was a reality to be valued for its own sake, its own "excuse for being," at the same instant that it organized within itself all possible spiritual reality; for Hawthorne, the rose, the man, or the machine was quite frankly used as a representation of a moral or religious truth.

The first result of such a method was a necessary simplification, and hence artificiality, of the natural surfaces of the objects that Hawthorne used to illustrate his pattern of feeling and belief. In place of the close attention to the objective appearance of the outer world, there was a conscious stylization of the object. Miriam in *The Marble Faun* spoke for the artist in general—for the allegorical artist—and defined something of Hawthorne's technique when she told Donatello: "We artists purposely exclude sunshine, and all but a partial light . . . because we think it necessary to put ourselves at odds with Nature before trying to imitate her."[52] All of Hawthorne's works excluded the sunshine, except for bright moments of contrast, in favor of the shade and the shadow and removed themselves from the complexity of nature. In *The Scarlet Letter* the claustrophobic streets of the New England village; the town square hemmed in by prison, graveyard, and church; the interior of the Governor's mansion; the rooms of Hester and Dimmesdale far outnumbered the scenes in the forest. When these latter were described, they were dark inward places, lit infrequently by the dazzle of deceptive sunlight. In *The House of the Seven Gables*, the brightest of his fictions, the settings continued the allegory of inwardness: they centered about the chambers of the house itself and especially about the parlor at the heart of the house, the chimney at the center of this heart, the secret recess within the chimney—hidden places within hidden places. Although *The Blithedale Romance* and *The Marble Faun* showed less reticence in confronting the landscape, they showed a similar emphasis on interiors: gatherings about the fire at Blithedale, scenes in the churches and villas of *The Marble Faun*. The inward settings were all used to allegorize the soulscape of Hawthorne's world; the most dramatic, and certainly a representative, setting was the catacombs, in which the torches of man illuminated "one small, consecrated spot" around which "the great darkness spread . . . like that immense mystery which envelops our little life, and into which our friends vanish from us, one by one."[53]

Hawthorne's characters as well showed the effects of the allegorical method and demonstrated its primary characteristic: the artificiality of its natural surface, which pointed immediately to some moral or metaphysical truth that it purported to represent. There were no fully developed or complex social personalities in his works. His women, to take the most important gender in his characterizations, were divided with neat artificiality between the dark and the light; here Hawthorne continued the emblematic tradition of the Puritans with regard to these colors. Hester's "dark and abundant hair" and "deep black eyes" and generously proportioned body were duplicated in Zenobia's "dark, glossy tress" and her ample proportions, "which irresistibly brought up a picture of that fine, perfectly developed figure in Eve's earliest garments," and again in the description of Miriam as a "dark-eyed young woman" with a "rich Oriental character on her face." These dark women are paired off against fair, or at best lighter-haired and always slighter, more delicate, girls, who were as persistently identified with "white" as their voluptuous sisters were associated with "black": Priscilla in *The Blithedale Romance*, Hilda in *The Marble Faun*. And these fair or brown-haired maidens were as consistently artificial in their correspondence to the spirit as their dark-tressed counterparts were one-dimensional in their embodiments of flesh, sense, and nature.

The allegorical method was evident, too, in the way in which the stylized, artificial constructions were used to represent a limited number of general truths in the world of human moral or religious commitment and in the logical, rational way in which these constructions could be understood. *The Scarlet Letter*, the most effective embodiment of Hawthorne's world view, can and must first be read on this simple level of an allegory of the Puritan-Christian metaphysic. There were several indications in the story itself to direct us to this reading and to support Hawthorne's prefatory assertion that strong traits of his ancestors' character had entwined themselves with his. He constructed his otherwise shadowy and indefinite work about a definite and important event in Puritan history, the death of Governor John Winthrop in 1649, and gave us the sense that his tale had to do with a moment of transition in the strength of the Puritan hold upon America—the passing of its literal power and its transformation into a symbolic power whose symbols would have to be reinvigorated by works like his own. Chillingworth's speech to Hester has the sense of summary in it: "My old faith, long forgotten, comes back to me, and explains all that we do, and all we suffer. By thy first step awry thou dids't plant the germ of evil; but since that moment, it has all been a dark necessity."[54]

In every detail the elements of the romance were manipulated to illustrate this "old faith" and its dark necessities. Neither the characters nor the fictional world they inhabit were given the complexity—the movement and development—of the world of actuality. Instead, they were thoroughly, beautifully, artificial creatures and things performing their part in a rigidly organized structure of meaning quite different from the American idea. The three major characters were bound in the Puritan chains of Original Sin, a sin that Hawthorne, following vaguer hints in Milton's *Paradise Lost*, felt to be deeply involved with the flesh of Eve and its attractions for Adam. Chillingworth was part of this complicity of sensuality, for he had taken a young wife to warm his old body; Dimmesdale and Hester had committed adultery, and there was in her "the taint of deepest sin in the most sacred quality of human life, working such effect, that the world was only the darker for this woman's beauty."[55] This original sin led to three varieties of actual sin in the process of the narrative itself. It prompted Hester's feelings of lawless independence: "She assumed a freedom of speculation . . . which our forefathers, had they known it, would have held to be a deadlier crime than that stigmatized by the scarlet letter."[56] It caused Dimmesdale's sin of concealment and his consequent prideful isolation from the rest of guilty mankind; Hawthorne drew from his experience the moral: "Be true! Be true! Be true! Show freely to the world, if not your worst, yet some trait whereby the worst may be inferred!"[57] Finally, it caused Chillingworth to commit the unpardonable sin that Hawthorne a little before had allegorized in "Ethan Brand"—the sin of intellectual curiosity and pride of knowledge, the sin, it would seem, of modern man. " 'We are not the worst sinners,' " Dimmesdale told Hester; it is Chillingworth who is far more, and irretrievably culpable: " 'He has violated, in cold blood, the sanctity of the human heart.' "[58]

Committing their actual sins, the three protagonists worked out their destinies toward the possible ends permitted them by the fatal necessities of their past. Hester abandoned her rebellion and came back to live within the restrictions and laws that are the necessary outgrowth of man's sinful nature; in doing so she found peace and life; Dimmesdale, mortally scarred by his crime of concealment, finally expiated his sin of isolation by exposure on the scaffold and found peace in death. Chillingworth, having committed the crime that Hawthorne, interpreting the Puritan tradition in a world of science and empirical knowledge, regarded unpardonable, was damned, his fate made visible in a physical deformity that shadowed forth his commitment to the devil.

Perhaps even more than the characters in Hawthorne's stories, the things of his tales were used to serve the purpose of his moral. Indeed, this equivalence of things and people in his fiction in some degree testified to his inevitably allegorical tendency. The novel is a story about seemingly literal people; the allegorical romance, as practiced by Hawthorne, is about frankly artificial entities, vastly oversimplified; and in this fictional world a letter, a house, or a flower—to name some of Hawthorne's favorite emblems—serves as well or better than do his characters to represent the general truths for which the author tries to find concrete equivalents. The scarlet letter itself was, of course, the most important of such emblems; it was used to depict with methodical rigor each aspect of the Puritan belief about the nature of Original Sin: its root in sensuality, its power to generate actual sins of pride and of intellect, its pervasiveness, its ineradicability. Not only did it stand for the first letter of a crime of sense, but its color and its almost voluptuous "Oriental" ornamentation allowed it to represent the satisfaction of physical sensual desires. In the way in which each of the characters reacted to it lay the expression of their actual sins of pride. Hester risked damnation when she took it off; Pearl, described as an animated scarlet letter, refused to allow her mother to remove it. Hester's salvation was finally made certain when at the end she returned to the village to live out the rest of her life with the scarlet letter still visible on her breast. Dimmesdale refused to wear it openly; instead he kept hidden on his flesh what may be either its stigmata or a self-inflicted scar in its shape. Chillingworth's quest, a quest that doomed him, was a search for the letter; and when he finally perceived it on the breast of his victim, his transformation into the satanic was complete.

Just as it is used to delineate the varieties of original and actual sin, so is the letter used to allegorize its pervasiveness and ubiquity. When Hester passed her neighbors, even the most exalted of the community, "the red infamy upon her breast would give a sympathetic throb."[59] Her needle, the same that sewed the scarlet letter, was used to make all the official garments of the community—from baby linen to the death shroud—including the ruff of the magistrate, the scarf of the soldier, and the band of the priest.

The necessary criteria for the allegorical method were thus met in every particular—the frank abandonment of lifelikeness, the identification of the stylized surface with a general meaning on the level of human moral and religious experience, and the rational way in which such general meanings can be understood by the reader. Yet although Hawthorne felt the force and the underlying truth of the Christian world view, he was no sectarian believer. He felt like a Puritan, but the time when an imagination like his could think like one was two hundred years past. The message Hawthorne received from reality was a series of broken hints. In weaving these together, he undertook "a task resembling in its perplexity that of gathering up and piecing together the fragments of a letter which has been torn and scattered to the winds."[60] He made this statement when trying to tell us of Miriam's relation to brother Antonio and there spoke of the "mystic utterances" that he would try to make coherent and of the "sadly mysterious" influences that motivated his heroine. The piece of triangular cloth that he claimed he found in the Custom House told him no clear truth but was a "mystic symbol," which communicated itself to his sensibilities but whose "deep meaning" evaded "the analysis" of his mind.[61]

These mysteries were evidently of two kinds, and Hawthorne's emblems stretched in two directions to become something more suggestive and, at the same time, more complicated and interesting than allegories: they took on both a metaphysical and psychological dimension. The metaphysical mysteries were concerned with the inexpressible, illogical, and inscrutable ways of God as he related himself to the affairs of men; and upon this subject Hawthorne had little of the certainty of Bunyan. "The mind wanders wild and wide," says Kenyon at the end of *The Marble Faun*, when he tries to speculate upon the meaning of the story of Monte Beni; he appeals to Hilda, the embodiment of pure faith: "O Hilda, guide me home!" She can but answer, "We are both lonely; both far from home! . . . I . . . have no such wisdom as you fancy in me."[62] The clue to the mystery, the story suggested, lay in the doctrine of the Fortunate Fall—the fall of innocent, amoral, Adamic man into humanity through sin: "Did Adam fall, that we might ultimately rise to a far loftier paradise than his?" Hilda rejected this solution in the strongest terms and forbade Kenyon to take even this perplexing comfort, even this mysterious solution to the "mysteries"; but it was this paradox that lay at the deepest levels of Hawthorne's romances and gave the allegory a metaphysical resonance.

In two of the earlier romances, there were other strong hints of a solution to the problem of evil in the doctrine of *felix culpa*. In *The Scarlet Letter* Hester's sin made her capable of sympathetic help to other sinners; the early sketch "Endicott and the Red Cross" suggested this ambivalence when it described the meaning of the scarlet letter as both "Admirable" and "Adulteress." The prettiness of Phoebe—after it was exposed to the evils of the House of the Seven Gables, to the knowledge of its past, and to the knowledge of lust and greed—deepened into true beauty as her maidenhood "passed into womanhood."[63] With the assertion of these paradoxes, Hawthorne's allegories took on a complexity that removed them from the simple category of static emblem.

The second level of mystery lay in the opposite direction—not in the cosmos, but in the microcosm of the individual mind of man. Hawthorne, like Poe and Melville, was exploring dramatically and aesthetically the dark and irrational human motives that the Enlightenment treated as aberrations to be cured by reason but that the morbid-minded believed to be the essence of the human condition. The dark labyrinth of mind was not only the labyrinth of metaphysical questing for the knowledge of God; it was as well the labyrinth of the recesses of the human unconscious. Hawthorne seemed aware of this correpondence between the concerns of the "psyche" and the concerns of the "soul" and hence of the correspondence between psychology and religion. After telling us of the curse of the Pyncheons and of the way in which those haughty aristocrats were, in the "topsy-turvy commonwealth of sleep," the subjects of the plebian Maules, he added: "Modern psychology, it may be, will endeavor to reduce these alleged necromancies within a system." [64] And Chillingworth's ministrations to Dimmesdale were the probings of a skillful investigator into psychic phenomena: "delving among his principles, prying into his recollections, and probing everything with a cautious touch, like a treasure-seeker in a dark cavern." Then followed so accurate a description of psychoanalytic therapy that an American historian of the science (forgetting that Chillingworth is described as diabolic and doomed) has called this passage the beginning of American psychoanalysis:[65]

If the [physician] possess native sagacity, and a nameless something more,—let us call it intuition; if he show no intrusive egotism, nor disagreeably prominent characteristics of his own; if he have the power, which must be born with him, to bring his mind into such affinity with his patient's, that this last shall unawares have spoken what he imagines himself only to have thought; if such revelations be received without tumult, and acknowledged not so often by an uttered sympathy as by silence . . . if to these qualifications of a confidant be joined the advantages afforded by his recognized character as a physician,—then, at some inevitable moment, will the soul of the sufferer be dissolved, and flow forth in a dark, but transparent stream, bringing all its mysteries into the daylight.[66]

In illustrating these dark places and caverns of the mind, Hawthorne's fictional constructions lost the firm, one-to-one correspondence to a clearly defined moral. His characters, seen in relation to these mysteries, were no longer one-dimensional outlines but became exceedingly complex congeries of meanings. Their motives became ambiguous; their value became problematical; their fates were in no sense directly and rationally related to their actions. Chillingworth's behavior was given a dimension that seems a startling premonition of Freudian ambivalence: "It is a curious subject of observation and inquiry, whether hatred and love be not the same thing at bottom. . . . Philosophically considered . . . the two passions seem essentially the same."[67]

And even the inanimate things of the story refused to be circumscribed by a superimposed moral. The scarlet letter, the controlling allegory of the tale, operated in many paradoxical ways. It made Hester more capable of sympathetic help to others (the early sketch "Endicott and the Red Cross" had already suggested this doubleness of the emblem's meaning). Even its concealment was similarly ambiguous, for it made Dimmesdale a more effective preacher; there is a strong suggestion of the connection among sin, disease, and art in Hawthorne's description of the way in which Dimmesdale's agony sinewed his performance: "This very burden it was that gave him sympathies so intimate with the sinful brotherhood of mankind, so that his heart vibrated in unison with theirs, and received the pain into itself, and sent its own throb of pain through a thousand other hearts, in gushes of sad, persuasive eloquence."[68] Finally, the letter, graven on the tombstone as a representation of the metaphysical and psychological mysteries, was the last thing we see in the story. It was a "device, a herald's wording of which might serve for a motto and a brief description of our now concluded legend. . . . ON A FIELD, SABLE, THE LETTER A, GULES." The sentence before had described the red letter in this heraldic device as "the one ever-glowing point of light" in the dark story; added to this description was the paradoxical assertion that this light was "gloomier than the shadow."[69] A light that is gloomier than the shadow, a light that sheds brightness and at the very moment darkens the blackness around it—this was not the stuff of pure allegory but something much more complex; and it was the kind of

nonrealistic device Hawthorne fashioned to create his patterns of meaning, his dark idea that was so different from the
dominant idea of his culture.

2. Poe

In a strange dialogue, "The Colloquy of Monos and Una,"
Edgar Allan Poe gave his view of the inadequacy of his
country's faith in the future. He posited a time near the end
of history when human aspirations, represented by the primal male of Monos and the primal female of Una, lay in their
common grave. The male "one" murmurs to the female a
reminiscence of the developments of man and describes
them as the exact reverse of the American idea. Western
man's story, he tells her, was a story of failure and decay;
furthermore, the failure was due precisely to the ability that
he prized most—his analytic reason. Two destructive impulses were let loose upon the world: the impulse to know
and the impulse to equalize. Reason and democracy, twin
components of the American idea, are the evils that have
ended in their only possible earthly conclusion: a purification by fire, a holocaust that cleanses the world of civilization
and returns it to its primitive Eden.

Indeed, this is the first unequivocal example of pure primitivism in our literature. However, it is a primitivism founded
not upon the Enlightenment's chaste and cerebral vision of
the radical goodness of man but upon the romantic glorification of pure, amoral sensuousness—the radical primitive worship of the undifferentiated impulse to pleasure. Its yearning
toward the past was absolute; it wished for nothing less than
a quite literal return to the Eden of prehistory —to the "holy,
august and blissful days, when blue rivers ran undammed,
between hills unhewn, into far forest solitudes, primeval,
odorous, and unexplored."[70] It was a primitivism back to
which only the intense and obsessive cultivation of one of
men's faculties—the faculty of "taste," which "holding a
middle position between the pure intellect and the moral
sense,"[71] was the indispensable human faculty—could lead
us. Yet this faculty was disregarded by civilization, whose
efforts, dominated by intellect and the moral sense, were
directed toward the annulment of "taste," the repression of

enjoyment; "the Earth's records," therefore, led Monos "to look for widest ruin as the price of highest civilization."[72] Mankind had ignored those few visionaries who had "ventured to doubt the propriety of the term 'improvement' as applied to the progress of our civilization"[73] and who had tried to tell them that man fell from Eden when he ate of the fruit of the tree of knowledge. The consequent attempt to master and control nature had led to the next great evil: "wild attempts at an omni-prevalent Democracy."[74] Man could not both experiment and democratize without succumbing: "Huge smoking cities arose, innumerable. Green leaves shrank before the hot breath of furnaces."[75] The inevitable result had been holocaust; the result of progress was disaster, the death of civilization.

The vision that led to the formation of the little world of Poe's illusions was another controlling idea, another imaginative alternative to the vision of reality in America. Like Hawthorne's, Poe's idea took its shape from the terms of its rejection of its culture's faith. It was a world that started with negation: it said "no" both to the idea of progress and to the moral goodness of natural man. Having thus emptied the American cosmos of its belief, it then tried to come to terms with the absolute need of every human to believe in something that will give meaning and value to his existence. Where Hawthorne found this "something" in the inscrutable God of a Hebraic-Christian universe, the disasters of which could be understood by the doctrine of Original Sin, Poe proposed that the meaning and value that lay beyond the world of social appearances was the principle of Beauty—of pure pleasure without the taint of moral or intellectual repression. This principle of Beauty was doomed, crushed by the world of American culture; the visionary who held to this principle was deemed mad and indeed, if madness be defined as a radical maladjustment to society, was actually mad. Madness and disease then become the norms of Poe's world; turmoil and decay, the principal movement; and death, the all-absorbing end. "The play is the tragedy, 'Man,'/And the hero the Conqueror Worm."[76]

The artist who had this vision of society as identical with *death*—with the repression of primitive sensual pleasure, which is defined as *life*—maintained that he was celebrating "life" when he concerned himself with the "death" of society and civilization. It therefore becomes the subject of some confusion when Poe talked of death. If he equated the "death" of civilization with death, then presumably he was celebrating the death of death and hence was celebrating life. Yet this way madness lies—whether absolute madness or the relative madness of a radical social deviant. If Poe's society, his American society, were neurotic and diseased, then he was sane and healthy. If it were sane and healthy, then he was neurotic and diseased. It is futile to argue which statement is true. We can observe that Poe, after rejecting his society's idea, wrote poems and stories whose major obsessions were madness, decay, and death.

This was not a necessary path for the radically primitive artist to follow. There is another—the wild celebration of the anarchic pleasure principle, which constitutes the work of a modern Dionysian like Henry Miller. That Poe did not take this path but instead remained obsessed with death suggests that he was far from consistent in his radical primitivism; his inconsistency had two causes.

First, he could not bring himself to locate "Beauty" in the actual, the material, world. Once, in "The Colloquy of Monos and Una," he suggested that the inhabitant of the Eden of Pleasure was a fleshly man. Usually, however, he accepted the Platonic supremacy of ideal or mind over body and the conception that there is a "Beauty above" that is eternal and apart from the material universe. The wild attempts of man to make beauty are struggles "by multiform combinations among the things and thoughts of Time, to attain a portion of that Loveliness whose very elements . . . appertain to eternity alone." Eternal beauty, the sole meaning and value of the universe, is not of the earth; the sadness we feel when we see or hear a beautiful work of art is our "petulant, impatient sorrow at our inability to grasp *now* wholly, here on earth, at once and forever, those divine and rapturous joys."[77]

The second reason for Poe's obsession with death was the agony induced by the intolerable and irreconcilable strife between his hatred of civilization and his religion of art. Poe found civilization worthless: the death principle itself; but poetry—art—is part of civilization; poems are the works of man, and "under the sun there neither exists nor *can* exist any work more thoroughly dignified—more supremely noble than this . . . poem per se—this poem . . . written solely for the poem's sake."[78] Art, then, is form—the forming of things in this world by an unnatural arrangement of the "things and thoughts of Time." And this, along with all of man's works, must be destroyed with the death of civilization. Furthermore, the loveliest of the things of time that can be arranged by the artist—the thing that captures most of the indefinable essence of beauty—is the earthly beauty of woman. And both these beauties must be destroyed by both kinds of deaths: the beauty of art destroyed by the death of civilization, which will herald the rebirth into the anarchy of Eden, and the beauty of woman destroyed by the decay of the grave and the tooth of the worm. No wonder that horror and agony were the normal conditions of Poe's poetic and fictional world, for all that it worshipped was doomed by the system of beliefs he set up to replace his emptied universe.

This system of beliefs, then, began with negation. Not only in this colloquy did he say "no" to the idea of progress. He repeated his negations again and again throughout his poems, tales, and sketches. Even in so light an exercise as "Morning on the Wissahiccon," he revelled in visions of other days "when the Demon of the engine was not" and when "the red man trod alone." For a moment this vision of Eden and the wilderness returned in the appearance of an old elk, which in his imagination embodied the idea of primitive pleasure: "I fancied the elk repining, not less than wondering, at the manifest alterations for the worse, wrought upon the brook and its vicinage . . . by the stern hand of the utilitarian." In an ironic turn the beast proved to be "a *pet* of great age and very domestic habits, and belonged to an English family occupying a villa in the vicinity."[79] In his critical reviews as well, Poe emphasized his opposition to progress. He chided William Cullen Bryant for sustaining "in the very teeth of analogy . . . a hope of *progression* in happiness."[80] The clearest and most biting of his negations, however, was in a poem he used as a prelude to his youthful long vision of the religion of Beauty, *Al Aaraaf*. This was the sonnet "To Science," the sharpest expression of his distaste for the analytic reason that "dims the mirror of our joy." The sonnet described science as the "true daughter of Old Time" —time that causes decay and death, that "alterest all things" with his "peering eyes." Just as in Al Aaraaf, where knowledge would be described as the "keen light" refracted from the "bounds of Death," so in the prefatory poem it was associated with disaster. It was a "vulture, whose wings are dull realities." It prevented the imagination from soaring; it had destroyed mythology and the mythological vision. It had taken the spirit out of nature, "the Naiad from her flood" and "The Elfin from the green grass." Finally, and most damningly, it had stolen from the poet his "summer dream beneath the tamarind tree."[81]

The scientific mind here excoriated was the science of Aristotle, Bacon, and Mill—the science of empiricism, the reduction of all knowledge to either deduction or induction from observed facts. Poe contemptuously referred to the first two fathers of experimental knowledge as Aries Tottle and Hog in his "Mellonta Tauta"; and in the same satiric fiction he scornfully described Mill's self-contradictory "axiomatic truth" that "contradictories cannot both be true."[82] For the kind of "scientist" who would use intuition as a mode of comprehension, who would devote himself to the workings of the mind, and who, above all, would reject utilitarian purpose in favor of elegant formulations from an imaginative combination of both psychic and physical evidence—for this kind of "scientist" Poe had sufficient respect to make one the main character of a new kind of prose fiction. Yet this new kind of fiction (he called it the fiction of "ratiocination"; we know it as the "detective story") was in every way symptomatic of his general rejection of the values of his society. It scorned bourgeois sentiments by its cold amorality and its absence of human feeling; it scorned society's organizations by showing the bumbling foolishness of its authorities: the police officer was always a dupe. Above all, it displayed its contempt for the commonplace values of the middle class by proposing as the central character a man without family, affection, or love, whose life consisted solely of a dehumanized selection and arrangement of the chaos about him into elegant solutions that satisfy his aesthetic sense.

Having emptied the poetic universe of "truth" as a supreme value, Poe also emptied it of "morality"—at least as understood by his culture. Again and again he insisted that poetry has only peripheral connections with the faculty of "Duty" and suffers fatally when it permits the "moral sense" to intrude upon it. Having set up the pleasure principle as the supreme goal of human striving, he felt that "he who pleases is of more importance to his fellow man than he who instructs." He admired Longfellow's effects but deplored in him his "didactics," which, he declared, were all *out of place*."[83] Poe's stories and poems deny all "conventional habits of thinking" with regard to good and evil. There are no moral perspectives as we know them—no heroes who stand for "right," no villains who stand for "wrong," as society understands these terms.

What was left in Poe's universe was Beauty, and this was the main value, the goddess of his cosmos. She presides over a realm of "holy" pleasure, and her worship was the religion that Poe substituted for both the conventional worships of Western civilization and the American secular faith in worldly advancement. "An immortal instinct, deep within the spirit of man, is thus, plainly, a sense of the Beautiful. . . . The thirst belongs to the immortality of man. It is at once a consequence and an indication of his perennial existence."[84] This virtue is *supernal*: it is not afforded to the soul by any existing collection of earth's forms, save perhaps the sad chord struck upon a harp.

The aim of the poet is to try "to attain a portion of that Loveliness"; having caught a fleeting glimpse of it, he struggles in his art to arrange the "things and thoughts of Time" in such a way that they remind us of the ineffable essence that is beyond human capacity to realize fully and to express. This much Poe said openly; but what is everywhere implied in his poems and stories is that one of the "things and thoughts of Time"—the physical love between man and woman—that other romantic poets, especially optimistic romantics like Whitman, had taken as the supreme symbol of eternal value is not a representation of beauty but is quite the opposite. Sex for Poe was not fulfillment, completion, and life but was death, a loss of form in chaos. There were no earthly love poems or love stories in him, for to him love—that is, the physical heterosexual passion—was a kind of death.

The above description of his cosmology is drawn from poems, essays, and stories published throughout his career. Yet like the attitudes of most romantics, his views were an intuition of his youth and received full expression in the long early poem *Al Aaraaf*. Standing alone in the chaos of a world that had abandoned him, finding no roots either in a family that was not his own or in a culture to which he felt himself alien (on a "surf-tormented shore"), haunted by the fear that "*all* that we see or seem/Is but a dream within a dream,"[85] he tried to grasp for grains of the "golden sand" of certainty as they trickled through his fingers. "O God! can I not save/ One from the pitiless wave?" he cried in final anguish. In *Al Aaraaf* he had described the one grain of certainty that he could save and that would save him: the art of poetry, which is the act of worshiping beauty. And, symptomatically, he described it in a poem that, at the same time, is a poem of death, of the inevitable trap into which an earthly worshiper of beauty must fall, of the trap of love—the "death" of aspirations to fuse with the beautiful.

The poem's vision was of a universe in four parts. There was a realm of God; but he never appears, and when he is heard it is with a "silent sound." There was the realm of ideal beauty—of the Goddess Nesace—and this was the realm of heaven, which is the concern of the poem. Somewhere, as vague as the precinct of God, there was a third realm—the precincts of hell and death—which refracted the light of death-dealing knowledge. And then there was the region of the physical galaxies in which lay the earth.

At one time Nesace visited "our star" (the earth), but now she resides only in her own star. When she visited the earth, it was God's favored place; now, however, it is a small fallen globe "in which sightless cycles run" and where God's "love is folly" and where chaos rules. At the time of her visit, she apparently inspired the great art of the ancients, but these have gone from the earth; their images exist only in another part of Beauty's realm, a twin star called "Al Aaraaf." (Here the geography is unclear; whether Al Aaraaf was a member of a double-star system, the other half of which was Beauty's abode, or whether it was another and gloomier part of Beauty's single star is not certain.)

The poem began with several restatements of the unearthly, supernal nature of Beauty's world; but after this disclaimer, there then came a description of it in terms of the essences of earthly flowers. Although this realm is presumably "lower" on the scale of celestial being than the realm of God, Poe revealed his allegiance to it by describing it as an "oasis in the desert" of heaven. Nesace (Beauty) hymns her fealty to God in the odors of the flowers and states her willingness to be his ambassador. His silent voice both affirms that she was the embodiment of his spirit ("Thine is my resplendency") and orders her to leave her home and fly to other worlds to "divulge the secrets of thy embassy . . ./ lest the stars totter in the guilt of man!"

Part II begins with a description of Al Aaraaf—a star that still lay in Beauty's "Therasaean reign." It was a region, the poet told us in his notes, between heaven and hell; its landscapes were like the beautiful ruined cities beneath the waves of the Red Sea. Here dwell the spirits of men and women who have not attained the realm of pure beauty, for they are guilty of the knowledge "refracted from Hell," guilty of love, and still bound by passion. "With the Arabians," Poe noted, "there is a medium between Heaven and Hell, where men suffer no punishment, but yet do not attain that tranquil and even happiness which they suppose to be characteristic of heavenly enjoyment." This medium he defined in a Spanish quotation as an unbroken dream, a pure day, happy, free; one would be free of love, of passion, of hate, of hope. Al Aaraaf is just such a place; there "sorrow is not excluded . . . but it is that sorrow which the living love to cherish for the dead, and which, in some minds, resembles the delirium of opium. The passionate excitement of Love and the buoyancy of spirit attendant upon intoxication are its less holy pleasures—the price of which, to those souls who make choice of 'Al Aaraaf' as their residence after life, is final death and annihilation."

The "bright beings" of Al Aaraaf are stargazers, for the stars are the eyes of Beauty. They lie, however, in a sweet death, the death of the love ecstasy, the "last ecstasy of satiate life." Nesace begs them to leave love's caresses, which are "lead on the heart." She calls upon a beautiful maiden "Ligeia," her "beautiful one," whose loveliness is identical with music and poetry; she asks Ligeia, the spirit of poetry, to breathe the life of art into the ears of the slumberers. Two of the spirits do not hear it, "for Heaven no grace imparts/To those who hear not for their beating hearts." The male spirit, Angelo, and his lover, Ianthe, reminisce about the moment he was transported from earth to Al Aaraaf. Al Aaraaf came close to earth at Nesace's bidding; at that moment the earth "trembled" with the same spirit as that with which Beauty herself trembles. Angelo left the earth at the spot where this beauty was concentrated—the Parthenon; as he left, he saw the earth hurled into chaos. Now he and his love sit in eternal night and murmur hopelessly to each other.[86]

Al Aaraaf predicted all of Poe's future works. The general tone was the melancholy derived from the vision of a bliss that could be glimpsed by man but from which his humanity, his passions as well as his reason, disqualified him. The world it created was ruled by Beauty; her principal handmaiden was named "Ligeia," a spirit who is identified with "number," "Rhyme," and "harmony." Man's shattered globe lay sterile, and the history of its development was not progress but devolution to a bleak chaos where all values were inverted, where God's wrath was scientifically explained away as a "thunder cloud," and where his "love was folly." Salvation in this universe would occur only through the worship of pure beauty to which we might be led by pure poetry. Beauty's essence for Poe was symbolized by the form of the perfect female and was concentrated particularly in her eyes.

The trap set for man, however, was sex; man was a spiritual being who had "fallen" into the knowledge of sensual love; he therefore could achieve not the realm of beauty but a kind of hedonist's purgatory; here in the halfway house he could feel but three pleasures: the highest of them was a sweet sorrow, which, significantly, resembled the "delirium of opium"; the other pleasures were the ecstasy of love and the intoxication of alcohol. The first pleasure was sacred; the latter two were considered "less holy."

Concerned then that his actual physical world of "reality" was chaos, convinced that pure ideal beauty was the highest value, certain that this beauty was unattainable on earth but that its essence was symbolized by the beautiful body of woman, anguished by the fear that man's sexuality doomed him to a passion that destroys this symbol, Poe wrote literary criticism, poetry, and prose fiction that were direct expressions of this "little world" of belief expressed in *Al Aaraaf*. His criticism began with the conventional romantic assumption that poetry begins with some insight into the world beyond the world of the senses—in this case with the vision of "Ligeia." Poe therefore called for a poetry of the imagination rather than of the fancy—to use Coleridge's distinction, which he had read and had approved. Having said it, however, he then cut poetic practice away from any tendency toward looseness and freedom to which such a theory had often led other romantics. The poet might be a divine madman (a poet is "but one remove from a fool,"[87] sententiously asserts the voice of society, the prefect of "The Purloined Letter"), but he must be a very crafty madman indeed. He must painstakingly select and arrange and organize the words that represent the objects of his physical world into the new forms and order of art. And since music is the handmaiden of Beauty, the sounds of these words are all-important; poetry becomes not "metre-making argument" but metres—not sound to imitate sense, but sound that is in itself divine sense. In short, a poem will not signify or point to any other meaning in the world of things but will be its own supreme meaning and the only possible glimpse into an otherwise hidden eternity. In this critical theory Poe supplied the program for the American artist who rejected the symbols of his culture: he must, said Poe, create his private symbols and then find ways to make them effective.

Applied to the works of his contemporaries, this doctrine led to a body of the most searching criticism we had yet had in America. It led to the theory of the short story as the perfect form for ratiocination, horror, or terror, in which every element would contribute to a single unified effect. It led to the measuring of American poets against the standards of the English romantics—Coleridge, Shelley, and Keats—and to the attack on nonromantic poetry as second-rate. He carefully measured the stanzas, the lines, even the single feet of his fellow authors to discover if every part belonged as a harmonic contribution to the whole. He scanned their verse for evidences of didacticism or utilitarianism and chided them if either seemed a substantial part of their verses. Above all, he condemned any suggestion of conformity or subscription to the idea of progress and democracy, an idea whose terms were as blasphemy to his religion.

Unhappily, as everything about this genius was unhappy, his poetry, the form he valued above all others, was his least successful mode. Its attention to "music" led to a crushing monotony; in "The Raven" 705 out of 719 feet are perfect trochees, 10 are doubtful, and only 4, the musically similar dactyls, have variance. Lowell's term "the jingle man" was not unearned. The persistently regular cadences invoke a hypnosis not unlike the holy pleasures of Al Aaraaf, but poetry is an intensification of the senses rather than an annulment of them. Poe's verse was most successful in shorter lyric expressions; and the poem that defines the object of his worship, the goddess of Beauty, was, not unexpectedly, the most successful. This was the theme of "To Helen."

"To Helen" was neither a poem of passion nor a verse in praise of a woman as a woman but rather a poem to an ideal beyond emotion. Poe's description was cool and dispassionate, and his terms were strangely generalized. The effect was a complete depersonalization, a transformation of sex into spirit. The first elaborate comparison was to a "Nicaean bark," which carried the "weary, way-worn wanderer" back to his eastern home from the risks, dangers, and uncertainties of the adventures of his ill-advised progression westward: Nice was a western outpost of Mediterranean culture, the "native shore" of antiquity where, as he said in *Al Aaraaf*, "beauty clung" around "a proud temple call'd the Parthenon." The value of Helen was not the value of a physical being but that of a disembodied means of returning to the realm of the aesthetic.

The second stanza repeated the metaphor and emphasized the desperation of the expatriate; the allusions to Helen's actual physical beauty continue to etherealize her. Three aspects of her body—her hair, her face, and her "airs"—are mentioned, but they are not described; in each case they are qualified by an adjective that removes them from particularity by directing attention away from their concrete being and toward some vaguely suggested realm of ideal pleasure. "Hyacinth," an indeterminate Homeric epithet, suggests the curl of a statue's hair; "classic," applied to "face," tells us only that beauty was to be associated with a lost Eden of pleasure. "Naiad," as a qualification to the very general "airs," does nothing to materialize this attribute but rather associates it with a spirit of ancient mythology. The classical culture in turn is, then, in its two major manifestations, identified by single adjectives: "grandeur" applied to Rome gives us a sense of size and also lends a feeling of anticlimax, a descent, a falling away from the value of the Grecian culture of which the term "glory" seems a richly suggestive summary, implying the height of religious devotion, embodying the essence of godhead. Having succeeded in transforming the earthly emblem of beauty into a generalized essence, Poe then devoted the last paragraph to setting his goddess—the "Psyche" from his Holy Land of ideal beauty—in the temple of his religion of art, to replacing the Virgin with a figure that is totally classical.

Although he considered the medium of prose inferior to that of poetry, Poe ironically achieved his greatest success in the short story. He thought so little of prose that he was quite willing to use it to satisfy a popular taste that was running toward the titillations of the Gothic tales introduced by Horace Walpole into English literature and popularized by Monk Lewis, Charles Maturin, and Mary Shelley. The German Gothic tales of E. T. A. Hoffman helped to increase the favorable climate for the horrible mingled with supernatural, while the Gothic novels of Charles Brockden Brown had made their way as the first substantial body of fiction by an American author. Poe's feelings about the chaos of the modern world, his identification of sex with death, his unresolved horror at the prospect of the corrupting grave—all combined to attract him to the Gothic tale. His "Berenice," which he said had originated in a bet that he could "produce nothing effective on a subject so singular," was an effort to capitalize upon public taste for the fantastic. This grotesquerie described a man haunted by the teeth of his beloved and ended with a ghoulish feat of dental surgery that left the narrator with thirty-two white mementoes of his love. Poe was convinced that his future success depended upon his writing this kind of material to which his fundamental commitments made him so sympathetic. "To be appreciated, you must be *read*," he wrote his editor, and he therefore proposed to continue to furnish him with tales that would sell. Earlier in the letter he described the nature of this form of fiction: "the ludicrous heightened into the grotesque: the fearful colored into the horrible: the witty exaggerated into the burlesque: the singular wrought out of the strange and mystical."[88]

He combined these elements into short tales and into several longer narratives that frankly capitalized upon the popularity of another form, the travel adventure. In the most elaborate of these, *The Narrative of A. Gordon Pym*, the fusion of the Gothic and the travel tale was complete; he used the hybrid form to demonstrate that the "terror is not of Germany but of the soul."[89] It was the "perfect form" for a depiction of the chaotic world of modernity where man, driven by forces he cannot understand or control—himself not the least of the horrors—and drawn inevitably to his doom, moves in an alien and hostile world. There is a turning of the tradition of travel against itself; since the Renaissance it had been a testament of affirmation, a testimonial to man's conquest and triumph: John Smith had told his story to demonstrate how man might achieve a spatial expansion commensurate with his inner dignity. In *Pym* Poe told a story of aimless, senseless, futile wanderings marked by horror at every stage and climaxing in total destruction.[90] True to his creed of art, Poe inverted each one of his society's beliefs and illusions to make a perfect form for dissolution. In place of the goodness of nature, he posited the fearfulness of the elements and of the carrion birds that drop gobbets of human flesh from their curved beaks; in place of the goodness of man, he posed the irreducible blackness of the human condition; in the place of the triumph of rationality, he proclaimed the supremacy of the irrational; in place of triumph and conquest, he portrayed the end of modern man in annihilation under the white shrouds of the universe.

Perhaps the most terrible of all the elements of this harrowing tale—the complete loss of what the Enlightenment regarded as "humanity" in the perspective of the narrator—is the least explicit. Pym was the central character; we can call him a hero only for the sake of identification. Completely selfish, totally amoral, he was superior solely because of a more heightened sensitivity and a greater self-awareness than the people about him. He is a member of "the whole numerous race of the melancholy among men," and he is drawn to his adventures by descriptions of "terrible moments of suffering and despair." To this perversity he adds an intense "hypocrisy pervading every word and action."[91] His abnormal sensitivity serves only to make him the first to think of cannibalism; his hypocrisy makes him the last to approve of the fearful proposal of the survivors of the shipwreck. He tries desperately to cheat his fellows when lots are drawn to designate the victim, and then, when the victim is dispatched, he partakes of the ghastly feast without a qualm. He turns to the reader as if he were addressing the *hypocrite lecteur* and advises, "Before any one condemn me for this apparent heartlessness, let him be placed in a situation precisely similar to my own."[92]

Locked in his selfhood, driven by a compulsion to self-destruction, the protagonist finds an outer world that matches the horror of his inner state. In his voluntary entombment, when he stowed away aboard *The Grampus*, he dreamed of "Every species of calamity and horror . . . demons . . . serpents . . . deserts," strange trees "crying to the silent waters for mercy, in the shrill and piercing accents of the most acute agony and despair."[93] He awakens to a real world even more terrible, to the scene of a murderous mutiny and an even bloodier suppression. The ship is battered by a storm, a "horrible, shrieking din and confusion."[94] A brig appears to rescue them; their delight turns into "triple horror" when the rescuing ship is revealed as a charnal barge populated by corpses, male and female, "in the last and most loathesome state of putrefaction."[95] Saved by a rational and kind captain, Pym perverts his rationality to his own ends as he despises the good man as "deficient in energy"[96] and urges him to the doomed, senseless voyage to the Pole. Poe invoked the Antarctic as an image of the unfathomable mystery of the universe, an image he had earlier used in "M.S. Found in a Bottle"; there he spoke of the icebound antipode as an awful region that embraced "some never-to-be-imparted secret, whose attainment is destruction."[97] So to annihilation Pym urges on his comrades as he leads them further and further south. Before destruction they pause at the heart of the blackness of things—the evil that lay at the bottom of humanity and that for him takes the shape of hideous Negroes who destroy the ship and all its crew but Pym and the half-breed, Peters. The Negroes, "wicked, hypocritical, vindictive," are in fear of a greater evil than their own—the horror of the whiteness that lay beyond their evil, the whiteness of the final mystery that embraces Pym in its shrouds.

"To Helen" was the identification of Poe's religion; *A. Gordon Pym* was his summary of the chaos of the world of contemporary beliefs and illusions. "Ligeia" was his attempt to demonstrate the role of poetry and art in this chaotic world and his desperate gloomy effort to express the "salvation" of the artist through the triumph of the artistic will. This short story, which he considered his best, transferred the scene from Al Aaraaf to the earth and described what happens when the ideal becomes part of reality, with its necessary attendant fall into the corruptions of the earth. Ligeia, the spirit of poetry, was seen in the short story communing with a mortal; the spirit was, as it must be, embodied in a beautiful woman: her expressions must be the expressions of humanity, but her aspirations must be the aspirations of the ideal. How this paradox may be resolved, how the triumph of the ideal of art may finally be achieved, and at what cost to the ordinary concerns of "sane," "rational," and "conventional" human commitments—this was the theme of the tale of which Poe was most proud.

Ligeia is the goddess of "numbers," "rhythm," and "harmony." In brief, she is poetry, the first handmaiden of the goddess of absolute beauty and chosen by her to whisper in the ears of the sleeping spirits of Al Aaraaf. Now she is on earth. According to Poe's cosmology, ours is a world that has received the full distortion of the light of "knowledge," which has transformed everything to its radical opposite: "truth" is "falsehood," "sanity" is "folly," and "love" and "life" are "death." Coming, as she must, from nowhere, with her parentage obscure, her paternal name unknown, Ligeia bears all the outward signs of her allegiance to the goddess of Poe's cosmos; she is herself very beautiful; she has the "hyacinthine" locks of the goddess personified in "To Helen"; above all she has the eyes of the goddess as she is described in *Al Aaraaf*, and her eyes are like twin stars.

However, coming into the world of men she necessarily partakes of the two inevitably damning faculties of man—his reason and his passion—and with her powers carries them to even greater extremes than those of which ordinary mortals are capable: "*all* the wide areas of moral, physical, and mathematical science"[98] become her province in a manner "gigantic" and "astounding"; and more than any other woman she is "a prey to the tumultuous vultures of stern passion." The sole possible end of knowledge and sexual desire is, according to Poe's vision, death; so Ligeia lies dying. The next to last gasp of her creative powers was the poem "The Conqueror Worm." In it she describes the "motley drama" of the world of physical things as containing "much of Madness, and more of Sin/And Horror, the soul of the Plot"; it is a drama that the watching angels affirm as "the tragedy, 'Man,'/And its hero the conqueror Worm." Having become mortal, Ligeia must die; having known knowledge and passion, the condition of mortality, she must pay for the guilt of her knowledge. Yet in her last breath she asserts the possibility of triumphing over her death by the power of the will.

With her death the narrator turns to opium as his solace. This is no vice—quite the contrary; Poe considered the opium delirium to be the nearest sensation to the "holy pleasure" of Al Aaraaf, the perceptive sorrow of him who knows that Beauty is his goddess but who knows also that he cannot reach her. The heightened sensitivity of the opium dream, then, is a permissible, although less satisfying, state than the heightened sensitivity of poetic awareness. In this demonic world all values are necessarily inverted; so it truly becomes an "accursed moment" (accursed from the standpoint of the religion of beauty, although the sacrament of the accepted faith of his culture) when he enters into what the "normal" world would believe to be a healthy love, his marriage to the Lady Rowena Trevanion of Tremaine, her fair hair and blue eyes the embodiment of sentimental conventional beliefs about the goodness of man and nature. He brings his new bride to a nuptial chamber whose decorations are those of a tomb: for Poe, earthly physical love was "death." The story then proceeds to describe how, through the effort of will of both the narrator and of Ligeia herself, the fair but never "beautiful" Rowena dies and Ligeia physically usurps her body. With a shriek the narrator acknowledges "the full, and the black, and the wild eyes—of my lost love—of the Lady— of the LADY LIGEIA."[99] The will has triumphed; absolute beauty, life, "the *true*, the divine Eros," asserts its supremacy in a world devoted to the powers of reason and passion, both of which are death; beauty, art, poetry come back into death in the act of coming back into life; the only possible reaction to this tragic paradox is the maniacal shriek of the narrator.

The method Poe used to present his controlling idea went a full step further away from the imitation of perceived reality than the method of Hawthorne. The ordinary world, emptied of meaning and significance, could not possibly supply the materials for his art, could not be the "things of time" that might be used to embody an ideal of beauty to which the ordinary forms and shapes were direct antitheses; the "thoughts of Time," the idea of his culture, could not remotely comprehend a system that made its faiths mockeries, its truths follies, its sanities madness—that, above all, made its belief in life and love a belief in death and annihilation. So Poe's imagination dealt in counters radically different from the common coinage. He had no sympathy with the transcendental urge to use the ordinary world of experiences as valid symbols of the transcendent world. Wordsworth, he declared scornfully, "has given immortality to a wagon, and the bee Sophocles has transmitted to eternity a sore toe, and dignified a tragedy with a chorus of turkeys."[100] Instead, Poe turned to the weird, the grotesque, the unusual —to the irrational, the mysterious—as the only suitable stuff for the making of his private illusions, which were substitutes for the idea of his culture.

3. Melville

Hawthorne replaced his culture's idea with a pattern essentially Puritan; Poe countered it with a pagan worship of absolute beauty; Herman Melville had "nothing" to offer in its place: nothing except the magnificent tormented expression of the condition of doubt, rescued from absolute despair only by the tragic triumph of the human spirit, which was capable of both facing and expressing the awful possibility of a meaningless universe. "The strongest guard is placed at the gateway to nothing," wrote a writer of the generation that rediscovered Melville. "Maybe," Fitzgerald continued, "because the condition of emptiness is too shameful to be divulged." Melville's was the first American imagination to break down these guards at the gateway to the possibility of a senseless world. And yet he never rested in even this precarious position but continued to question, to doubt; and what we have in his romances and short stories are various phases of that doubt of both God and man—of the traditional Christian faiths and of the American idea as well. Hawthorne's description of him in 1856 remains definitive: he could neither believe nor rest easy in his unbelief but persisted in wandering over the wastelands of questioning and speculation.[101]

He was a child of his times, however, in his willingness to start, as a point of departure, from his society's chief structure of feeling: its pride in the present, its faith in the future. If there could ever be a solution to the problem of the painful earth, Melville would have seen it as an American solution, based upon the principles of democracy and equalitarianism, which he felt were more highly developed in America than in any other part of the Western civilized world: "We Americans are the peculiar, chosen people—the Israel of our time," he wrote in *White-Jacket*. "We bear the ark of the liberties of the world . . . the Political Messiah . . . has come . . . in *us* . . . national selfishness is unbounded philanthropy; for we cannot do a good to America but we give alms to the world."[102] And a year later, when he wrote his masterwork, he called for inspiration upon the "just spirit of Equality," the "great democratic God" who "didst pick up Andrew Jackson from the pebbles."[103] In his collection of poems on the Civil War, he tentatively expressed something close to a belief in progress: "With certain evils men must be more or less patient. Our institutions have a potent digestion, and may in time convert and assimilate to good all elements thrown in, however originally alien."[104] This was in 1866, and it echoed the more positive declaration he had made years earlier: "In the Past is no hope; the Future is both hope and fruition."[105]

It is clear from these examples that the American secular faith—the faith in progress, the belief in a democracy founded upon the conception of man's essential goodness—was one of the possibilities that Melville allowed himself to entertain, but with small enthusiasm and no tenacity. Furthermore, Emerson's romantic invigoration of those beliefs was another of the possible truths that Melville speculated upon, and not with entire disapproval. Although the bulk of his testimony is vigorously critical of Emersonian optimism, although his dominant mood was approval for those who thunder "no" and scorn for those who say "yes," he echoed in his fiction some of the praise he had expressed in a letter to Evert Duyckinck, where he described Emerson as a "thought-diver" and averred his love for all men who *"dive."*[106] In three of his works where Emersonian ideas are advanced, these ideas do not, in the final analysis, fare badly. They are incorporated in the doctrines of Plotinus Plinlimmon in *Pierre*, who preached the doctrine of a virtuous expediency based upon transcendental convictions: to live by absolutes in a world of relative values and contingencies is fatal—so ran the theory of this practical idealist; and the tragic outcome of Pierre's titanic attempt to live by absolutes would seem at least partial testimony to the truth of Plinlimmon's philosophy. Captain Amasa Delano in "Benito Cereno" was an embodiment of transendental optimism; and although his sanguinity made him incapable of reading the signs of his world correctly and prevented him from smashing through the pasteboard masks of experience to the truth behind them, still, as Benito Cereno pointed out to him, his innocent optimism saved them both from disaster. In *The Confidence-Man* Mark Winsome, a thinly disguised portrait of Emerson, was the only man on the Mississippi who could beat the fraudulent con man at his own game; his brand of "virtuous expediency," it would seem, was the one that worked in an ambiguous world.

However, it was a deceptive world that Melville saw and that he made the world of his fictions; he found no solace in the thought of an inscrutable God from whose grace humanity had fallen; nor could he find rest in a religion of art. Instead, like Taji in *Mardi*, he spent his life wandering over the seas of speculation with the prow of his canoe pointed out toward the horizon and refused to harbor in any faith. His wandering brought him perilously close to the border of total despair, to the "gates" of nothingness. What he left behind was a record of an imagination willing to face the appalling possibility that all faiths were impossible—that the faith in God was lost forever and that the American faith in the progress of radically good men in a beneficent natural world was equally false. Their withdrawal left only the most unbearable of all truths: "the colorless, all-color of atheism from which we shrink."[107]

That the cult of progress was incapable of supplying Melville with a sustaining faith early became clear. Despite the vigorous hopeful chauvinism of the passages about America as the new Israel in *White-Jacket* and despite corresponding statements about the natural goodness of natural man in *Typee*, the experiences of Melville's youth and adolescence and early maturity made him skeptical of the faith in human virtue and human advancement. Not that his earliest difficulties—the financial disaster of his family, the early decay and death of his father—were necessary determinants of his later attitudes; but they at least made him wary of an easy optimism. And the contrast between the industrial city of Liverpool and the Polynesian culture of the Marquesas Islands, which he observed in his early manhood, made him dubious of the moral superiority of the civilized and the Christian over the primitive and the pagan. In Liverpool he saw the ravages of industrialism, as yet unfettered by the reform movement that would moderate the conditions of laissez-faire economics. While there is no certainty that, like his fictional counterpart Wellington Redburn, he saw a mother and her children dying of starvation on the streets, there is no doubt that this image, real or imagined, was symptomatic of the evils of civilization, which "for every advantage she imparts, holds a hundred evils in reserve." And by contrast "the Polynesian savage, surrounded by all the luxurious provisions of nature, enjoyed an infinitely happier, though certainly a less intellectual existence, than the self-complacent European."[108]

In this avowal of the happiness of the Typees, there was a strong element of the "primitivism" of Jean Jacques Rousseau, whose name he invoked to define the reason for Polynesian felicity. The cause of their high degree of social order was the "inherent principle of honesty and charity towards each other," their government "by that sort of tacit common-sense law which, say what they will of the inborn lawlessness of the human race, has its precepts graven on every breast. The grand principles of virtue and honor, however they may be distorted by arbitrary codes, are the same all the world over: and where these principles are concerned, the right and wrong of any action appears the same to the uncultivated as to the enlightened mind."[109]

However, this was no sustained and unquestioned faith in the goodness of man and nature, upon which it might have been possible to erect an optimistic faith; rather there was at the very outset a deep sense of the doubleness—of the deceptiveness—of the world of appearances, a sense of the mystery and the depths of darkness that lay at the core of man's existence, be he civilized or savage. Civilization, indeed, was not condemned as such: "The naked wretch who shivers beneath the bleak skies, and starves among the inhospitable wilds of Tierra del Fuego, might indeed be made happier by civilization, for it would alleviate his physical wants."[110] The happy conditions of the Typees was a function of their unique geographical and climatic situation. In this condition both happiness and real virtue were more easily attained, by far, than under the conditions of Western civilization. Yet in both situations, that of the Typee as well as that of the wretch in Liverpool, there was an underlying horror, a fact of their existence as humans. Living under conditions that have been spared "the penalty of the Fall,"[111] the Polynesians showed more of the potentialities for goodness that are a universal part of the human condition. Yet they showed, too, the equally fundamental savagery of human nature. And, more than that, their paradise was one in which, if he allowed himself to be pulled back into it, the already fallen civilized man would find himself descending to an even greater darkness of unnamed evil.

This was Melville's fear as he wrote of it in *Typee*; lying indolent in an Eden of pleasure, he found that the proposed tattooing, which would make him part of that Eden forever, was a prospect of absolute horror. When the native artist showed a "painter's enthusiasm" for scarring a white face, Melville became "half wild with terror and indignation." He never penetrated the mystery of the ritual scarification; he knew only that it was connected in some dark way with "superstitious idolatry" and that this worship, which pervaded "the most important as well as the minutest transactions of life," compelled the savage to live "in the continual observance of its dictates, which guide and control every action of his being."[112] From that moment he lived in dread of the "odious operation" that would make him, like the white stranger in *Omoo* who was tattooed across the face with a blue shark, "a renegado from Christendom and humanity. . . . Far worse than Cain's—*his* was perhaps a wrinkle, or a freckle, which some of our modern cosmetics might have effaced; but the blue shark was a mark indelible, which all the waters of Abana and Pharpar . . . could never wash out."[113]

For Melville tattooing meant a fatal fall from civilization into savagery. In *Israel Potter* John Paul Jones's arm, scarred like "a New Zealand Warrior," was, Melville wrote, an indication of the "primeval savageness which ever slumbers in human kind, civilized or uncivilized."[114] When to the threat of tattooing was added the suspicion that the Typees practiced ritual cannibalism, Melville's craving to escape from Eden was overwhelming; and when he succeeded, he described his flight to sea as a flight from the clutches of barbarism:

These savages, unlike the feeble swimmers of civilized countries, are, if anything, more formidable antagonists in the water than when on land . . . the savages were spread right across our course . . . Mow-Mow . . . would have seized one of the oars . . . I dashed the boat hook at him. It struck him just below the throat . . . never shall I forget the ferocious expression of his countenance . . . one other of the savages reached the boat . . . the knives of our rowers . . . mauled his wrists.[115]

This double attitude toward primitivism continued through Melville's career, with the emphasis falling more and more upon the evil and darkness, rather than the goodness, at the heart of the human condition. In "Benito Cereno" Captain Delano's complete blindness was nowhere more apparent than in his view of the Negroes: "There's naked nature, now; pure tenderness and love,"[116] he said of the malevolent and murderous slaves. The same sentimental primitivism was the target of Melville's attack in *The Confidence-Man*. The basic lie that the cheater sold to the travelers aboard the *Fidèle* was "confidence in nature, confidence in man." And two of his disguises were specific allegories of the falsity of these dual beliefs at the heart of the American faith. The crippled Negro, appealing to a sympathy for the "common, familiar, and low," was the first of the frauds; and another of his disguises was that of an herb doctor whose argument runs: nature is health; health is good; nature cannot work ill. The last utterance of Melville's artistic life, "Billy Budd," demonstrated the operation in human affairs of a basic, natural malignity, a depravity that is as natural as goodness; the scorpion, Melville points out, is the sole responsibility of the Creator.

Along with his rejection of that part of the American idea that posited the essential beneficence of nature and man, Melville rejected his culture's faith in the possibilities of secular improvement. He continued, it is true, even after 1850 to maintain some feeling for the westward movement as an evolution in human affairs: "the Western spirit is, or will yet be (for no other is, or can be), the true American one."[117] Yet, as the muted tone of even this comment on his culture's faith indicates, his perception of the radical evil in man, "civilized or uncivilized," made him skeptical of men's societies and of the possibilities of their improvement through the use of reason; with Hawthorne and Poe, Melville was convinced that man's Faustian reason, and his attempted advancement through technology, was not to be his salvation but his doom. He shrewdly recognized that Benjamin Franklin was a summary of the American idea and attacked both his culture's faith in progress and its principal spokesman in his portrait of Franklin in *Israel Potter*. Franklin, he wrote, was "the type and genius of his land." He was "everything but a poet."[118] Melville described him sitting in his study surrounded by all the "hangings and upholstery of science."[119] In a cheerful voice Franklin called upon Israel to trust in man, for "an indiscriminate distrust of human nature is the worst consequence of a miserable condition."[120] Franklin, a hardheaded practical man of affairs—as Melville saw him—warned Israel: "Never joke at funerals, or during business transactions."[121] And Israel ended his association with "the type and genius of his land" by throwing his little bible, *Poor Richard*, aside and exclaiming, "Oh, confound all this wisdom!"[122]

Through Melville's shorter tales, too, there ran a constant vein of romantic rejection of progress and its principal nineteenth-century handmaiden, technological progress. Although the lightning rod salesman in the little sketch named after him represented religious orthodoxy rather than scientific faith, still the connection between him and the first American to explain the nature of lightning was probably more than fortuitous. And more specific in its analysis of the inevitable disaster of the cult of progress was "The Bell-Tower." Melville set this parable at the time of the Renaissance, which he described as the birth of the "jubilant expectation of the race."[123] It was the time of the discovery of America as well. Bannadonna—the great Renaissance figure "enriched through commerce with the Levant," demonstrating the modern pride in self-reliance by his status as an "unblest foundling"—was a "great mechanician," and he built a campanile taller than any other so that he might stand "erect, alone": he dared to poise himself higher than any that had stood before because, resting on each stage of the tower's growth, he had gradually ascended and finally had mastered the dizzy heights without fear. He cast an enormous bell, but in its molding was the flaw of human sacrificial blood. He made a mechanical monster to strike the bell; the monster slew its master, the bell cracked, the tower fell. Bannadonna, "asking no favors from any element or any being," had proposed to rival and rule nature: "He stooped to conquer. With him, common sense was theurgy; machinery miracle; Prometheus, the heroic name for machinist; man, the true God."[124]

"Man, the true God"—this *hubris*, for Melville, led inevitably to damnation. The belief in progress is a belief in the perfectibility of man; only God is perfect; the cult of progress is then the erection of man into God and the modern proof that the deadliest of the sins is pride: so ran his argument. One of the disguises of the devil in *The Confidence-Man* was therefore as a salesman for the Black Rapids Coal Company, and he urged his fellow travelers to invest in America's material technological progress. (Mark Twain and Charles Dudley Warner later used coal mining as the representation of the best in American activity, one of the many complete reversals of Melville's attitudes that was typical of Twain.) Then in *Clarel*, the long poem that broke his long silence, Melville described a debate between a believer in progress and a disbeliever. The spokesman for modern optimism answered the question "Whitherward does the surge impel?/ The end, the aim?" with the ready answer: "Through all methinks I see/The object clear; belief revised,/Men liberated —equalized/In happiness." Derwent concluded with an almost flippant rejection of the dark uncertainties that haunted Melville: "No mystery,/Just none at all; plain sailing." Opposed to this simple-minded spokesman was one whose sober and searching skepticism of the new cult of human betterment stood in sharp contrast to Derwent's shallow blitheness. The skeptic described how the "impieties of 'Progress'" speak scornfully to God and ask, "'How profits it? And who art Thou/That we should serve Thee?'" With the same pride that Bannadonna evidenced the "Impieties" declare: "Of Thy ways/No knowledge we desire; *new* ways/We have found out, and better." These false counselors conclude with this admonition to the Almighty from the self-sufficient believers in progress: "Go—/Depart from us." The humble pilgrim then asks, "And if He do?/ . . . Is aught betwixt ye and the hells?"[125]

With the idea of "God departed" and without the belief in secular improvement to replace him, there was only his art—his ability to dramatize his inner torments—between Melville and the hells of despair. His whole life was a quest for certainty, and he very early set himself the task of finding a faith. In the most sacred place of the land of the Typees, there had been evidence of a religious observance that seized Melville's imagination: the effigy of a dead chief in his canoe, "holding his paddle with both hands in the act of rowing, leaning forward and inclining his head, as if eager to hurry on his voyage. Glaring at him for ever, and face to face, was a polished human skull, which crowned the prow of the canoe. The spectral figurehead, reversed in its position, glancing backwards, seemed to mock the impatient attitude of the warrior."[126] The place had a mysterious charm for Melville. "I hardly know why," he said, "but so it was."[127] It was the first satisfying externalization of his own inner aspirations and of his knowledge that his creative life was to be a voyage of his soul in quest of an absolute, that the voyage was endless, and that it was in the quest itself, and not in its achievement, that lay the only fulfillment of the human condition.

In *Mardi* Melville wrote an allegory of his discovery of these truths. He described himself as a young man on a thoroughly earthbound whaling voyage who stepped off from certainty and from the world of the normal and the natural into the grey mists of the boundless Pacific to become Taji, a "half-and-half deity," who travels among the ideas of the past in search of absolute goodness. In this new guise he addressed America directly and told it the meaning of his literary growth: "Oh, reader, list! I've chartless voyaged. With compass and the lead, we have not found these Mardian Isles." The world of Mardi, he told us, was "the world of the mind, wherein the wanderer may gaze round with more of wonder than Balboa's band roving through the golden Aztec glades." The absolute in this world of mind was a "phantom-future" created by the desperate yearnings of man. The verdict must be, then, that "the golden haven was not gained" and never could be; "yet, in bold quest thereof, better to sink in boundless deeps, than float on vulgar shoals."[128] At the end Taji's companions, one after the other, had accepted the haven of some island of belief; but Taji, with "eternity . . . in his eye," turned his "prow into the racing tide."[129]

In *Mardi*, too, Melville speculated upon the subject and style that would embody his newly chosen theme of the endless quest of man for meaning: the subject would be "God's creatures fighting, fin for fin, a thousand miles from land, and with the round horizon for an arena"—a subject that, he decided, "is no ignoble subject for a masterpiece."[130] The style of this masterpiece would be one in which the natural surface would incorporate many meanings. It would not employ commonplace facts as symbols, in the way in which Emerson and Whitman used them—and by so using them expressed their convictions about the immanent meaning and value of the commonplace world of their experience; neither would it be the allegorical or emblematic mode in which artificial constructions are used as representations of truths and meanings that can be closely defined. Rather it would be in the style of Babbalanja's "nursery tale," which told of an "immense wild banyan tree . . . its thousand boughs striking into the earth"; and concerning that tree, "it had long been a question which of those many trunks was the original and true one. . . . But the tree was so vast . . . that it was quite impossible to determine the point." Babbalanja then described how nine blind men each claimed the root that he put his hand upon to be the "true" one; but they are chided by meeting a guide who declares, "The tree is too much for us all." Mohi thereupon exclaims, "What . . . mean you by your blind story!" And Babbalanja answers, "It is a polysensuum, old man."[131] And the construction of "polysensua," of patterns and figures that embodied the significance that was "too much for us all" and that had as many meanings as the thousand-rooted banyan tree, was, for Melville, the method to contain and express his radical doubt.

The "polysensuum," or many-meaninged story, is the style of Melville's *Moby-Dick*, his masterwork, and of "Benito Cereno" and "Billy Budd," his two most successful shorter tales. Each of them took as its basic plot an incident in history: the smashing of the *Essex* by Mocha Dick, a mutiny aboard a Spanish merchantman in 1799, an incident in the British navy of 1797. Each maintained itself on the natural surface, was solidly dimensional, and existed as a presumed imitation of "reality" as that reality has been perceived by the experience of mankind. This reality, however, was not of the commonplace but of the conditions of extremity: of men facing ultimate tests of courage, endurance, decision, and disaster. These tests, these extreme conditions, were then treated—by allusion, metaphor, and all the devices of plot and characterization—so that they represent larger and larger areas of human experience and become the only means of knowing whatever there can be known about the ultimate.

The White Whale was the most compelling of the objects Melville treated, and the story through which the Whale swims was the most significant of his "polysensua," for the Whale represented no less than the entire subject of Melville's life and works: the timeless quest for ultimate meaning, the meaning that lies behind "the pasteboard mask" of appearances. The motley rabble aboard the *Pequod*, representing every race and most of the conditions of the world, is a representation of mankind "in pursuit of those far mysteries we dream of . . . in tormented chase of that demon phantom that . . . swims before all human hearts."[132] The Whale was a hieroglyphic, but not the reassuring, uniform hieroglyphic that the leaf of grass was for Whitman; instead it was an "awful Chaldee" that Melville put before the reader and challenged him to "Read it if you can."[133]

The meaning behind the mask of appearances was proposed as a number of alternatives, all of which the Whale and its story hold in suspension. The meaning could be that there is a good, although mysterious and inscrutable, God; he can, as another alternative, be an evil God who torments man, the cruel God of Shelley in *Prometheus Unbound* or of

Byron in *Manfred*. Or he can be a God who is simply impersonal nature, careless of man; or he can be a bumbling God,
unable to control the mechanism he has created. Each of
these four possibilities is contained in *Moby-Dick*: there is
evidence for them all, and an attempt to fix one of them as
the final exclusive answer is as doomed to failure as is the
quest of Ahab itself.

The first kind of God was a constant possibility of the tale;
indeed, he was that "spirit of Equality" from which the
narrator begged for inspiration for his epic; he is the God of
Love who gave one of his sons, Queequeg, for the salvation
of man; Queequeg died so that his body—his coffin, which
was tattooed to resemble exactly his own skin—might buoy
Ishmael up. He was the God of righteous wrath as well, who
punished Ahab for the "unpardonable Sin" of hubristic pride
with which, to the exclusion of humanity and its concerns,
he pursued his fixed idea.

All the other possibilities of the ultimate meaning of God
were there too. Ahab, in the perspective of a universe dominated by a malignant deity, changed from an unpardonable
sinner to a great champion of man against God, a Prometheus
who defended humanity against the malevolence of the universe. Or, if the ultimate truth be that "God goes 'mong the
worlds blackberrying"[134]—and this is the vision that Pip,
the divine mad boy, brought back from the depths of the
sea—then Ahab was no less the champion of humanity, the
believer in a "prouder if a darker faith,"[135] a "bigot in the
fadeless fidelity of man,"[136] striking a doomed blow for human dignity in the face of the "oblivious gods." God himself,
then, was like the ship's Carpenter, a man without a "duplicate," a "manmaker" whose "impersonal stolidity . . . so
shaded off into the surrounding infinite of things, that it
seemed one with the general stolidity discernible in the
whole visible world."[137]

Ahab, seen in these latter, dark perspectives, howled at
the Whale as either "agent" or "principal"; and Ahab would
seek out the Whale—either the evil God (the principal) or a
representative of the evil God (the agent)—and burst his
heart's hot shell upon it. Furthermore, as he worked on the
manuscript, Melville identified himself more and more with

Ahab. The motto of the romance, he declared immediately after its completion, might well be Ahab's cry that he baptized his harpoons, not in the name of the Father, but of the devil. And in a letter he wrote while he was deep in the final version of *Moby-Dick*, he declared that the admirable thing about Hawthorne was his powerful embodiment of "a certain tragic phase of humanity"; he defined that phase as "human thought" in its effort to know the "absolute condition" of things, which declares itself "a sovereign nature . . . amid the powers of heaven, hell, and earth. He may perish; but so long as he exists he insists upon treating with all Powers upon an equal basis." Up to this point he had used the third person. Then he shifted to the first person, and, where before he had been talking about Hawthorne, he then talked about himself: "If any of those . . . Powers choose to withhold certain secrets, let them; that does not impair my sovereignty in myself, that does not make me tributary."

The letter did not stop there, and neither did the implications of *Moby-Dick*. The letter went on to sound the deeper horror, the deeper anguish, the deeper doubt: "And perhaps, after all, there is *no* secret. We incline to think that the Problem of the Universe is like the Freemason's mighty secret, so terrible to all children. It turns out, at last, to consist of a triangle, a mallet, and an apron,—nothing more! We incline to think that God cannot explain His own secrets, and that He would like a little information upon certain points Himself. We mortals astonish Him as much as He us." And then Melville broke into something near to incoherence with the final cry: "But it is this *Being* of the matter; there lies the knot with which we choke ourselves. As soon as you say *Me*, a *God*, a *Nature*, so soon you jump off from your stool and hang from the beam."[138]

This was close to Babbalanja's cry in *Mardi*: "Where is the Ultimate? Ah, companions! I faint, I am wordless. Something —nothing—riddles."[139] A good but inscrutable God, an evil God, a bumbling God, a careless God—these were some of the possibilities that *Moby-Dick* contained. The first possibility was a gloomy faith but one that had the seeds of the ultimate optimism of Hawthorne; the other possibilities were fearful, but none were so terrible as a last alternative, which is also part of this many-meaninged tale, a meaning that had been suggested by Babbalanja's broken gasps and by Melville's equally tormented letter to Hawthorne. It was the possibility that there is *nothing* behind the pasteboard mask; nothing behind the blank wall of appearance. This possibility was the underlying horror of *Moby-Dick*: this the whiteness of the Whale bodied forth. The sea contained the "image of the ungraspable phantom of life";[140] the overwhelming head of the great Whale himself was the key to its meaning; and both its meaning and the phantom itself may be "nothing," a nothingness whose only valid symbol is whiteness.

Melville devoted his most highly charged chapter to "The Whiteness of the Whale." After hinting at what the whale was for Ahab, Ishmael tried to describe "the thought, or rather vague, nameless horror concerning him."[141] It was a horror both "mystical" and "ineffable." He despaired of putting it into words but identified its most appalling feature as its "whiteness." He further declared that he must try to explain this ineffable mystery in whatever "dim, random way" he could command, "else all these chapters might be naught." What was it that this whiteness signified? What was the meaning of this color, without an understanding of which the whole work would be futile? After describing the other embodiments of the horror—the white bear of the Poles, the albatross, the white pony of the plains, the albino man, the White Friar and Nun, the White Andes—he speculated, first, that it had something to do with the truth that "though in many of its aspects this visible world seems formed in love, the invisible spheres were formed in fright."[142] This, however, would account for the horror of blackness, not whiteness; so "not yet have we solved the incantation of its whiteness." Then he asked the final, rhetorical question: "Is it that by its indefiniteness it shadows forth the heartless voids and immensities of the Universe?" It is the "colorless, all-color of atheism," the proof that "deified Nature . . . paints like the harlot, whose allurements cover nothing but the charnel-house within." Of all this he said, "The Albino Whale was the symbol."[143]

Fortunately for his art, the years between 1846 and 1850, between the publication of *Typee* and the writing of *Moby-*

Dick, were years given to the appreciation of the best of literary models. Not only Spenser, Milton, Browne, Rabelais were grist for his mill and supplied him with allusions and language and cadences; but Shakespeare, above all others, left him glowing with a near-religious fervor: his name Melville would couple with that of Christ. And in the pattern of Shakespearean tragedy, he found the form that was capable of controlling and containing these wild exuberances of many-meaninged artifacts in a significant work of art.

Melville seemed to have known instinctively that the classical tragic form, as reinvigorated by the Elizabethans, was capable of controlling and ordering the wild range of meanings that he raised as possibilities: from the possibility that a good and just, if difficult, God ruled the universe to the possibility that the universe was mere mechanism or mere whim. As Aristotle had analyzed the effects of tragedy, it was seen as a form that affirmed the dignity of man in a meaningful universe. For it proposed that the fate that overtakes the protagonist is clearly the result of an inner weakness, a flaw in his greatness, a crack in his perfection that widens into destruction. Evil (the "flaw") overcomes good and must be punished by a higher good. A generation before Melville, Hegel suggested a variation upon this interpretation of the effects of tragedy, a variation that even more strongly affirmed the existence of a just and omnipotent deity and accounted for the paradoxical "uplift" and affirmation one feels at the conclusion of any great tragedy. High tragedy, Hegel said, was not the result of the conflict between evil (the weakness of a great protagonist) and good but was the result of the conflict between two partial "goods," each of which tries to assert its supremacy over the other and both of which must, lest they become God, be cancelled in catastrophe.[144]

Both theories of the tragic effect supply ways of reading *Moby-Dick* and Melville's subsequent major works. The Aristotelian analysis must have been strong in Melville's own consciousness, for he gave his tragic hero both the trappings of greatness that Aristotle insisted were necessary and an Aristotelian heroic flaw, an obsession with revenge, made startlingly palpable in the great angry scar that ran down

Ahab's face and trunk like the scar left by lightning on an oak. A monomania that blotted out his humanity, the flaw doomed Ahab and lesser men with him. Pierre's disregard for humanity (his rejection of Lucy) in his frantic obsession to live by absolute standards corresponded to Ahab's monomania and led to the same results. Billy Budd's stutter, his incapacity to communicate, was a flaw in his perfection if we regard the story as Billy's tragedy; or, if we look upon Captain Vere as the tragic protagonist, Vere's commitment to the letter of the law, his conservative protection of society against threatened anarchy, was the fatal weakness in an otherwise great personality.

In each case, however, it is possible to read the fables as Hegelian rather than as Aristotelian tragedies. Ahab's revenge then becomes not an evil but a "partial good," for it is an attack upon the forces of evil and a defense of human dignity. This good conflicts with another, his human sympathies; Ahab, we are told, is not without his humanities; and as they must be, each partial good is cancelled out in a catastrophe that affirms the existence of a higher "goodness." Pierre's obsession with the Absolute, when seen in this light, becomes not an "evil" but the "good" of dedication to universal principle. Billy Budd's failure to communicate is "innocence" rather than weakness; it is his "unconscious simplicity" that his fellows revere; Vere's legalism becomes a dedication to the necessary laws of man. Indeed, "Billy Budd," in this sense, is the most Hegelian of Melville's tragedies, for it projects the tragic dilemma of Creon in *Antigone*, the work that Hegel thought the most exemplary of the Greek tragedies.

Whether read as Hegelian or as Aristotelian tragedies, Melville's romances were tragic forms suitable for an affirmation of the existence of significance and value in an ordered universe. Yet there is another possibility and an alternative analysis of the impact of the tragic form that would enable it to contain the other extreme of possibilities that Melville explored in his quest for absolute certainty. Emerson, we have seen, was the theoretician who had described this possibility a few years earlier: the possibility that there is "no over-god to stop or to mollify this hideous enginery that grinds and thunders, and snatches [men] up in its terrific system." This sense of fatality, Emerson wrote, is not "divine will" at all but "an immense whim." The conception of a brute order, heedless of man, operating, not as universal reason, but as universal chaos, he said, is "the only ground of terror and despair in the rational mind, and of tragedy in literature." With typical optimism Emerson averred that "antique tragedy, which was founded on this faith can never be reproduced."[145] Whitman, too, had seen tragedies as the contortions of the soul in the throes of nihilistic despair; he had even made the hunt for the Whale the symbol of skepticism when he had written of the "bloody flukes of doubters."

This vision of "universal whim," no longer part of Emerson's or Whitman's world of consciousness, was symbolized by "whiteness" in the profoundest depths of Melville's meanings and was almost the final word of both his major tragedies: *Moby-Dick* and "Billy Budd." Indeed, if we consider the stories without their epilogues, "whiteness" *was* the last word. This was almost the ending of *Moby-Dick*: "A sullen white surf beat against its steep sides [the sides of the vortex which sucked down the *Pequod*]; then all collapsed, and the great shroud of the sea rolled on as it rolled five thousand years ago."[146] This was almost the ending of "Billy Budd": "And the circumambient air in the clearness of its serenity was like smooth white marble in the polished block not yet removed from the marble-dealer's yard."[147]

These were not the last words in either work. Both contained short codas, brief descriptions of salvation and redemption through human love and sympathy. The epilogue of *Moby-Dick* described how Ishmael was buoyed up by the "body" of Queequeg (the tattooed coffin) and was rescued by the *Rachel*, which was cruising for her missing children. The last paragraphs of "Billy Budd" told us that the seamen of the British navy regarded a chip from the boom on which Bill hung as "a piece of the Cross." These were reminders that the disasters that destroyed Ahab and Captain Vere were results of their tragic choices of higher imperatives over human love; their destruction, then, demonstrated universal order, and not cosmic whim. In this shifting back and forth between belief and skepticism, Melville demonstrated that in his last tragedy as well as in his first his only resting place was doubt, relieved by a glimmer of hope. In *Moby-Dick* he had written that we all pass through "infancy's unconscious spell, boyhood's thoughtless faith, adolescence's doubt (the common doom), then skepticism, then disbelief, resting at last in manhood's ponderous repose of If." We are, he declared, "infants, boys, and men, and Ifs eternally." Then in a significant metaphor he compared our souls to the "orphans whose unwedded mothers die in bearing them: the secret of our paternity lies in their grave."[148]

Melville, then, found high tragedy the only form this side of the grave capable of embodying all the possibilities of the meaning of our paternity. Since a vision of the universe as "whim" was one of the viable alternatives, true comedy became impossible. There was a kind of laughter in Melville, however, and even one attempt to write a "comedy": *The Confidence-Man*. There is a radical difference, however, between Melville's laughter and Mark Twain's, between true comic laughter and the gasping explosion of derision from the rictus of irony. True comic laughter is of two kinds, both of them affirmative, both of them paying eventual allegiance to a sense of health and order in the universe. One is the joyous laugh—the laugh that is part of the approval of life and sex; the laugh we give when we see a healthy child. The other is the satiric laugh: the laugh that follows our perception of the gap between a true reality and some appearance that deviates from that reality, while we envision the possibility of the reform of the error or the vice against which we direct our laughter. Moral or social health, then, is the concern of satiric laughter, just as physical health is the concern of joyous laughter. A comic joke always contains an ultimate vision of health and wholeness that the individual instance, the butt of the joke, contravenes.

What if there is no vision of health or wholeness? What if the possibility is entertained that there is no cosmic meaning against which we can measure man's individual absurdity? Then the whole universe becomes a "vast practical joke." These were Melville's words, and the chapter in *Moby-Dick* in which they appeared bore a title that suggested the kind of laughter that follows such a "joke." The chapter was called "The Hyena"; its tone was the maniacal yawp of the obscene beast. In the context of his tragedy, Melville's tone was genial enough when discussing the "queer times and occasions" when all of life and death seem "only sly, good-natured hits, and jolly punches in the side bestowed by an unseen and unaccountable old joker."[149] When the time came when he regarded nihilism as the only truth, he wrote what he termed a "comedy," but it was far more terrible and far more negative than his tragedies. Unlike the tragedies this "comedy" held no affirmative possibilities but portrayed the universe as a vast joke played by a cosmic trickster. The laugh was neither the joyous laugh nor the satiric laugh but the "black, brightening,"[150] the cackle of "moody madness muttering in the corner,"[151] the laughter of irony. Where the satirical vision sees an order, observes the individual from the standpoint of that order, and uses laughter as the weapon to bring the individual back into that order, the ironical sees no order but, quite the contrary, sees the entire universe as an absurd joke.

And this is the world of the *Fidèle*, the world of *The Confidence-Man*. In it Christ must be considered "an imposter . . . from the East"[152] and his Father, an old man mumbling over the Bible in the cabin below. The Confidence Man, the cosmic joker, plied his trade unhampered. Confidence, trust, love, sympathy, belief in man, belief in God, belief in nature—all were as worthless as reason and progress, because the entire universe was meaningless and absurd, and in an absurd universe none of these can have significance. The hyena laughter of irony was the only true reaction: it was the laughter of the one-legged custom inspector and the Missouri bachelor. The Confidence Man, quite naturally, hated it: "Something Satanic about irony," he ironically says. "God defend me from Irony."

Irony, then, was Melville's style in the depths of his despair, the lowest depths reached by nineteenth-century negation of the American idea. Its concluding scene was a masterpiece of this style. The *Fidèle*, we are sure, is the world. It is a "ship of fools."[153] Its cabin, the cosmos: the circle of light at the center of the cabin is a "solar light"; the outer edges of the cabin are in "planetary" darkness. Under the circle of light sits a white-robed bearded old man reading from the Bible. A confidence boy has sold him a false counterfeit detector. After extinguishing the dying lamp, the Confidence Man himself takes the old man by the hand and leads him off. And thus ended Melville's "comedy"; God the Father, doddering, duped, is led off by the devil into outer darkness. Melville had fashioned the necessary style for the rejection of his culture's idea and the creation of symbolic black comedy as the form that would answer the hyena laugh of the universe.

VI ~ The Idea in an Industrial Age

1. William James

The writings of the generation that followed Melville and Whitman, Lowell and Holmes—the works of those authors who were born between 1835 and 1845—continued to take their shape from the interaction of the individual sensitivities of the artists with the idea of American optimism. Like the writers of the preceding generation, those who came to their maturity in the years of the Civil War either accepted the basic tenets of the culture's faith—the possibilities of man and his capacity for continued progress—or rejected them; and whether they affirmed or denied, the forms they made were one with that acceptance or denial. By the time of the birth of William Dean Howells, of Mark Twain, of Henry James, and of Henry Adams, the official faith was firmly enough fixed so that it was a part of the atmosphere that they breathed. Henry Adams, looking back upon 1840 from the perspective of 1900, definitively described his culture's idea as it was fully constituted in the years before the Civil War. "Viewed from Mt. Vernon Street," Adams wrote, in describing the climate of his youth, "the problem of life was as simple as it was classic. Politics offered no difficulties, for there the moral law was the surest guide. Social perfection was also sure, because human nature worked for the Good, and three instruments were all she asked—Suffrage, Common Schools, and Press. On these points doubt was forbidden. Education was divine, and man needed only a correct knowledge of facts to reach perfection."[1]

Adams's was a shrewd summary of the idea. He spoke of it as a religion: the term "divine," the phrase "doubt forbidden" expressed a commitment beyond the intellect, a conviction at the level of the emotions as well as the mind, which defines a culture's meaning and its place in the universe. In short, he was describing an "official faith." The essence of this faith, as he observed it at the beginning of his spiritual odyssey, was the belief that the universe is dominated by moral law. We note the essential deism of the faith: God was not mentioned; there was no sense of his dramatic immediacy; there was instead the generalized sense of order of nature, the sanctity of the laws of physics and chemistry, and the way in which, by analogy, the affairs of men are governed by corresponding moral laws. There was a conviction about the value of man as well as nature: "human nature worked for the good." Man was not fallen; he was not alienated from universal goodness; there was no feeling of a terrible aboriginal calamity, which for Augustine and Cardinal Newman as well as Thomas Hooker and Jonathan Edwards had been the only way of accounting for the agonies of the human condition. Indeed, there were no agonies that could not be surmounted on the way to a better future. This sense of the future, this hope for a better world, was the third cardinal element of the American idea as Adams so well defined it: "Social perfection was also sure." The future would be achieved by essentially good men applying their human reason to the problems of the material and moral universe; education therefore was "divine." The method used by human reason was the method of inductive empiricism, the new instrument that Bacon had given to the modern man: "a correct knowledge of the facts" was all that was needed to improve the world.

This was the faith of Bryant, Longfellow, Lowell, and Holmes, and it was the basis of the faith of two men who reshaped it to meet the demands of an industrialized and continental society: William James in philosophy and William Dean Howells in imaginative literature. Philosophical pragmatism and literary realism were the vehicles for expressing

American optimism during a period in which the developing complexities of American society were compelling serious reevaluations of the articles of that faith. The major changes that William James and Howells made in the idea were in the direction to which Oliver Wendell Holmes had pointed: the removal of the belief in natural goodness and in human perfectibility from the realm of mythology and the substitution of a far more contingent and conditional optimism. By the time they had completed their work, they identified the cult of progress, not with the belief in the nobility of savage man, but with the potentialities of all men to rise above their animal state; and the belief in perfectibility was coupled not with some rigid metaphysical formula for the future but with the possibilities of man to meet the challenges of his environment as a free agent—free to choose between alternative possibilities, knowing that his choice will always be partial and inadequate but certain that he has the capability of making choices in which the good will outweigh the bad. It was, in short, the conception of the "Open Universe," which was the essence of nineteenth-century pragmatic optimism.

This sense of an open universe was connected with a continuing, and even an increasing, emotional rejection of a European past and a dedication to an American future. Although both Howells and William James would be severely critical of the inadequacies of their society and culture, their fundamental commitments to its values remained unshaken. Although William James, for example, would sometimes deplore the American scene as "naked" and "vacuous" and would protest the "skinniness and aridity" of its scenery and the "strange thinness and femininity"[2] of its landscape, his more typical reaction was that of his father, who had often told his children that he was glad that his lot was cast in a land that was not obsessed with death and with the past. He said he had always been restless in Europe and had ended by pining for the land of the future. William continually responded to the relation between the Old World and the New in favor of the New. He identified a worship of Europe as a "gaping at . . . grandfathers' tombs"; he called the weight of the past "fatal" and even paraphrased the excessive words of Tennyson: "Better fifty years of Cambridge [and he was, of course, talking about the American Cambridge], than a cycle of Cathay!" He ended the letter to his sister that contained this exaggeration with the signature, "Your brutal and Philistine brother,"[3] for he knew just how brutal and philistine his brother Henry, as well as his sister, would consider such an assertion. With Howells—and with Robert Frost, who in our own times has said how "unterribly" life goes on in America—William usually protested that the country consists mainly of the quiet round of ordinary events and not of the real, but abnormal, horrors reported in the newspapers. Although he frequently found the American scene thin and arid, he usually expressed the feelings that should Henry drop his "English ideas and take America and Americans as they take themselves," he would "certainly experience a rejuvenation."[4]

This rejection of the past, and this concentration upon the present and future, was part of William James's general rejection of absolutes. All but one. His attitude, and that of Howells and Mark Twain, was predicated upon one absolute, one metaphysical principle without which their world would collapse—indeed, without which the world of Mark Twain did collapse at the turn of the century. This was the Emersonian absolute, the principle he proclaimed, the truth he insisted upon, and for which James said, "Posterity will reckon him a prophet." This *a priori*, without which pragmatic affirmation could not exist, was that "the point of any pen can be an epitome of reality; the commonest person's act, if genuinely actuated, can lay hold on eternity."[5] The reality of the external world, of society, of the things of the phenomenal universe—the sense that the external world is "no mere bare fraud" but plays "*some* positive part"[6] in the scheme of things—the deep, intuitive affirmation that there is significance and value in the physical world of external reality—this was the unreasoned belief upon which American pragmatism, which otherwise spurned the absolute and the metaphysical, was firmly based.

Yet after this one, and all-important, *a priori* belief James's pragmatism tried to rule out all others. For his was an attitude toward the universe that dwelt upon the supreme value of facts and of action and that insisted that both reality and worth lay in the realm of experience, and not in the realm of an absolute idea. Whatever its philosophical label, this insistence upon the thing and the deed could not be mistaken for other than what the nontechnical mind would call "realism," and it was the counterpart of the school of fiction by that name that grew in America after the Civil War. The basic attitudes of both realists in literature and pragmatists in philosophy were the same. They both gave the same answers to the fundamental questions about the nature of the universe, about the means of knowing truth, and about the nature of good and evil. What is the external world? James answered that it was no mere show or delusion but a part of fundamental reality. How can we know this world? We can know it through our involvement with it, through the interaction of our senses with an objectively existing and real outer world. Sense perception, not intuition, became the prime pragmatic tool of knowledge. The accent was on seeing, smelling, tasting, touching, hearing: upon experiencing and upon drawing working hypotheses from the experience as a guide to subsequent experience. The basic account of James's world was contained in the preface to his monumental psychology, which emphasized the physiological reality of emotions and which refused to discuss any of their metaphysical implications. This attitude toward feeling, he said, must be based upon certain fundamental assumptions about the nature of reality; then he listed three points upon which the pragmatic world view was predicated: "Psychology . . . assumes as its data (1) *thoughts and feelings*, and (2) *a physical world* in time and space with which they coexist and which (3) *they know*."[7]

James was aware that this accent upon brute perception and upon the inductive method was not the final answer (indeed, in his "Open Universe" there were no final answers); he acknowledged that bare induction was inadequate to explain the processes of knowing the physical universe. However, it was the best method for his generation as it took its place in the progressive development of mankind's powers. In an appreciation of Louis Agassiz, who, too, was concerned with the "facts," James wrote:

The causal elements and not the total are what we are now most passionately concerned to understand; and naked and poverty-stricken enough do the stripped-out elements and forces occasionally appear to us to be. But the truth of things is after all their living fullness, and some day, from a more commanding point of view than was possible to any of Agassiz's generation, our descendants, enriched with the spoils of all our analytic investigations, will get round again to that higher and simpler way of looking at Nature.[8]

This awareness of the way in which his "realism" and "empiricism" constituted a phase in the development of more inclusive ways of knowing led him later to hail Bergson's achievements as a "great system," part of "a really growing world."[9]

James also knew that his beliefs, based upon the supremacy of the fact, comprised but an individual view, part of the plurality of views that could be believed in with equal justification; and he was similarly undogmatic about the "values" to which he subscribed. His answer to the question "What is good?" was as relativistic as his answers to the questions of "What is the world?" and "How do we know it?" His pluralism insisted that the facts and the values of life need many perspectives to take them in, that there is no absolute, universal point of view. Yet all the worths that he ever talked about were human values and natural values, rather than suprahuman or supernatural values, and they all were a function of their capacity to make human life fuller, more generous, more decent, more tolerant. Values were tested, and indeed were identified, solely by the results of actions, by their ability to enrich the lives of the humans who held them. Value, which makes life significant, is a translation of ideals into action. Ideals themselves are not absolutes but are relative to the men that hold them.[10] They consist of an intellectual conception that carries with it a feeling of well-being and that contains some element of novelty. True meaning and true value, then, consist of a fusion of such an ideal with the courage and will to carry it into action, to realize it in the external world of things. Only in the results of such actions lies the test of whether either ideal or action was valuable. And when the fusion is "good," the results are an inner joyfulness springing from the divination that there lies in the world about one some cause for "a little more humility upon our part, and tolerance, reverence, and love for others."[11]

James's empiricism and his humanism were typical, both in their refusal to deny the religious impulse and in their essential optimism. He believed deeply in the "religious hypothesis"; and the way in which he defined it showed his fundamental commitment to the American idea. Religion, he said, consists in the belief that "the best things are the more eternal things" and that they are "the things in the universe that throw the last stone."[12] He believed further that the endless process of pluralistic attempts to know the truth and to accomplish the good was part of the universal triumph of "the best things." Normally urbane and tolerant, he reserved his contempt for intolerant pessimisms that contravened his radical optimism; when he spoke of the philosophies of despair, he sounded like Oliver Wendell Holmes speaking of Jonathan Edwards. Let the "orientalists and pessimists" say what they will, James averred; "the thing of deepest . . . significance in life does seem its character of *progress*."[13] He detested Schopenhauer, whom Melville had admired. James felt that the author of *The World as Will and Idea* "studiously lived for no other purpose than to spit upon the lives of the like of me and all those I care for," and he maintained that the German philosopher's "loud-mouthed pessimism was that of a dog who would rather see the world ten times worse than it is, than lose his chance of barking at it."[14] However, James's inveterate sanguinity, even more than Emerson's, was no shirking of evil; James acknowledged evil but held that "little by little, there comes some stable gain; for the world does get more humane, and the religion of democracy tends towards permanent increase."[15]

However, in his fortress of optimistic pragmatism, he was assailed by the same vision that had frightened his earlier English counterpart, John Stuart Mill, nearly out of his wits. Mill had suddenly found himself confronted with the thought of what the world would be were all his utilitarian dreams realized; the fulfillment of his hopes, he had realized with terror, would be a nightmare of spiritual poverty. James came to this same vision by confronting a contemporary scene. He visited the Assembly grounds at Chatauqua and felt himself "in an atmosphere of success" where the air was pervaded by "sobriety and industry, intelligence and goodness, order-liness and ideality, prosperity and cheerfulness." This, he realized, was the "middle-class paradise, without a sin, without a victim, without a blot, without a tear." And it filled him, not with joy, but with a kind of horror. It was, he said, as if all the "pessimism about our civilization were, after all, quite right. . . . And, to get human life in its wild intensity, we must in the future turn more and more away from the actual, and forget it, if we can, in the romancer's or the poet's pages."

Then, at the sight of a workman laboring on a high iron structure, he perceived in a flash of insight where he had been mistaken in this lapse into pessimism. He had been languishing in a state of what he had called "ancestral blind-ness," the prejudice that prevented him from seeing the Emersonian truth that there were "great fields of heroism" in the ordinary and commonplace world of the daily lives of all men. "Not in the clanging fights and desperate marches only" is glory to be found "but on every railway bridge and fire-proof building . . . on the decks of vessels, in cattle-yards and mines." The vision led him at first to the sentimen-tal Victorian fallacy of locating human heroism only among the poor; as the scales of ancestral blindness first fell from his eyes, it seemed to him that the only genuine virtue was "virtue with horny hands and dirty skin." However, he quickly perceived that the worth to the universe of "courage, kindliness, and patience" is just as great if the possessor be a man of education and power as it is when the man is "an illiterate nobody, hewing wood and drawing water."[16]

2. William Dean Howells

The sympathy between pragmatism and an imaginative lit-erature devoted to the actual world became quickly apparent. Novelists and poets, James wrote, should "fill us with a better insight" into the heroism and virtue of the common-place and wean us from "that spurious literary romanticism on which our wretched culture . . . is fed."[17] And just as the European novelist to whom he most frequently alluded was

Tolstoi, so the American novelist who most nearly met his specification was the man who humbly tried to achieve a small measure of Tolstoi's particular kind of greatness, William Dean Howells. For twenty years before the appearance of James's *Psychology* and thirty years before his *Pragmatism*, Howells had instinctively been translating the entire range of attitudes summarized by "pragmatism" into intelligent and enormously influential fiction.

Howells started with the one *a priori* that was the foundation of pragmatic affirmation: the conviction that the commonplace world of normal experience was significant and valuable. "Ah! poor Real Life which I love,"[18] his early fictional spokesman sighed, and Basil March went on to express the hope that he could help others to know and to love the ordinary and the common. Almost untouched by the searching doubts of Melville and Hawthorne and reacting scornfully against the gloomy neuroticism of Poe, Howells turned rather to Emerson as "a presence of force and beauty and wisdom, uncompanioned in our literature."[19] And while Howells, like William James, spent most of his life exploring the physical, the immediate, the social, his exploration was always conducted with the unexpressed, but powerful, commitment to the metaphysical value of the commonplace world of experience—the *a priori* of pragmatic thought.

Then after accepting this one absolute, Howells formed his fiction on the supposition that all other preconceptions, all other rigid formulae imposed on life, were a threat to moral health. William James used the term *romantic* to denote a kind of fiction that begins with a preconceived premise about men and motives, and Howells, too, fell into the habit of calling it thus. Unlike William James, however, Howells was uncomfortable with the assumption that romanticism was all bad. This assumption had grown in America since the time of Oliver Wendell Holmes, because *romantic*, as an adjective, had come to be associated with a certain low form of literary expression for which, to distinguish it from serious literature, we prefer the term *sentimental*. Sentimentalism—the kind of writing whose purpose is to arouse conventional and expected emotional responses—was corrupting America's taste and dulling its sensibilities as Howells grew to literary maturity in the years immediately after the mid-century. Sentimentalism was the reinforcement of the "ancestral blindness" that William James pointed out as the barrier to true perception. And Howells's first impulse, as part of his commitment to pragmatic optimism, was to satirize this ancestral blindness, this barrier to human improvement. Beginning with his first sketches in 1870 and 1871 and continuing on through his posthumous novel of 1920, he made this opposition to sentimentalism an important motive of his work. Sometimes it was incidental to larger considerations—in *The Rise of Silas Lapham* and *A Hazard of New Fortunes*. In these works, whose major themes were a defense of pragmatic morality and a criticism of society, antisentimentalism was an important minor motif. In *Silas Lapham* he described the dangers of Penelope Lapham's sentimental attitude toward courtship and love: Penelope wished to give up Tom Corey to her sister Irene and thereby satisfy the demands of sentimentalized morality; the pragmatic minister, David Sewell, pointed out that this would serve only to make three people miserable instead of one, and by his common sense Sewell helped to bring reason and order into the chaos of sentimentality. In *A Hazard of New Fortunes*, an attack upon sentimentalism had a similarly important, if minor, place. In a charmingly unexpected characterization, Howells drew a portrait of Miss Woodburn, a southern belle, a type that in sentimental fiction was stereotyped as hopelessly frivolous; Howells made her a hardheaded, sensible, shrewd critic of sentimentalism in the South, which tries to live according to the ideals of a world that never existed.

More often, however, the attack on ancestral blindness was not the subordinate, but the major, motive and meaning of his fiction. Indeed, it was at the center of his two best works written before 1885: *A Foregone Conclusion* and *Indian Summer*. *A Foregone Conclusion* was an international story— the first of its kind—to which Howells turned after his autobiographical novels on American themes: *Their Wedding Journey* and *A Chance Acquaintance*. It was the story of Don Ippolito, an Italian priest, who succumbs to a fleshly love for a handsome American girl. Howells treated the theme, not for its potentially shocking nature, but as an illustration of the way in which a sentimental attitude toward the world brings tragedy and disaster. "Helplessness, dreamery, and unpracticality"[20] are the key words used to describe the failings of Don Ippolito, who, in turn, always complains about the "practicality" of Americans. Yet in the story precisely this "practicality"—that is, the testing of all human attitudes by the standard of their operation in the ordinary world of human involvements—is shown to be morally right and the sentimental withdrawal from reality is shown to be morally, as well as practically, wrong.

Howells again took up this theme of the conflict between varieties of ancestral blindness and commonsense empiricism in *Indian Summer*, the most successful of his antisentimental novels. It was a good-humored story, filled with a comic sense of the possibilities of human reason together with an appreciation of human weakness. The ancestral blindness in this case was the mistaken view of love and marriage held by Imogene Graham, the beautiful young ingenue of the tale. She had derived all her knowledge from bad romances and silly poems and tried to apply it to the reality of human relationships. She sentimentally imagined that she had a mission with regard to Colville, the middle-aged hero who had had a shattered love affair. Imogene placed herself in the role of a self-sacrificing heroine, who would make up to this attractive older man the wrong done to him long ago by one of her sex. Flattered by her attentions, Colville, lonely and at loose ends in Florence, allowed himself to be pleasantly deceived into believing Imogene loved him. Mrs. Bowen, the sensible, middle-aged heroine, was prevented from interfering in the affair by the operation of another form of sentimentality; she can only watch passively as the delusions of young girl and middle-aged man threaten to turn into the painful realities of an unsuitable marriage.

However, Howells believed in happy endings,[21] and as an indication of the general optimism at work behind his pragmatic vision, the universe took its hand in resolving the plot: a lucky accident saved them. Colville was trampled by a horse as he melodramatically tried to save Imogene; the shock of the near catastrophe shook the sentimental chaos into order. Colville came to consciousness in the comfort, quiet, and orderliness of Mrs. Bowen's home, and he knew he would like to stay there forever. Through this resolution Howells left no doubt that, like William James in philosophy, he was trying to teach his generation, through literature, to turn away from false ideals and sentimental *a priori* to the good of empirical and practical solutions. Mr. Waters, like David Sewell, a New England Unitarian divine dedicated to the ideal of the Social Gospel, summarized the meaning of the story: "We are a long time learning to act with common-sense or even common sanity in what are called matters of the affections."[22]

The attack on "ancestral blindness," then, was one of the principal motifs in American literary realism and the first of its affinities with American pragmatism. Like the philosophical movement it affirmed at the same moment that it rejected; its rejections were gestures of affirmation. Its attack on the false was an implicit defense of the real: venerating the hard bedrock of actuality as a stratum of significance that had been covered over by the effluvium of sentimentality. Since the ordinary life of ordinary men and women was both significant and valuable, the problem became not one of imposing some *a priori* form or pattern upon it but of finding literary means of allowing the forms and the patterns of reality to find expression—a vehicle that would impose least constraint upon the meanings that were the texture of life itself. The discursive antimythic narration, the form of Cervantes and Fielding and Defoe, had been the response to just such an affirmation of reality in the mainstream of the novel; it was the form that Howells reinvigorated for the American nineteenth century. He saw it, at its best, as involving the dramatic method of description and dialogue combined with the loose, epic technique of plotting. He created a fictional world as if it were a stage: the setting described so that the reader might visualize it, the characters portrayed so that their personalities and their actions might speak for themselves. He described such details of an actual environment and recorded such snatches of "overheard" conversation as would give the illusion of a section of contemporary reality that is seen and heard directly by the reader. Such objective visualization became a major purpose of fiction. Regional writers, whose main purpose was to describe an area of America in all its physical detail, to record the manners, and to set down with fidelity the speech of the natives, began to crowd the literary scene; Mark Twain was but the best of them.

In such a literary program the plot—the fable—of a narrative was its least part. That the story "goes it alone" became Howells's favorite phrase of approval, for a well-regulated plot smacked of the *a priori*—of some absolute scheme imposed upon the lives of people. On the contrary, the events in the realistic novel should be so selected and arranged that they seem the probable causes of antecedent actions and partake as well of the sense of the uncertain, the fortuitous, the unrelated, which we know is also a part of the world of common experience. In other words, the world of fiction that Howells tried to make and that he tried to encourage others to make was the world as the pragmatic psychologist believed the world really to be: "a physical world in time and space" with which "thoughts and feelings . . . coexist" and which men's thoughts and feelings really "know."

The first positive motive of realistic fiction, then, was the identification, the affirmation of the observed world as significant and valuable. Its motive was part of the general sense of nineteenth-century optimism that saw the world as meaning intensely and meaning good. Through 1884 and 1885 this normality, this commonplace, was the normality of middle-class America, the America of Howells's experience, of the small professional—the journalist, the editor, the teacher, the occasional leisured scion of small means—and, more importantly, their culturally influential wives and daughters. In these years Howells began to be concerned about the same kinds of people to whose lives William James began to be sensitized at almost the same time; these were the men of "horny hands and dirty skin." When the lives of these men and women began to be of serious concern to Howells, he became aware of the terrible inequities and injustices of the system of laissez-faire capitalism that had grown up in America; and he then turned his realistic fiction to a new purpose: to destroy a particular and pernicious kind of ancestral blindness, blindness to the wrongs and the evils of a good system that was going bad. To show what was wrong with things as they were so that people could give heed to making them better—this was the new purpose of Howells after 1886, and he pioneered this new native ground for serious American fiction with *Annie Kilburn* and *A Hazard of New Fortunes*.

The kind of realism introduced into American letters by these works—a realism that criticized the society of which it was a part—had been developing in France, and several years after *A Hazard of New Fortunes*, Emile Zola defined in *Le Roman Experimental* the relation of this kind of art to a belief in progress. Zola's shrewd point was that socially critical fiction could be called "experimental" because it performed the function, in the area of society and of morals, of a laboratory of mankind in which the individual may watch experiments in human relations and from these experiments may induce the laws that govern human affairs. Far from being an excursion into pessimism, then, the narrative devoted to social criticism—like its comic counterpart, the satire—exposed evils so that man might reform them. There is always a double kind of optimism at the heart of such social criticism—optimism about the nature of society and optimism about the nature of man. Society is, if cankered, at least curable; man is, if deceived, at least capable of enlightenment. There is assumed a standard of health and sanity from which both group and individual have deviated and to which both can be recalled; the deviations and the evils can be cured if they are identified; potentially good men of good will can be trusted both to understand the evils and to reform them. The artistic commitments of "critical realism" are to the pragmatic idea of the open universe, a universe in which progress is, at least, possible.

Howells was considered the father of this movement in America: Hamlin Garland, his devoted disciple, pointed to *A Hazard of New Fortunes* as the first American work in this genre. Other fictions had dealt with social protest, but *A Hazard of New Fortunes* was far superior to them in range and power. Profoundly impressed by Dostoevski, Howells was, nevertheless, far more influenced by Tolstoi and by his reverence demonstrated his basic allegiance to the "healthy minded." (Between the two of them, Thomas Mann has observed, Dostoevski and Tolstoi divided up the world, Dostoevski embodying its darker half and Tolstoi its side of sun and light.)[23] Howells was attracted to the sunshine: Henry James said of him that there was a "whole quarter of the heaven"[24] upon which his back was turned. Although Howells could admire Dostoevski's insight into the dark places of man and nature, he was far more responsive to the vision of Tolstoi who, like Emerson, combined a mystical idealism with a reverence for the commonplace physical embodiment of that ideal and whose anguished awareness of the evils of man and the inequities of his system was surmounted by a faith in a significant and valuable universe.

A Hazard of New Fortunes, the seminal work of American critical realism, then, expressed the hopefulness of the American idea. Yet it embodied the idea in its newer, more open, pragmatic form: the form of William James rather than the form of Longfellow. It was a complicated story involving the complicated moral choice that men are forced to make in a complex modern society. True to his fundamental devotion to experience, Howells chose the only area of the conflict between capital and labor that he knew well—the world of editing and publishing. Basil March, the main figure and a fictional counterpart of Howells himself, was editor of a magazine whose owner, Dryfoos, demands that a socialist employee be discharged. March's friend and partner, a typical entrepreneur probably modeled after Sam McClure, urges that the radical be sacrificed. The owner's saintly son, Conrad Dryfoos, has been drawn into sympathetic involvement with the socialist and with the working men whose painful grievances finally broke into open and violent strikes. And the owner's daughter is entangled with a fortune-hunting, self-serving artist, Angus Beaton.

The way Howells handled these four plots was symptomatic of his essential optimism, even in his deepest doubtings of the way in which American society was developing. The old capitalist is taught Christian humility and forgiveness by the sacrifice of his son; Angus Beaton, the typical uncaring, selfish opportunist, loses everything, including his right to be dignified into a figure of tragedy: the pistol with which he thinks of shooting himself goes off harmlessly. These are the unhappy endings of two of the four strands of story. While unhappy, in neither case do they illustrate the universe as careless whim. Rather they suggest the operation of moral law, sometimes mysterious, sometimes complex but always inexorable. The private selfishness of Beaton is a counterpart of the public selfishness of Dryfoos, and each receives its punishment. Egocentric, uncaring, his acknowledged artistic brilliance no compensation for his lack of disinterested love, Beaton wanders purposelessly through the pages of the novel. Dryfoos is unable to extend his love for the members of his immediate family to those remote from him; he is incapable of the extension of sympathy from the individual to the social: he regards the strikers as "lazy devils" who "ruined business." When Conrad defends the workers, Dryfoos strikes him and wounds him on the temple. And after his son's death, he bows over the coffin and sees it—"the wound that he had feared to look for, and that now seemed to redden on his sight. He broke into a low, wavering cry, like a child's in despair, like an animal's in terror, like a soul's in the anguish of remorse."[25]

The endings of these parts of the plots that display the tragic curve, the fall from high place to unhappiness, were not expressions of pessimism or of hopelessness in a disordered universe; on the contrary, they affirmed an essentially moral cosmic scheme in which man's acts are justly punished or justly rewarded. The fates of the actors in the two other strands of the fable were even more an indication of Howells's fundamentally optimistic vision. For in this book, profoundly felt and closely observed, written immediately after the death of his daughter and the wounding of his hopes for a just and democratic America by the civic murder of the Haymarket anarchists, Howells could still work out the novel's structure so that at the end the decision of Basil March to stick by his principles resulted in his material as well as his moral advancement; and the practical good sense of Miss Woodburn was rewarded by her happy marriage to the likeable, if overly aggressive, Fulkerson. At the end, after observing the two unhappy and the two happy endings, Basil March could state, no longer with the certainty of a

Longfellow or a Bryant, but with the contingent and tentative tone of a William James, the essential terms of the American idea in its modern form: man is worthwhile; "God did not make us despicable"; the universe is significant; "I don't know what it means, but I believe it means good."[26]

3. Mark Twain

There has been no closer literary relationship in America than that between Howells and Mark Twain. The cry of grateful joy that Twain gave when he read Howells's praise upon the appearance of *The Innocents Abroad*[27] was but the first in a series of expressions of gratitude with which Twain indicated his fealty to most of the ideas and almost all of the literary theories that Howells had been trying to make into the program for a school of American fiction. Although they were not identical in their reactions to all of the elements of the civilization about them, their friendship was strengthened by their similar, intuitive responses to the values of their culture. Like Howells—even more than Howells and certainly with a more instinctive grasp—Twain believed that truth and worth lay where his culture's idea believed them to be: in the possibilities of democratic man and in his worldly progress. Twain's position in American letters is unique in his ability to summarize the deepest commitments of most of his contemporaries. He could be an unashamedly popular writer without being a sentimental one; he could reach the numbers of American people that he did, and that he still does, because he expressed their fundamental convictions with a completeness that came from his own commitment to them. Out of this deep and unexamined commitment came his major work; when his faith in the beliefs that constituted the American idea was shattered, the talent that gave us *Huckleberry Finn* ended with it; the flow of his genius slowed to the turgid eddies of *The Mysterious Stranger*.

Mark Twain was above all else a comic writer: this is the first thing that must be said about him; it is an assertion that would have been crushing in its superfluity in his own age but that must be made in ours. Like all great comedians he contains depths of pathos and of anger that give dimension to his humor. His writing evokes the two kinds of true comic response: the affirming laugh of the joy of life, youth, vigor and the derisive laugh of satiric ridicule that forces us to perceive the deviation of the average man from the true and the real. His satiric laugh expressed, however subtly, a fundamental allegiance to the thing or person laughed at; he believed that society could be cured, that man could be reformed. When Twain lost his faith in the idea of his culture, his laughter became the rictus of cosmic irony that sees the whole universe as a colossal joke. Yet Mark Twain—the essential Mark Twain, we may say, the Mark Twain of *The Gilded Age*, *Tom Sawyer*, *Huckleberry Finn*, *Life on the Mississippi*, and *The Connecticut Yankee in King Arthur's Court*—was the American true believer in the idea that sustained his culture, and these works are best understood as his comic response to his contemporary society: a joy in its accomplishments, a satiric ridicule of its failings so that it might be made healthier and better.

This comic response was possible because of Twain's automatic sympathy with the twin premises of his culture: its belief in the essential goodness of man and of his consequent possibilities for advancement. The outcries against man's evils and stupidities, which he sounded from the beginning and which grew in number and intensity at the end, were the undertones to the optimistic tenor of his typical and most creative work. Expressions of negation in his early career often verged upon misanthropy; but they never drowned out the dominant sounds of a devotion to the youthful, to the untutored, to the childlike, combined with the corresponding dedication to a belief in material progress—a combination of commitments that is the substance of the American idea.

Dedication to the value of innocence is clear from the beginning of Twain's career: admiration for the unsophisticated is implicit in the triumph of both the language and the wit of the folk in "The Celebrated Jumping Frog of Calaveras County." And this admiration was more evident in his first major work, *The Innocents Abroad*. With his characteristic instinct for grasping a national mood, he summarized in his title the worship of the simple, the primitive, and struck the true satiric note when he called Americans in Europe the "Innocents" and included himself as one of the unknowing. He would make fun of them and of their lack of knowledge, but more often he would make the primary object of his ridicule not their simplicity but the Old World's pretentiousness.

The double tone of a defense of innocence and a self-implication in whatever ridiculous features might be found in lack of sophistication is sounded in the preface. The narrative that follows, Twain wrote, "is only the record of a picnic," but its purpose is "to suggest to the reader how *he* would be likely to see Europe and the East if he looked at them with his own eyes. . . . I make small pretence," he continued, "of showing anyone how he *ought* to look at objects of interest beyond the sea."[28] The identification with American innocence is complete. His will not be the observation of a sophisticate; he will leave that task to others who are "more competent." Instead he will be the typical man from Missouri, taking nothing on faith except the virtue of the useful, accepting no story secondhand unless it has been checked and verified by the testimony of the senses.

His ridicule is often directed at his own kind, but only when they cease to be true innocents and pretend to be something more. Simplicity and homeliness masquerading as worldliness are as detestable to him as sophistication itself; and on this kind of pretense he turns scorn as withering as that he leveled on Old World culture. He reports his uneasiness with a loud and coarse American tourist who "ordered wine with a royal flourish and said, 'I never dine without wine, sir.'" After this "pitiful falsehood" the pretender told the world at large: "'I am a free-born sovereign, sir, an American, sir, and I want everybody to know it!' He did not mention," Twain concluded, "that he was a lineal descendant of Balaam's ass."[29] Far more frequently, however, the satire is directed at sophistication itself, not at innocence pretending sophistication. Twain found sophistication, as embodied in the traditions of the Old World, mainly humbug, and with a pride in naivete scarcely to be matched in our literature, he derided the traditions, the institutions, the artwork, even the geography of Europe and the Near East.

Traditions he found generally to be an accumulation of falsehood and deceit—colorful on the outside, corrupt at the core. The Portuguese fishermen who swarm aboard the *Quaker City* at the Azores had, he reported, "brass rings in their ears" but "fraud in their hearts."[30] When a guide repeated the story of extravagant deeds in a medieval castle, he commented: "Splendid legend—splendid lie."[31] When a work of art seemed to him merely a blob of faded colors, which was his impression of *The Last Supper* as it mouldered on its damp wall, he ridiculed the feigned ecstasies of the onlookers who, he insisted, were not seeing reality with their own eyes but with the eyes of sentiment. However, when a work of art appealed to his childlike love of the large, the extravagant, and the costly, he admired it unreservedly. The cathedral at Milan, he reported, was "surely . . . the princeliest creation that ever brain of man conceived," and he revelled in "the driest details" of the great structure: "the building is five hundred feet long by one hundred and eighty wide, and the principal steeple is in the neighborhood of four hundred feet high. It has 7,148 marble statues . . . one thousand five hundred bas-reliefs . . . one hundred and thirty-six spires . . . the bill foots up six hundred and eighty-four millions of francs."[32]

Even the scenery of the Old World, measured against that of the New, faded into insignificance. Lake Como was nothing compared to Tahoe; and as for the "celebrated Sea of Galilee," not only was it smaller, but when "we come to speak of beauty, this sea is no more to be compared with Tahoe than a meridian of longitude is to a rainbow." Significantly, he found the contrast not only in the physical aspects of each but in the mood they generated: "Silence and solitude brood over Tahoe; and silence and solitude brood also over this lake of Genessaret. But the solitude of the one is as cheerful and fascinating as the solitude of the other is dismal and repellent."[33]

Howells greeted the work with joy, and the rest of America immediately took Twain to its heart. For Howells it was the explosion of false myth and the direct confrontation of reality in which he rejoiced; for the rest of America it was the presentation of this iconoclasm in a form reassuring to their faith: it told them that they were better than the Old World and that their cherished innocence and simplicity afforded the better means of knowing the truth. It also hinted at the way in which a worship of the time of childhood and youth could be made an emotional part of the worship of progress and advancement, for it suggested that we could look back upon the time of childhood with a distorting optimistic vision that would see most of the joys and few of the tragedies of that time of life: "School-boy days are no happier than the days of after life, but we look back upon them regretfully because we have forgotten our punishments at school, and how we grieved when our marbles were lost and our kites destroyed—because we have forgotten all the sorrows and privations of that canonized epoch and remember only its orchard robberies, its wooden sword pageants and its fishing holidays."[34] This was Twain the rationalist speaking, knowing that childhood was never any better, or worse, than maturity. Yet he knew, too, that there was a certain sense in which the falsehood about happy innocence was true: it reaffirmed the optimistic conviction about man's goodness, for it told of the variety of ways in which childhood and youth, with its rebellion against convention and constriction, were seedtimes of the future and suggested that the worship of innocence was a celebration of the possibilities of remaking the world.

For Americans this celebration had a particular poignance. After the Civil War they could look back not only upon the youth of their individual private lives; they could look back, too, upon the youth of their culture when, before the rise of industrialism and the cities, the work of society went on in an agrarian or small-town atmosphere where, as Howells observed later, the simple faiths of Jefferson and Franklin were better suited to the facts of social and economic life than they ever would be again. The generation of writers who were born between 1830 and 1840 had lived their own childhood and adolescence in this period of their culture's childhood and adolescence; when this time had become, as Twain put it, an "enchanted memory," they could write hymns to childhood that were filled with a sense of this golden time in a society that matched the golden time of most men's youth. Thomas Bailey Aldrich's *The Story of a Bad Boy* was the first of them, and when it appeared, Howells, and a wide reading public, hailed it as a significant contribution to the country's literary heritage. However, Aldrich's work was soon eclipsed by Twain's masterpiece in the same style: *The Adventures of Tom Sawyer*.

The lasting adult interest of this book for boys is in Mark Twain's creation of a character that best represents the typically American belief in the goodness of the natural man. This is, of course, Huckleberry Finn; his character is given to us only in general outlines in the work that concentrated on Tom Sawyer, but the basis is there. He is uneducated; he has received none of the nurturing of school, of church, or of society. Yet he is fundamentally and ineradicably good. Faced with the injustice of the wrong man's conviction for murder, he risks his own skin to right the wrong. Confronted by the possibility of Injun Joe's harming the widow, he alerts the Welshman, who comes to her rescue. His virtues have nothing to do with the refinements and manners and customs of society. They are pure, aboriginal. And therefore the resistance of this kind of natural boy to those refinements is the purest kind of comedy. He was

introduced . . . into society—no, dragged . . . into it . . . and his sufferings were almost more than he could bear. The widow's servants kept him clean and neat, combed and brushed, and they bedded him nightly in unsympathetic sheets that had not one little spot or stain which he could press to his heart and know for a friend. He had to eat with knife and fork; he had to use napkin, cup, and plate; he had to . . . talk so properly that his speech became insipid in his mouth; whithersoever he turned, the bars and shackles of civilization shut him in and bound him hand and foot.

He bravely bore his miseries three weeks, and then one day turned up missing.[35]

The rebellion was not against the values of the Widow's "civilization" but against the superficial trappings of that society; and America could laugh at the rebellion because it was not directed against its fundamental commitments but against the show, the surface, the external forms—the protest of the innocent against cleanliness, order, customs, manners;

the perennial protest of the child against maturity; and a perpetual affirmation of the value of the natural. In *Huckleberry Finn* Twain added a second great character to Huck himself as the symbol of natural goodness; this was, of course, Nigger Jim; and these two humble heroes stand as affirmations of the faith in natural man, a faith the Connecticut Yankee later would state convincingly: "A man *is* a man . . . Whole generations of abuse and oppression cannot crush the manhood . . . out of him."[36] And the fundamental meaning, as well as the fundamental value, of *Huckleberry Finn* is the persistence of basic human goodness despite the operations of a corrupt and coercive society.

The nature of this society must be clearly identified, for a failure to identify it has led to the major confusions about the meaning of *Huckleberry Finn*. This work is central to the American idea, because it affirms not only the basic goodness of natural man but the possibilities of an American society such as the one visualized by Jefferson and Franklin and carried into the nineteenth century by the New England liberal tradition of Bryant and Longfellow, Holmes and Howells and William James. With this society Twain identified completely, and his major work came out of the fusion of its values with the vigor of his Western experiences. The institutionalized deviation from its values constituted the "society" that perverted the conscience of Huck and against which the attacks of *Huckleberry Finn* are directed. It was not directed against the society of middle-class, republican America.[37]

By the time he wrote the endearing "enchanted memory" of *The Adventures of Tom Sawyer*, Twain had married and had settled into this society, of which his wife, whom he adored, was a complete embodiment. It was the culture of Howells and Thomas Bailey Aldrich and Charles Dudley Warner, the optimistic humanitarian culture now scornfully referred to as "the Genteel Tradition," and it was this culture that Twain always had in mind when he thought of the best possibilities of society. When he described the interaction between innocence and this kind of society, he was at his most cheerful: the Widow Douglas is their spokesman, she who agreed that Huck had "good spots in him" and "meant to give Huck a home under her roof and have him educated; and that when she could spare the money she would start him in business in a modest way."[38] This kind of decent, homely, middle-class American society, with its religion of social improvement, was a society toward which both Mark Twain and Huckleberry Finn yearned with all their Missouri hearts. After the gang ran away, the boys one by one became homesick for the families they had left, and "Huck was melancholy too." He eyed the departure of the other boys for home and finally said: " 'I want to go, too, Tom. It was getting lonesome anyway, and now it'll be worse. Let's go, too, Tom.' "[39] And at the end, made miserable by the unaccustomed constrictions of social behavior, he is persuaded by Tom to stay and "be respectable"; he will, he says bravely, "stick to the widder till I rot . . . and if I get to be a reg'lar ripper of a robber, and everybody talking 'bout it, I reckon she'll be proud she snaked me in out of the wet."[40]

For the civilization that snakes people out of the wet, a joyful, truly comic acceptance of the youthful antagonism to all restrictions and manners was a natural and easy indulgence. Yet a totally different kind of civilization was also sketched out in Twain's book on the glories of youth. This was the narrow, restrictive, hypocritical "civilization" whose representative in *Tom Sawyer* was the Calvinist minister who "dealt in limitless fire and brimstone, and thinned the predestined elect down to a company so small as to be hardly worth the saving."[41] And this kind of civilization would become one of the two evil aspects of culture that were targets for Twain's wrath and that provided him with a quite different kind of foil for the celebration of innocence. The widow's kind of civilization Huck will find comically uncomfortable; the minister's kind will be something from which he will flee for his life, or, when cornered by it, he will trick it and with comic triumph subdue it. This corrupt society of hypocritical hard-shelled Calvinism, the decayed tradition of the Puritans, was represented in *Huckleberry Finn* by a significant addition to Widow Douglas's household, the goggle-eyed Miss Watson. Twain had probably thought to make Nigger Jim the Widow's slave; he so alludes to him in the section lifted out of the manuscript of *Huckleberry Finn* and inserted into *Life on the Mississippi*. If he had kept to this relationship, however, he would have had Jim and Huck fleeing from the American idea. So he introduced Miss Watson—whose God is the God of Jonathan Edwards, not Benjamin Franklin—and Huck said: "I could see that there was two Providences, and a poor chap would stand considerable show with the widow's Providence, but if Miss Watson's got him there warn't no help for him any more." And then he added wistfully, hopefully: "I thought it all out and reckoned I would belong to the widow's, if he wanted me."[42]

It was the society of Miss Watson, not the society of Widow Douglas, from which Huck fled. And the warped theology of the corrupt society that threatens the natural man was matched, even exceeded, according to Twain, by the warped morality of the slave-holding, feudal culture of the South, a culture that could coerce a boy like Huck into believing that to steal a Negro slave was an evil act. The prime villains in this system were the aristocratic planter and slaveholder who maintained the evils of feudal chivalric ideas in then contemporary America. Outwardly attractive, charming, and gracious, the representatives of this level of the false society were capable of a brutal killing such as that of poor Boggs by Colonel Sherburn or of Buck Grangerford by the feuding Shepherdsons. And when this culture imposed its morality, with none of its outward charm, upon its lowest levels, the result was the poor-white trash—represented, at their ugliest, by horrible old man Finn, whose company is objectionable even to the filthiest pig and who rants on about the official faith, which has made possible a "govment" of justice and equality: " 'Oh yes, this is a wonderful govment, wonderful. Why, looky here. There was a free nigger there, from Ohio; a mullatter, most as white as a white man. . . . And what do you think? They said he was a p'fessor in a college, and could talk all kinds of languages. . . . .And that ain't the wust. They said he could *vote*, when he was at home.' "[43]

The decayed, pseudochivalric culture of the South produced, according to Twain's analysis, the whole class of old man Finns—the poor whites. They do their lynchings "in the dark, southern fashion." Their sport is tying cans to dogs and seeing the poor beasts run themselves to death. Twain made it clear that this kind of system will produce this kind of man in any age. A few years later he described the knights of King Arthur's England who engage in precisely the same sport; and in the blind allegiance of the lower classes of the sixth century, he portrayed exactly the same degradation of humanity; the peasants, he said, reminded him "of a time thirteen centuries away, when the 'poor whites' of our South who were always despised and frequently insulted by the slave-lords around them, and who owed their base condition simply to the presence of slavery in their midst, were yet pusillanimously ready to side with the slave-lords in all political moves for the upholding and perpetuating of slavery."[44] The portraits of the cowardly mobs in *Huckleberry Finn* are no illustrations of a belief in the essential evil in man; they are descriptions of the way in which an ugly society makes ugly men; and as a constant foil to this ugliness, we are presented with the inherent, ineradicable beauty of the vulgar boy and the vulgar man who preserve their inner, natural glory.

Twain preserved at least this belief in natural goodness even into the last decade of the century. The figure in the past who appealed most consistently to his imagination was Joan of Arc, and when he wrote her story in the next decade, after he had been sobered by his financial failures but before he was permanently embittered by the death of his daughter, he made it clear that Joan was the eternal symbol of the glory and goodness of the innocent. For Joan is the supreme historical representation of the virtue of the vulgar. Her father was a constant reminder that "peasants are not merely animals, beasts of burden put here by the good God to produce food and comfort for the 'nation,' but are something more and better."[45] The "humble eye" of the Dwarf could see the great truth where others failed. The greatness of Joan was in her gathering together, in her own spirit, the wisdom and insight of the folk: "She was a peasant. That tells the whole story. She was of the people and knew the people. . . . We make little account of that vague, formless, inert mass, that mighty underlying force which we call 'the people'—an epithet which carries contempt with it. It is a strange attitude; for at bottom we know that the throne which the people support stands, and when that support is removed nothing in the world can save it."[46]

The belief in the natural goodness of natural man, a belief enshrined in the history of Joan of Arc as well as in the "hymns" to the boyhood of Tom Sawyer and Huckleberry Finn, fused without seam in Mark Twain's most creative years with the second necessary half of the American idea: the expectation of human progress. Like most men in his culture, he habitually felt himself part of a significant and valuable historical process, the advancement of man through the progressive development of improved ways of shaping both nature and society. One of the few admirable Europeans in *The Innocents Abroad* was the Russian Baron Ungern-Sternberg, a "boisterous, whole-souled old nobleman," who was "a man of progress and enterprise—a representative man of the age." Typically, the Baron's progressivism was demonstrated in the fact that he was "a sort of railroad king. In his line he is making things move along in this country."[47] It would be unfair not to add that Mark then went on to poke some fun at both Russian and American character; but the main point of the passage is that it so calmly and easily and completely accepts the equivalence of progress and virtue and significantly uses technology—specifically the railroad—as the touchstone of both.

Appropriately, the key work of Mark Twain's most creative years was a book whose meaning and structure IS the American idea—the fusion of the dream of innocence with the belief in progress. This is *Life on the Mississippi*. Like the official faith its structure is double. Its first part is a celebration of the joys of America's youth, which is Mark Twain's youth—the era before the Civil War, the era of the steamboat making its dangerous trip down a river whose treachery and beauty provided the maximum opportunity for the experiencing of individual glory. It was written in 1874 at the behest of Howells, who wanted an account of a hitherto unexplored literary corner of the America to whose activities he was devoting his editorial and creative career. *Old Times* is full of a sense of the romance of the river before the Civil War. Yet it already contained within itself the germ of the second section, written in 1882 after he had returned with notebook in hand to the Mississippi to observe its changes; for in *Old Times* he describes how, even then, in the naive age he was celebrating, he understood the difference between the romance of innocence and the reality of progress. As he learned the truth about the river and found out its secrets, he could better do his job as the pilot of the steamboat; but he found, too, that "all the grace, the beauty, the poetry had gone out of the majestic river!" With knowledge came disenchantment: "All the value any feature of it had," he went on, was "the amount of usefulness it could furnish toward compassing the safe piloting of a steamboat."[48]

The germ of the second part of the book was already there in its first section, for the second part is a sympathetic treatment of the contemporary America, with its bustle and progress, with its scientific and technological advancement, as the same kind of maturing toward usefulness that the pilot's own knowledge represented in another context. The proposition reads something like this: even in the days of primitive innocence before the Civil War, the acquisition of knowledge by the pilot and the application of this knowledge to the physical world meant at the same time an increase in well-being and a loss of romance. In the same way the acquisition of knowledge by society and its application to the advancement of the nation meant the increase in well-being at the necessary expense of the romance of the individual: in this case the riverboat pilot. In discussing the pilot's association, he told how it seemed indestructible; and yet "the days of its glory were numbered." The railroad took away most of its passenger trade, and a "vulgar little tug-boat," towing a dozen barges, took away its freight trade, and "behold, in the twinkling of an eye, as it were, the association and the noble science of piloting were things of the dead and pathetic past." The terms of that last sentence are worth pondering, for they give us the essence of Mark Twain's acceptance of the American style: piloting was "noble"; it was an occupation that affirmed the essential nobility of man, who was capable of facing the world with his own intuitions; but it was destroyed by the necessary advancement of human reason and its applications to the physical world about man and therefore quite properly became a thing of the "dead and pathetic"[49] past.

The second part of the book, added in 1882, was largely the description of what happens when one society tries to live by the values of a "dead and pathetic past." This, of course, was the postwar South, and his trip through it was a trip past the "sports" of cockfighting and dogbaiting, past the sham "House Beautifuls" with their false pretensions of Georgian grandeur, past the society whose ruling class was an aristocracy with its senseless *code duello* and whose lower classes were the gaping and gawking poor whites with the vicious morals of their masters and with none of their charming, if outdated, manners. The southern attempt to sustain "maudlin Middle-age romanticism" in the nineteenth century, the "plainest and sturdiest and infinitely greatest and worthiest of all the centuries the world has seen,"[50] was one result of this confusion between reality and myth; and another was the cult of Sir Walter Scott and his code of chivalry. Scott became the "enchanter" who had checked "the wave of progress" and had held the South asleep, incapable of awakening to "the genuine and wholesome civilization of the nineteenth century."[51]

The journey south, through a civilization held in bondage to the past, took up most of the work; the northern trip was a coda, for during it he is satisfied merely to describe, by contrast, from St. Louis northward "all the enlivening signs of the presence of active, energetic, intelligent, prosperous, practical nineteenth-century populations" whose "people don't dream; they work."[52] Their cities are "brisk" and "handsome"; there are canals over dangerous rapids, whose "masonry is of the majestic kind . . . and will endure like a Roman aqueduct"; the communities are "fine and flourishing"; they are "belted with busy factories"; they breathe "a go-ahead atmosphere which tastes good in the nostrils."[53]

The idea for *A Connecticut Yankee in King Arthur's Court* may have been in Twain's consciousness as early as the writing of *Life on the Mississippi,* for in the earlier work he not only identified the South's problems with its sentimental medievalism, he at one point quoted the frantic irrationality of a southern reporter who identified the sick yearnings toward the medieval with the court of the Round Table: the southern belles, this commentator wrote, wore " 'the colors of their favorite knights, and were it not for the fact that the doughty heroes appeared on unromantic mules, it would have been easy to imagine one of King Arthur's gala-days.' "[54] *A Connecticut Yankee* is the last of Mark Twain's major works, and it is the last major work in which the twin commitments of the American idea are completely the terms in which Mark Twain viewed his world through fiction. His "natural man" has grown up; Huckleberry Finn has become Hank Morgan; Hank, like Huck, is a representative of the folk, the true "nation." His ancestry is significant and typical: the son of a blacksmith, the nephew of a horse doctor, he has been both himself; now a maker of machinery, he will try to speed up progress, the progress of the sanest and healthiest century the world has seen, by bringing it to the Western world thirteen hundred years too early. He will be trapped by historical necessity, and his dream will be destroyed by superstition and reaction. However, he will have enacted a drama of the struggle of the forces of the Enlightenment with the forces of darkness, which Twain felt could be a lesson to his contemporary world. He wanted it to speak to people everywhere who were struggling for republicanism. "These are immense days!" he wrote Howells in 1889, immediately after its appearance. "Republics and rumors of republics, from everywhere in earth. There'll be plenty to sneer and depreciate and disenthuse—on the other hand, whoso can lift a word of the other sort, in the name of God let him pipe up! I want to print some extracts from the Yankee that have in them this new (sweet) breath of republics. . . . I want the book to speak now when there'll be a listening audience, alert and curious to hear—and try to make that audience hear with profit."[55] And as late as 1895, he felt that of all his books it had the greatest chance of survival because '"some powerful political and social lessons are cleverly interleaved with the satire of the story. It should be,' he added in this statement to an Australian reporter, 'a power in the democratic colonies of Australia.'"[56]

The tragic ending of *A Connecticut Yankee*—with the "Enchanter" Merlin finally triumphant over Hank Morgan, the man of the Enlightenment—was dictated by historical necessity; progress and democracy had not, after all, come to the

Western world in the sixth century. And there are undoubtedly some of the stirrings of uneasiness with the validity of
the American idea, an uneasiness that would deepen into
pessimism and then into the nihilistic despair of his later
years, when his sense of the inevitable determination of all
things by antecedent events resulted in a sense of fatalism
and futility. This was not yet the feeling projected by *A
Connecticut Yankee*.

It must be agreed, however, that one of the major problems in assessing Mark Twain's optimism is the accounting
for the sense of determinism in his thought and his works
from the very beginning. Taught his Calvinism at a very
early age, he dropped its theological aspect very early but
seemed to cling to the sense of inevitability that was part of
the Presbyterian world view, a kind of truncated Calvinism,
predestination without God.

One more evidence of Mark Twain's complete representa-
tiveness is the way in which he took a potentially pessimistic
theory—that of determinism—and assimilated it into an optimistic view. This is not unusual for either Europeans or
Americans in this century. The argument runs something
like this: what causes men to act as they do? A theological or
religious viewpoint ascribes it to God or to some metaphysical
principle. A naturalistic viewpoint assigns the cause to the
world of things and to a sequence in the past that leads up to
the present reality. Both the place and the time—the world
and its past—as the location of significance and cause may
lead to optimism. If the events of *this* world are solely responsible for happenings, then the reason for happenings
can possibly be changed by man. If the chain of events *in*
time, rather than out of time, is responsible, then we may
hope—by changing the events of time, by changing a present
that becomes the past—to control at least part of our destinies.
This fundamental optimism of naturalistic determinism operated as a major motive in the critical realism of Howells. It
operated even more conclusively in the works of Mark
Twain—even as late as 1900, when there seemed to be very
little optimism left in him. For that year, when he wrote his
"What is Man?", he answered that man is a mechanical part
of a mechanical world; but he still gave, as an answer to what

man should then do, the melioristic response that he must devote himself to deeds that most contribute to the possible happiness of most men. In contrast to the "out of Space, out of time" location of causality, Twain located significance and purpose in space and in time and therefore held out some hope that man might coerce both space and time to his advantage.[57]

Mark Twain, then, realized his world in terms of his culture's controlling idea, and his own little illusions of art took their strength from their uncanny ability to give this idea its expression. Pudd'nhead Wilson remarked that we should cling to our illusions, for when we lose them, we die. When Mark Twain lost his illusions, he was dead—dead as a great writer; and the record of his last twenty years is the record of dismal and abortive attempts to make literature out of the shattering of his beliefs.

However, during his most creative years, the years from *The Innocents Abroad* to *A Connecticut Yankee*, his creative work was a defense of, and not an attack upon, the basic commitments of his culture. These commitments were pervasive in the expressed content of his works up to 1890; they just as surely determined the form of his fiction, for they affected the design and the outcome of his plots, the characters he created, and the language that embodies them all. The plots of realistic fiction are a direct outgrowth of a fundamentally comic view of the world; the rambling, loosely constructed adventures of a character as he moves physically through space become the representation of the sequence of man's life as it moves through time; space sequence represents time sequence: this is the only way the writer can compress the events of life into the events of art. By accepting this looseness of life itself and imitating it in his fiction, the writer pays allegiance to the immanent meaning of the external events. He imposes a minimum of direction and coercion upon them. He tries to write a species of personal history. Selection, arrangement, and structure are minimized, even deprecated; Twain threatened with suit, bodily harm, or murder the reader who would try to find motive, moral, or plot in *Huckleberry Finn*.

Yet the selection and arrangement are there; and one of

their results is the conclusion of plot in "happy endings": in life, not death; in triumph, not disaster. For the first time in the American nineteenth century, the choice of the happy ending was typical of the fictional worlds that serious American writers were constructing. Serious literature as well as sentimental literature after the Civil War was suddenly seized with the cult of the happy ending. What had been chiefly the technique of the sentimentalist before the war became the technique of those tellers of tales whom we regard as honorable. In DeForest's *Miss Ravenel's Conversion* northern homely virtue prevails over southern romantic decadence, and Miss Ravenel is converted from secession to loyalty, from false romanticism to sensible realism. The same pattern is true of *Kate Beaumont*, where the young mining engineer of the North asserts the supremacy of reason over the dark and false traditions of a southern code. Even Henry James—who would soon find the tragedies, the tall stone walls that fatally divide us, more to his conception of reality than the comedies—even James near the outset of his career, when he wrote of the impact of Europe on America in *The Europeans*—showed us the triumph of the light of New England over the dark of the wicked, although charming, Baroness and constructed a happy ending when the American heroine is united with her American hero. For Howells, the most representative novelist of his era, the possibility of the triumph of human reason and insight over the problems of the world was an article of faith never seriously challenged, even in the depths of his despair and doubt after the Haymarket Riot and the death of his daughter. His typical work involves the *rise*, not the *fall*, of the Silas Laphams of America. From the beginning of his career to the end, Howells showed the possibilities of the triumph of human reason.

In Mark Twain's work before 1893, there is a dominance of the comic, rather than the tragic, plot. *The Gilded Age*, like *Kate Beaumont*, ends with the victory of the hardheaded mining engineer and his sweetheart, a woman physician, and with the failure—but a failure without tragic overtones—of the forces of greed, corruption, and speculation. When Twain returned to the theme of *The Gilded Age* in *The American Claimant* (1892), he once more demonstrated the victory of modern practicality over sentimental dreams: Sally Sellers, who led a double life—during the day "American . . . and proud of her head and hands and its commercial result" and during the evening living in a "shadowland" of "feudal fantasy"—ends in a happy marriage and a healthful return to the real world. Colonel Sellers at the outset of the novel is shown temporarily defeated: "Three dollars a week," he tells Washington Hawkins mournfully. "It's just human life . . . just an epitome of human ambition; you aim for the palace and get drowned in the sewer."[58] However, this mood does not last for long. Soon his wounded spirit heals, and he and Washington "make things hum"; and his fortunes take a turn for the better as—happy, expectant, triumphant—he careens out of the novel.

Above all, in his masterpiece, *Huckleberry Finn*, Twain embodied his culture's official faith in the happy ending—in the ability of a boy to use his combination of natural good-heartedness and acquired shrewdness to triumph over the forces of material and man-made evil. This needs emphasis at a time when *Huckleberry Finn*, like its great predecessor *Don Quixote*, is in danger of revision at our modern hands. We find it difficult in our age to realize that a work of art can be both affirmative and great. Just as Unamuno revised *Don Quixote* to meet the needs of tragic modern Spain, so modern American critics stress the many pessimistic notes about man in society that are the minor, not the dominant, tones of *Huckleberry Finn*. In depicting his fable of two American flights toward freedom, freedom from the enslavement of southern institutions and of moral traditions, Mark Twain wrote an optimistic book. The plot of *Huckleberry Finn* ends in two triumphs, Nigger Jim's physical freedom and Huckleberry Finn's moral freedom, after Huck's decision to substitute the saving grace of modern pragmatic humanism for the authoritarian morality of Miss Watson and all she represents.

Not only is the whole movement of the book an affirmation of the possibilities of escape from evil, but the structure of each subordinate episode is correspondingly the comic structure of triumph of enlightenment over darkness, of realistic common sense over sentimental aberration, of life over death. Caught in the nonsense of the Grangerford-Shepherdson feud, Huck is the instrument by which the lovers of the two opposed families are united. Involved in the shameful duplicity of the Duke and the Dauphin as they attempt to swindle Mary Jane Wilks, Huck snatches the victory from them as he returns common sense to the deluded town and gold to the bereaved family.

The purely financial terms that are part of the happy endings are not the most important, but certainly are the most revealing, of the proofs that Twain's identification was with middle-class values. Money gained honestly is worthy of care and respect; it is to be guarded against thievery or fraud and the inflation that comes from speculation. There is a gentle satire of Jim's desire to get rich by putting his money out to deposit at impossibly high interest rates. Yet there is wholehearted authorial approval of Huck's cleverness in saving the principal and earning legitimate rates of interest, 6 and 7.5 percent, on two important sums of capital that figure in the narrative at its beginning, at the climax of its next-to-last adventure, and at the very end. When, at the beginning of the novel, Huck hears that Pap is in town, he runs to the judge, for he knows with precocious acumen that he must place his money—it is $6,000, half the share of the reward for the capture of Injun Joe—beyond the legal reach of his parent. He begs the judge to "take" the money as a gift. The judge, understanding the ruse, gives him a legal lesson by "buying" the property. We learn at the same time that the money has been earning a safe rate of interest—6 percent.

In the climax of the last adventure, the Duke and Dauphin have succeeded in stealing the inheritance of the Wilks orphans. The sum is announced as $6,000. Yet not quite, for when the frauds count it, they find it short $415, just about the amount they had swindled previously from the villagers. In order to allay suspicions, the Duke and the Dauphin put in the $415 to make up the expected sum, and it is this total of $5,585, plus 7.5 percent "interest," that Huck is able to restore to Mary Jane and her sisters. Then at the end the importance of money is again emphasized when the safety of Huck's capital provides the solid financial underpinning for the traditional happy ending. The good fortune is in terms of freedom, of the triumph of common sense over romantic foolishness, and of love and friendship over hate. However, it is also in terms of dollars and cents and interest duly earned. Just before Pap's death is revealed, Huck thinks glumly that his father has most likely pried the money away from the judge. " 'No he hain't,' Tom tells him; 'it's all there yet—six thousand dollars and more.' "[59]

Even when the plots of most serious novelists of the era involve the most scathing and seemingly bitter condemnations and apparent negations of the world of social appearance, the condemnations are based upon a fundamental affirmation of the underlying order of the external world and the ability of man reasonably to understand and improve the world. There is a radical difference between the consistently unhappy endings of Henry James and Henry Adams and those of Howells—between Garland's angry short stories and angrier novels or Howells in *Annie Kilburn* and *A World of Chance*, on the one hand, and Adams's *Democracy* or James's *Princess Casamassima* on the other. In James and Adams the tragedy, the frustration, is built into the informing spirit of the fictional world and becomes the artist's statement of his lack of faith in the outer world of contemporary history. The disillusionment of Mrs. Lightfoot Lee in *Democracy* lies not in the fact that she discovers a corruption of democracy but in the fact that democracy is inherently and radically corrupt. The inability of Esther in the book that bears her name to accept the man of science, the man of religion, or the man of art is not a temporary difficulty of choice but a permanent and inescapable failure of these three major possibilities in a modern world. Science is impossible and verifies only that chaos is the truth of the universe and order is the dream of man; religion was at one time unity, but for Adams in his later life the virgin of Chartres looks down "from a deserted heaven, into an empty church, on a dead faith." This satire of "lost values . . . is a self-destructive literary form. Unable to comprehend the meanness he discovers, the satirist seems to argue that the world he represents is hallucinatory instead of real."[60]

The other brand of criticism—the kind to which Parrington

gave the name of "critical realism" and that was a dominant mode of the era—is a quite different attitude. In every case we find that the unhappy endings are meant as good medicine to cure a sick but not irreparably diseased body, both social and politic; it is antimythic, opposed to false myths that, according to the writer, obscure the perception of truth. The works of Howe, Kirkland, and Garland were attempts to explode the "myth of the garden"—the false myth of the agrarian West as inherently better than industrialization and civilization. Garland's critical creed was that "the veritist is really an optimist. . . . He sees life in terms of what it might be, as well as in terms of what is; but he writes of what is, and, at his best, suggests what is to be by contrast."[61]

The part of the fictional world of the novel that we term *plot* either emulated the basic optimism of the world outside of the novel in nineteenth-century America or else arranged events so that the reason or the cause for the unhappy ending for these events would be identified and presumably corrected. In either case the arrangement within the novel was an implicit affirmation of the probability, or at least the possibility, that the larger world could progress toward betterment. Furthermore, the characters with which writers of fiction after the Civil War began to people their little worlds show a similar response to the major official cultural faith that made sense of the outside world of American nineteenth-century experience.

The American secular faith as seen in Franklin and Holmes was pervaded by a belief in the value and beneficence of the scientific method as applied to human and social problems. In this they were in direct contrast to American romantic writers, who had used their art to attack the scientific attitude. For Melville the man of applied science and invention had been the dispenser of lightning rods who would lure man from the hearth of human sympathy or the manufacturer of a mechanical iron monster that would destroy both its own maker and the bell tower of human creativity. For Hawthorne the scientist had been the vile empiric committing the unpardonable sin of intellectual pride as he searched for limitless knowledge. Although in his last unfinished work he created a kindly apothecary, Dr. Dolliver, who could maintain the continuous chain of human sympathy, Hawthorne's earlier works had consistently portrayed the scientist as villain. He had fashioned two physicians: Chillingworth, whom the historian of American psychoanalysis has called the first psychoanalyst, and Rappaccini—both diabolic invaders of the sanctity of the human mind and body. And these men of medicine had their counterpart in Melville's infamous surgeon of the Neversink who inhumanly murdered his patient in the interest of pure science.

The novelists who made our significant postwar fiction, on the other hand, almost invariably treated physicians and scientists as heroes. They had before them the example of Dr. Oliver Wendell Holmes—shrewd, witty, commonsensical. "The attitude of modern science is erect," Holmes had declared. "Her aspect serene," he had said, "her determination inexorable, her onward movement unflinching."[62] With customary charming conceit this staunch believer in human progress had used a physician as the intelligent commentator of his novel *Elsie Venner*, and seven years later DeForest portrayed the benign Dr. Ravenel, father of the deluded Lily, who won his daughter from secession to loyalty by his reasonable good sense. In this pioneer work of American realism, the physician was described as one "who had been plotting for the benefit of the human race . . . one of those philanthropic conspirators . . . who, for the past thirty years had been rotten egged and vilified at the North, tarred and feathered and murdered at the South."[63] Captain Colburne, the young hero, had been the son of a doctor with whom Ravenel had studied mineralogy; Colburne had been quite young when, as Ravenel says, "science had the misfortune . . . to lose his father."[64] DeForest, like Sydney Lanier and like Robert Penn Warren and John Crowe Ransom two generations later, identified the North with the empirical and rational attitude and the South with the emotional and the intuitive. For DeForest, however, the South was obsessed with false emotion and sentimental intuition, personified by the romantic, dashing Colonel Carter. A small conversation between Colburne and Carter underscores their contrasting attitudes toward science. Colburne praises his younger professors at the new Boston University; these new teachers, he tells Carter, "accept geology . . . and discuss Darwin with patience." "Don't get out of my range," replies Carter scornfully. "Who the devil is Darwin?"[65]

Four years after Miss Ravenel and the warfare over her by the contending forces of science and sentiment, Charles Dudley Warner collaborated with Mark Twain on *The Gilded Age*, a novel whose purpose was to expose the emptiness of speculation and the value of applying reason to the human and natural resources of the country. They decided to make their heroine a doctor and their hero an engineer. The good sense of the girl and her lover's spirit of experimental inquiry enabled their part of the fiction to reach a happy ending. Twain's friend and guide, William Dean Howells, frequently used characters of scientific profession or leanings to resolve the chaos threatened by false sentimentalism. Although Dr. Breen of *Dr. Breen's Practice* was something less than a paragon of intelligence, she was beautiful and attractive and was guided in the right path by Dr. Mulbridge, who viewed her "out of grey eyes that, if not sympathetic, were perfectly intelligent, and that at once sought to divine and class her."[66] There was the Reverend David Sewell, of *The Rise of Silas Lapham* and the *Minister's Charge*, a sensible humanist and a devoted admirer of the Harvard geologist Louis Agassiz; there was the Reverent Dr. Peck in *Annie Kilburn*, who praised the skepticism of science as God-given and God-directed. And there was the physician Edward Olney of *An Imperative Duty*, who brought reason to bear upon an incipiently tragic situation, for he knew that "vice is savage and virtue is civilized."[67]

Through 1893 the heroes of Mark Twain's fiction are similarly skeptical and experimental; they reject tradition and convention unless experience proves the tradition true. The Pauper questions the conventions of royalty and its mode of living when it outruns economic realities; his suggested answer to the problem of state deficit is to move the court to a cheaper house; he knows just the place: one that "standeth over against the fish market."[68] Huck Finn is confronted with two extravagant views of the world. One is Tom Sawyer's: men can get rich easily; rub a lamp and a genie will come. Huck, the embryonic scientist, does not reject the hypothesis out of hand: "I got an old tin lamp and an iron ring and went out in the woods and rubbed and rubbed till I sweat like an Injun, calculating to build a palace and sell it; but it warn't no use, none of the genies come. So then I judged that all that stuff was only just one of Tom Sawyer's lies."[69]

This passage gives us some clue about Twain's cheerful willingness to accept the magical but not the superstitious or the religious. As Frazer points out, the magical view and the scientific view are essentially the same, with one developing out of the other. Both assume a reasonable, if unknown, natural connection between one natural event and another. A pin stuck in a doll will result in a pain in an enemy's body; certain sounds and certain gestures will result in the falling of rain. Jacques Ellul has seconded Frazer's insight: "Magic is the first expression of technique."[70] Superstition, as opposed to magic, means an unreasonable fear of the supernatural. For superstition Twain always had unreserved contempt; for magic he always had a certain condescending sympathy and understood that it was an incomplete or imperfect science. Huckleberry Finn and the Connecticut Yankee are one in their belief that the answers to all things are empirically found. Huck with his magic, Huck Finn believing that his bad luck comes from a snakeskin and continuing his belief when misfortune follows his adventure with the rattler, Huck Finn testing the story of the genie by rubbing the lamp is but a rudimentary scientist. Like Hank Morgan he is a man of the people. Huck and Hank are "vernacular" heroes—the one expressing the folk wisdom and empiricism on an earlier level of prescientific development, the other expressing all the belief in technics and machinery of a scientific stage of development.

The Connecticut Yankee, of course, is the paragon of the applied scientist, the engineer. Much has been made of the fact that Mark Twain referred to the Yankee as an "ignoramus"; from this has flowed a modern critical attitude that is beginning to invert completely the meaning of *A Connecticut Yankee* in the same way that modern Spanish critics have inverted the meaning of *Don Quixote*. For Mark Twain, however, "ignoramus" is no uncomplimentary word; he considered himself just such an ignoramus and, like the Yankee, strived to be nearly "barren of sentiment" or of "poetry,"[71] which, he said, were the same things. And more often than not Hank is a mask for Mark himself and represents what Twain considered to be the right way of looking at the world of experience. Despite the sadness and ambiguities that are there in the ending of the work, the book as a whole and the Connecticut Yankee himself are not ambiguous but are straightforward presentations of Mark Twain's devotion to an age that "knows how."

After Hank Morgan, Twain's next major hero was Pudd'n-head Wilson, whom Roxie knows to be "the smartest man in dis town." Pudd'nhead is called "a great scientist"; he is a member of the free-thinkers society and "interested himself in every new thing that was born in the universe of ideas, and studied and experimented upon it at his house."[72] And like Huck Finn and Hank Morgan, Pudd'nhead faces the stupidity, the ugliness, the decayed tradition of the town and proves himself superior to them.

However, there is a strange note in "Those Extraordinary Twins," the appendage to *Pudd'nhead Wilson*: the town's doctor is a "fool"; his prognosis for Angelo's wound, if left unattended, is that " 'exudation of the aesophagus is nearly sure to ensue, and this will be followed by ossification and extradition of the maxillaris superioris, which must decompose the granular surfaces of the great infusorial . . . system . . . ending unavoidably in the dispersion and combustion of the marsupial fluxes and the consequent embrocation of the bicuspid populo redax referendum rotulorum.' " Upon which Brother Joe says to himself, " 'The baptising's busted, that's sure.' "[73] This scorn for a man of medicine was symptomatic. Three years later, in 1895, when Harold Frederic finished the definitive story of America's fall from the paradise of innocent faith into the world of painful knowledge, he created a much more sinister figure, Dr. Ledsmar of *The Damnation of Theron Ware*; and with Ledsmar the wheel has turned full circle, back to Dr. Rappaccini. Ledsmar, the representation of empirical science, shows Theron a "Chinaman," upon whom he has been experimenting, asleep in a dilapidated summer house. Ledsmar, who has been drugging him daily, explains with a "whimsical half-smile": " 'I am increasing his dose monthly by regular stages, and the results promise to be rather remarkable.' " Remembering what Celia Madden has told him, Theron thinks the doctor is "a beast."[74] The portrayal of a villainous man of science is one of the several elements of style that indicate Frederic's uneasiness with the official faith. However, this was already 1896, and we were already over what has been called the great "watershed"[75] in American history.

Now what of the *"things"* with which the writers of fiction in the age of Mark Twain filled out their microcosmic worlds? The environment of the real world of Americans, of course, was dominated above all else by the appearance of the machine. The way in which the writer of fiction took the machine into his smaller world became another indication of the relation between the patterns of fiction and the pattern of history. As a point of reference, once more, we may observe the way in which Nathaniel Hawthorne used the machine; Hawthorne's romances were pervaded by negative imagery of the mechanical. "The image of the machine and machine power," it has been pointed out, "were widely employed as emblems of America's future."[76] Rejecting the idea of progress, rejecting the conception that mankind could turn his back upon his past and face a new and hopeful future, Hawthorne quite naturally rejected a positive image of the machine. His celestial railroad of progress was hell-bound; its engineer, a fiend. Smooth and easy as it seems, comfortable and modern as it promises to be, it is yet diabolical: its fumes and fires, those of the underworld. The train that carries Hepzibah and Clifford away from their past, away from the House of the Seven Gables, away from the involvement of man with Original Sin, leads finally and drearily to the end of the road—to an old church and another dark house.

There is, however, a change when we read of the machine in the works of the postwar realists. Listen to John DeForest's two heroes in *Miss Ravenel's Conversion* discuss the advances of civilization: " 'Weak spirits are frightened by this change, this growth, this forward impetus,' muses Dr. Ravenel; and then he tells the story of the Georgia 'cracker' who had been in mortal terror of his first train ride. 'Now that is very much like the judgment of timid and ill-informed people on the progress of the nation or the race,' the doctor says. Colburne laughs and agrees: 'On our train,' he says, 'on the train of human progress, we are parts of the engine and not mere passengers. I ought to be revolving somewhere.'"[77] And this, in general, remained the dominant conception of the machine through much of the fiction during the remainder of the century. The men who made the machines, the men who made and ran the railroads and the factories, could be—and often were—excoriated, but the machine itself generally remained an image of the triumph of progress.

It was, for example, the crowning achievement of the Yankee in the series of improvements Hank Morgan achieved for sixth-century England:

Slavery was dead and gone; all men were equal before the law. . . . The telegraph, the telephone, the phonograph, the type-writer, the sewing machine, and all the thousand willing and handy servants of steam and electricity were working their way into favor. We had a steamboat or two on the Thames, we had steam war-ships, and the beginnings of a steam commercial marine; I was getting ready to send out an expedition to discover America.

We were building several lines of railways, and our line from Camelot to London was already finished and in operation.[78]

A Connecticut Yankee remains, in general, the summary of the idea of progress in a work of art in nineteenth-century America. This is not to gainsay the troublesome note of ambivalence that creeps into the final part of the work, a note that, like the one in *Huckleberry Finn*, has been taken up and amplified in an attempt to read the work in exactly the opposite way from that in which it was intended. Faced with the necessity of reconciling his wishes and hopes with the hard historical truth that democracy and science had not, after all, actually come to sixth-century England, Twain was compelled to write a cataclysm to the end of his fable of the advantages of progress and so provide the period with its happiest hunting ground for revisionist critics and seekers of ambiguity. Beginning with Gladys Bellamy, who found the book "a fictional working out of the idea that a too-quick civilization breeds disaster," critics have dwelt upon such statements as these: "Unsuspected by this dark land, I had the civilization of the nineteenth century booming under its very nose! It was fenced away from the public view, but there it was, a gigantic and unassailable fact—and to be heard from yet, if I lived and had luck. There it was, as sure a fact and as substantial a fact as any serene volcano, standing innocent with its smokeless summit in the blue sky, and no sign of the rising hell in its bowels."[79] Taken together with the horror of the last scene, when the Yankee, barricaded in his cave behind his concentric circles of electrified barbed wire, destroys the massed hosts of chivalry, this passage has been the basis for an attempt to assert that we are meant to read *A Connecticut Yankee* as a bitter diatribe against the destruction of human values by the coming of the machine tended by the Yankee. Yet the man who could in 1889 still talk about an inventor as a sublime magician of iron and steel[80] was not one to respond with sentimental aversion when faced with achievements of the industrial revolution. Mark Twain's feeling of revulsion for the mechanical would have to wait until the deeper, truly tragic moods of his later years. In these years life for him would become a dream, a nightmare, with the ugliest part of the illusion that of a hopeless mechanistic world. He would write of a universe dominated by malignancy that appears on earth only to torment the pitiful creature man. The machine would become for him an example of the total mechanism of the universe of which man is but a hopeless and helpless mechanical part. The mechanism itself would be but a dream, and man, a homeless thought wandering forlorn in the empty spaces. He would describe life's journey as a ship voyaging among the molecules of a tiny drop of water. As the ship proceeds, it is sucked into a vortex of intermolecular forces, toward the blinding white glare that turns out to be the glare in an illuminated field of a microscope, through which peers a scornful god. This comes close to the terror of Poe's A. Gordon Pym, who found the center of meaning a shrouded, blank whiteness of nothingness or of Melville, whose Confidence Man leads a bumbling, senile God into outer darkness.

At the time of Twain's growing pessimisms, the literary

scene was marked by the appearance of Harold Frederic's *The Damnation of Theron Ware*, a novel written under the influence of William Dean Howells and following, in many ways, the generally realistic method of portraying American life—the style suited to the expression of the official American faith. Yet despite its involvement with the dominant tone of the preceding age, *The Damnation of Theron Wade* was, after all, the story of a fall, and not a rise. Its ending was uncertain and ambiguous. The healing of Theron seemed no final salve to his soul but a temporary way stop on the road to the dark hell of knowledge.

The torment of Theron struck a new note—the note of a modern tragic irony that regards man and society as mere delusive appearances and the cosmos as hostile and malignant. For Theron the world became "all black" and "plunged in the Egyptian night"; he found himself "alone among awful, planetary solitudes," where the universe holds him "at arm's length as a nuisance."[81] His question at the end—"Was it a sham . . . or isn't there any God at all,—but only men who live and die like animals?"[82]—introduces a terrible cosmic doubt, the same doubt that Stephen Crane expressed shortly before in *The Black Riders*, where the world is a "ship . . . forever rudderless . . . going ridiculous voyages."[83]

Two years later Mark Twain began his first sketches of *The Mysterious Stranger*; Henry Adams soon contemplated the jackals creeping down the desert ruins and saw in the picture the essence of man's plight in a waterless wasteland of an age of unbelief. This was the new tone that insinuated itself into Frederic's story of the progress of America through enlightenment and knowledge. Just as the novel is prescient in tone, so does it look forward in its use of imagery. It gives evidence of a shift in technique—away from the realistic and toward the symbolic and the mythical, away from the social and toward the individual. Frederic, like Crane and Norris, found himself interested in primitive passions, unconscious stirrings, racial memories in a collective mind; like other writers of the new generation and like Henry James, a writer of the old generation who had not participated in the realistic acquiescence, Frederic experimented with techniques for revealing his insights into new dimensions of mind and character. The very title, in which the theme of the Faust legend advanced from the dim recesses of allusion to complete overtness, signaled these changes. Just as the Titan of innovation, of the fire-bringing Enlightenment, was for Hawthorne double in nature, both fiend and angel, so the illumination of Theron Ware was also a great darkness and a moral disaster. Herbert Spencer's admonition to write as simply and clearly as possible, an admonition heeded by Twain and Howells and Eggleston and John DeForest, was no longer persuasive. The play upon the function of seeing and upon the word *light* had ambiguities enough to please the admirer of metaphysical poetry. When Theron's eyes were closed to knowledge, the biblical heroes glowed with a poetic light. When his eyes were opened, "this light was gone." As well as this paradox, there is the insistence upon the magic of numbers; *three* began to be the pattern of fictional experience, much as it had been in *Moby-Dick* or *The Scarlet Letter*. Theron was involved with three women; the temptations presented to him were three. Nature and the seasons began to play their role once more in this poeticizing of prose fiction. Alice Ware's garden was indeed a garden of the modern world; and when the serpent of knowledge came into her life, the "gaiety and color of the garden were gone, and in their place was a shabby and disheveled ruin."[84] The presence of the diabolical was as clearly indicated as it had been in the romance: after Ledsmar witnessed the fall of Theron, he held a lizard with a "pointed, evil head" and murmured to it: " 'Your name isn't Johnny any more; it's the Rev. Theron Ware.' "[85]

The technique of Frederic, then, was one of the landmarks in a change from a fiction that unobtrusively used symbols and allusion to reinforce the natural surface of a narrative to a *symbolism* that insisted upon itself as the embodiment of the fable's otherwise obscure significance. This shift in technique of using imagery and allusion was another element that had gone into the makeup of the fictional world, the microcosms created by the artists of nineteenth-century America. And it serves to verify the observations of Hauser, Abell, and Malraux, which have been restated by Professor Levin in terms of the literary art, that realism in the West has been grounded on "an experimental attitude toward nature."[86]

4. Adams and James: Toward the Waste Land

Mark Twain's series of financial disasters was capped by a crushing personal tragedy in 1896 when, on a lecture tour to recoup his lost fortunes, he received word of the death of his daughter Susy; and with this blow the accumulating doubts he felt about the goodness of nature and of man precipitated into an anguished hopelessness. He described the change in a beautiful, heart-rending letter to Howells, where he summarized his life as "one long lovely stretch of scented fields, and meadows, and shady woodlands; and suddenly Sahara!"[87] "Suddenly Sahara." Suddenly the Waste Land of disbelief—the empty stretches of an arid and hopeless universe and the alternation between moods of black rage, when he was convinced that malignity dominated the universe and trapped and tortured man, and moods of blacker despair, when he was convinced that man himself was evil and malign. And then occasionally he would sink into the utter hopelessness of the solipsistic last words with which he ended one of his tormented fragments of fiction: "Nothing exists but You. And You are but a *Thought*—a vagrant Thought, a useless Thought, a homeless Thought, wandering forlorn among the empty eternities."[88] His faith had been the faith of his culture; when it was gone, he had nothing to replace it.

His contemporary Henry Adams had gone through just such an experience; at the beginning of the twentieth century, he made his personal history into the definitive story of the decline and fall of American optimism. The purpose of *The Education of Henry Adams* was to answer the question "What could become of . . . a child of the seventeenth and eighteenth centuries when he should wake up to find himself required to play the game of the twentieth?"[89] Adams had been born and bred into the American idea that "the problem of life was as simple as it was classic," that "social perfection was . . . sure because human nature worked for Good, and three instruments were all she asked—Suffrage, Common

Schools, and Press."[90] *The Education*, narrated in the third person, was the record of a "mannikin" as he went through successive disillusionments with the country's middle-class, deistic, pragmatic world; it pictured a little representative microcosm of intellectual America. The certainty that "England's middle class life was the ideal of human progress"[91] was his point of departure, and it was there that the mannikin received the first of his disillusions. After watching his father struggle unsuccessfully to enlist Britain's support for the Union, Adams turned back to America, for he had discovered, in the home of the utilitarian faith, that "the whole business of society and diplomacy was futile. He meant to go home."[92] Yet at home, in the America of the Gilded Age, he found that if congressmen were hogs, then the question "What is a senator?"[93] raised itself. The presidency, he discovered, was an illustration of the devolution, rather than the evolution, of mankind: the fall from Washington to Grant made a mockery of the idea of America. Not only did he find the conception of progress based upon a belief in man's goodness a falsehood, but he discovered that progress based upon a belief in science was equally false. The nineteenth century had absorbed Darwinism into its optimistic belief by simply projecting upward the straight line from animal to man. However, Adams discovered the *Pteraspis*, the primordial, rapacious shark that has existed through the eons as a refutation of the advancement of the species and a permanent proof of the primordial evil that lies under the surface of events. The great white shark swims through the pages of *The Education* as the great White Whale swam through the mind of Ahab: a symbol of the irreducible evil and malevolence at the heart of human affairs.

And along with the progressive disillusion with the twin elements of the American faith, with progress based upon natural goodness, the mannikin that was Adams and was all Americans made a succession of discoveries about the nature of the universe: the only truth about it was its lack of meaning. He began first with the discovery that the study to which he had dedicated his early career was worthless, that history was "incoherent and immoral"—and anyone who tried to deny it was a liar. As empty as the study of the past was the study of the present. The whole business of diplomacy and society was futile. And then finally, after the death of a loved one—in *The Education* reported as the death of his sister but undoubtedly a screen for his otherwise unbearable memory of the suicide of his wife—he saw nature, as well as society, for what it was: "a chaos of anarchic and purposeless forces."[94]

The last lesson, the sum of his education in the nineteenth century, was "the denial of God, the illusion of the senses." In the twentieth century he tried to find in the newer sciences of atomic physics and molecular chemistry some order and pattern, and he discovered here too that the only law was chance. He explored the edges of the new psychologies and found that the only truth was "the chaos below."[95] And so the eighteenth-century man, having traversed the nineteenth century, emerged into the modern world to find one sole unalterable verity: "Chaos is the law of nature, order the dream of man."[96] This he had learned; this he confronted with the new faith of the twentieth century: the invention of order in a meaningless world, the making of a sustaining illusion out of the fact of nothingness. "Every man must invent a formula for his Universe, if the standard formula failed."[97]

The metaphors Adams used to depict his loss of faith in the American idea were revealing. Speaking of this faith at the beginning of his career, he observed that "no sandblast of science had yet skimmed off the epidermis of history, thought, and feeling."[98] Coming back to the America of the Gilded Age, he observed that "the American people were wandering in a wilderness much more sandy than the Hebrews had ever trodden about Sinai."[99] At the conclusion of his nineteenth-century education, he heard the news of the outbreak of the Spanish-American War while he was on the Egyptian desert, and in a gesture that summarized the exhaustion of the idea that had sustained his century and his country, he "leant on the fragment of a column in the great Hall at Karnak and watched a jackal creep down the debris of ruin."[100]

Henry James, whose fiction was the product of the same rejections of his culture's official idea, used the same imagery to express the same attitude: "Oh art, art," he cried in his journal, "without thee, for me, the world would be, indeed, a howling desert."[101] The major premise of James's fiction was the failure of the formula by which his America had made public sense of its universe and the need for the construction of a private formula, or, to translate it into James's equivalent terms: the way in which—amid the chaos of modernity, in the jungle of human instincts, and in the desert of his unbelief—man can achieve a tiny supersensual illusion of freedom through the artful imposition of order upon his world. This was the lesson his heroes and his heroines of his last great novels learned. Each went through an education out of innocence and into knowledge and learned that the only good is the artful pose in an impossible world. What Richard Chase has observed about *The Ambassadors* was true of all of James's major novels: their protagonists started out as William Dean Howells and ended as Henry Adams; they started as innocents and believers in the fundamentally virtuous nature of man and the universe, they learned the existence of evil and necessary tragedy at the core of the human condition, and they achieved their only possible salvation by imposing their own patterns upon the world about them.

This movement constituted the pilgrimage of Lambert Strether, of Millie Theale, of Adam and Maggie Verver in the novels of James's last and greater phase, just as it provided the basic motif of the earlier *The Portrait of a Lady*. These four works—*The Portrait of a Lady*, together with *The Wings of the Dove*, *The Ambassadors*, and *The Golden Bowl*—comprise the legacy of this consummate artist, and they take their shape as a result of his perception of the inadequacy of the American idea and the need for making an illusion of art that might replace it. Isabel Archer, whom Ralph Touchett often called "Columbia," began by feeling that one "should move in a realm of light, of natural wisdom, of happy impulse, of inspiration gracefully chronic."[102] She had "a fixed determination to regard the world as a place of brightness."[103] She liked better "to think of the future" than the past;[104] she could "never rid herself of the sense that unhappiness was a state of disease—of suffering as opposed to doing." Her two

American friends, Henrietta Stackpole and Caspar Goodwood, were representative of their culture; but unlike Isabel they never change. Henrietta was "a kind of emanation of the great democracy." Ralph Touchett, in one of his rare uncharitable moments, emphasized that she "does smell of the future."[105] Caspar Goodwood—an engineer, a doer of deeds, a builder of better contrivances—insisted that "we can do absolutely as we please," because "the world's very big." At the end of her painful education, however, Isabel had grown to know the truth: that "the world's very small"[106] and that her dream of "an infinite vista of a multiplied life" turned out to be "a dark, narrow alley with a dead wall at the end."[107] She renounced Caspar with a kiss; like Ralph Touchett she had learned to live "not a successful life—but a beautiful one."[108]

The story of an American's education out of the idea was even more explicit in the late novel James thought his best, *The Ambassadors*, where the journey of Strether was treated as a voyage of discovery, a pilgrimage from Woollett to Paris, from the faith of the New World to the faith of the Old. Waymarsh's mission was salvation: the saving of Strether's soul for the American religion of progress. And Strether felt that he had finally come to worship at some "monstrous alien altars" when he accepted the European faith of aesthetic perception as the highest good. Mingled with these references to a religious journey were the overwhelmingly dominant allusions to the little illusions of art. The center, the germ, of the novel was expressed in terms of the French art of the kitchen; life, Strether told little Bilham, is at best a jelly poured into a mold: the mold can be either dreadfully plain, or fluted and embossed; it is the fluting and the embossing that makes the difference between nothingness and wholeness of the spirit. This revelation took place in the garden of Gloriani—the supreme artist, whose name recalled the language James used to describe his first initiation into the religion of art at the *Galerie d'Apollon*, where in the recurrent dream of his youth, he had breathed "a general sense of *glory* . . . the world, in fine, raised to the realest and noblest expression."[109] In the garden of the glory of art, Strether had the premonition that he would never know anything until he rid himself of "his odious suspicion of the aesthetic."[110] When he reached his final discovery of the nature of Chad's relation to Madame de Vionnet, he lived as if he were within the frame of a painting. In his youth he had seen the canvas and had rejected it; at the climax of the novel, he actually became a part of it, and he moved as if "from clever canvas to clever canvas."[111] And finally he approached Madame de Vionnet in a scene that fused the allusions of religion and references to the arts into the meaning of his pilgrimage: he had traveled to the shrine of the religion of art in the howling desert of nothingness, for art was the sole salvation in the wasteland of the modern world.

Even in his earlier phase, best represented by *The Portrait of a Lady*, Henry James had developed an extension of the realistic mode of fiction through a treatment of objective reality that was decidedly different from the imitation of Howells and Twain. Although drawn to Hawthorne's vision of the universe, James yet disliked Hawthorne's allegorical method; he found that for it "almost nothing can be said."[112] And so he began to work toward a treatment of the world about him that imitated objective reality but in which allusion and adjective extended the reference of people and objects far beyond their actuality. His names ranged from an almost outright allegorical expression—"Bantling, Goodwood"—to the subtler suggestiveness of "Stackpole" and "Touchett." He was unafraid to make references to settings, colors, objects that so strongly suggest moral conditions that they seem to carry us into the technique of *The Scarlet Letter*. Isabel Archer's interior, for example, was "like a garden," and she began her story at Gardencourt in the spring; but "there were other inner recesses that were dusky, pestiferous tracts";[113] and so she ended her pilgrimage of discovery in Rome, the Rome that Hawthorne used earlier as the epitome of the darkness of the past.

And then in his last phase James added one more dimension to this style and transformed the writing of Anglo-American fiction. He deliberately attempted to make an artifact that would take the place of reality—a form that would carry the observer past perception into a realm of ineffable truth. He attempted to make each novel "a little world" and to make this world so tha' it would "bristle"[114] with meanings. Yet more than that, each little world—completely free of the author—would exist in space, with its meanings not only multiple but endless; for its meanings did not merely extend outward but doubled upon themselves to become ambiguous and even contradictory, with all the unpredictability that is the essence of life.

In writing about *The Wings of the Dove*, he used two metaphors to describe this process, and both suggested the construction through words of a spatial object independent of its creator that would exist to perform a service that neither the objective outer world nor its faithful imitation by the "realistic" novelist could perform. One metaphor was of fiction as a bridge, a span, of which the author created only the piers; if the piers were placed rightly and sunk deep enough, then the bridge "spans the stream" in complete independence of these properties. The piers "were an illusion for their necessary hour; but the span itself . . . seems by the oddest chance in the world to be a reality; since, actually, the rueful builder, passing under it, sees figures and hears sounds above; he makes out with his heart in his throat, that it bears and is positively being 'used.' "[115] The other comparison was that of fiction to a medal so made that, like the bridge, it hangs freely and magically in space; like the span it is independent of its creator, so that "its obverse and its reverse, its face and its back would beautifully become optional for the spectator."[116] Both metaphors suggest the two elements that radically distinguish James's style from the literary techniques of the novelists and poets of the idea. The novelists and poets whose vision of reality was monitored by their acceptance of the idea of their society used symbols, employed the objects of the natural world, to illustrate the significance of that world and of its controlling idea. James made artifacts, constructed "little worlds" that, like the medal, would show the necessary and irreconcilable doubleness of palpable reality and that, like the bridge, would carry the reader across the stream that separated chaotic actuality from the realm of eternal art.

VII~Optimism in the Twentieth Century:
Saul Bellow

"I don't pretend that my position is easy. We are survivors in this age, so theories of progress ill become us, because we are intimately acquainted with the costs."[1] This is Saul Bellow's Herzog speaking, summarizing the fifty years since Adams and James set the dominant tone for American writing of the twentieth century. Herzog's, and Bellow's, "position" is a defense of the "quotidian and ordinary" as "too great, too deep," for the "Wasteland outlook."[2] Bellow's stance, like Herzog's, has not been easy, even though it has been supported by poets of the glory of the commonplace like Robert Frost, Hart Crane, William Carlos Williams, and novelists like Sinclair Lewis, John Dos Passos, and John Steinbeck. Sounding over, and now all but drowning out these affirming voices, writers of alienation and despair, who express their rejections of the idea of America through non-representational forms, have created an "adversary culture" that counters the dominant pattern of feeling and belief that sustained Americans in the eighteenth and nineteenth centuries. However, Bellow—the most active and consistent, and possibly the best, novelist to appear in the fifties and sixties—has tenaciously affirmed the meaning and value of the American "quotidian and ordinary" and has continued to use traditional forms of social and psychological realism to express his unity with the controlling idea of his culture.

Like Herzog, Bellow has been "spared the chief ambiguity that afflicts intellectuals, and this is that civilized individuals hate and resent the civilization that makes their lives possible."[3] Herzog goes on to describe the modern writers' allegiance to "an imaginary human situation invented by their own genius and which they believe is the only true and the only human reality." A major theme of Bellow's novels is the opposition between the values of the quotidian American world and the alternate worlds that intellectuals sometimes comically, sometimes tragically try to create and to live in. Bellow's reality is the world "out there," as well as the world of noumena. His fiction is of a world sober and scarred; his characters are conscious of the cries of modern despair and full of the human cruelties that generate that despair. Yet, his protagonists cry, *yet* it is a world in which the same struggles go on that have gone on for centuries and in which there are precisely the same possibilities for tragedy, for glory, or— most likely and most heroically—for stoic survival. "We must get it out of our heads," writes Herzog, "that this is a doomed time, that we are waiting for the end, and the rest of it, mere junk from fashionable magazines." The doctrines of despair "take us in the wrong direction," he goes on, "and those of us who remain loyal to civilization must not go for it."[4] "I cannot agree with recent writers," said Bellow, "who have told us that we are Nothing. We are indeed not what the Golden Ages boasted us to be. But we are Something."[5]

There's a particular emphasis in the vision of Bellow's heroes who are, like Bellow, second-generation American Jews, sons of fathers who have recently reenacted the frustrations and fulfillments of the American dream of progress, who bring to contemporary circumstance the unique historical perspective of a people who have always known that the world is difficult but that society and community, not alienation and anarchy, enable them to survive and are the proper human conditions. "When the preachers of dread," writes Herzog, "tell you that others only distract you from metaphysical freedom then you must turn away from them. The real and essential question is one of our employment by other human beings and their employment by us."[6] With this Jewish consciousness, Herzog is able to face the depths of human degradation, a battered child, and the impulse to rage at the meaninglessness and unrelatedness of the universe with "one of his Jewish shrugs" and the almost forgotten Yiddish phrase, " 'Nu, maile' . . . Be that as it may."[7] Consciousness, Herzog adds, " 'when it doesn't clearly understand what to live for, what to die for, can only abuse and ridicule itself.' "[8]

Herzog, when he was class orator at McKinley High School, took his text from Emerson: " 'The main enterprise of the world, for splendor . . . is the upbuilding of a man.' "[9] An Emersonian vision of the significance, value, and beauty of the commonplace is the vision of Saul Bellow's fiction. Like Herzog, Bellow understands that we are the "survivors" of a hundred years of historical disillusion and are educated to a perception of the dark side of the human condition. He has been down in the mire of post-Renaissance, post-Cartesian dissolution—next door to the void. Next door, but never in it. "But we mustn't forget," Herzog writes after his acknowledgment of the temptations of nihilism, "how quickly the visions of genius become the canned goods of intellectuals. The canned sauerkraut of Spengler's 'Prussian Socialism,' the commonplaces of the Wasteland outlook, the cheap mental stimulants of Alienation, the cant and rant of pipsqueaks about Inauthenticity and Forlornness." Herzog, and Bellow, simply "can't accept this foolish dreariness."[10] Bellow's novels often deal with intellectuals struggling in the mire of post-Renaissance dissolution—either sinking into it or, in the case of some protagonists, struggling out of it, but in either case demonstrating that their tragedies, comedies, disasters, triumphs are precisely the same precious human stuff as those of mankind's presumably more heroic ages.

Fully conscious of modernist ironies that make affirmations difficult and slightly ridiculous, Bellow's novels are modern explorations of the idea of America and invigorations of Emersonian optimism. His one nonrepresentational novel, *Henderson the Rain King*, is a parable of the modern search for significance and of a rediscovery of the meaning of America. "Here comes Henderson of the U.S.A. . . . a restless seeker," Bellow writes, "lifting up his call to heaven for truth."[11] Henderson tells King Dahfu, " 'Change must be

possible. . . . Americans . . . are willing to go into this. . . .
You have to think about white Protestantism and the Constitution and the Civil War and capitalism and winning the
West.' "[12] The problem of the contemporary American, Henderson goes on, is that "the major tasks and the big con-
quests" are done; so it is the destiny of his generation of
Americans "to go out in the world and try to find the wisdom of life."[13] Enormously powerful, enormously wealthy,
enormously idealistic, Henderson, the eponymous, bursts
with desire to spend his power, wealth, and ideals; and
lacking any object commensurate with his desire, he goes to
Africa; every man has his Africa of the mind, Bellow tells us.
In the dark continent Henderson suffers, struggles, learns,
and finally returns home to America; leading a lion cub and
bearing in his arms an orphan child, he rediscovers the
"Newfoundland."

In this his only fable, the sole exception to his otherwise
realistic fiction, Bellow used a romantic mode to defend a
commonsense realism, a realism that is an Emersonian affirmation of the actual world and insists on the significance
of the commonplace because it is one with the spirit. Henderson leaves America (reality that has lost its sense of spirituality—let us call it "materialism") for Africa (the land of
romantic mindstuff without anchorage in the quotidian):
"The world was not itself," says Henderson when he arrives
in Africa; "it took on the aspect of an organism, a mental
thing, amid whose cells I had been wandering. From mind
the impetus came and through mind my course was set."[14]
However, when King Dahfu takes William James's brilliant
Emersonian psychology, where mind and body are shown to
be indistinguishable, and converts it into the pure idealism
of seeing nature simply as mentality, Henderson realizes that
"his brilliance was not a secure gift, but like this ramshackle
red palace rested on doubtful underpinnings."[15] Henderson
himself, a modern Innocent Abroad, is proud that "there
aren't many guys who have stuck with real life through thick
and thin, like me." And then he says, "It's my most basic
loyalty."

Henderson, more than most of Bellow's heroes, is a mask
for the author and expresses Bellow's "most basic loyalty":[16]

a loyalty to the kind of realism that has traditionally formed the aesthetic counterpart of the controlling, ordering idea of American culture. With the exception of *Henderson the Rain King*—a nonrepresentational form to describe the education of the protagonist into an acceptance of reality—Bellow's works are squarely in the tradition of Western realism; autobiographical, picaresque, dealing with people and places remembered or observed, it is a fiction of actuality, history personalized and clarified. Yet like all great literature of its kind, it is also a "poetry of fact." Indeed Bellow goes further than the realists before him in making his fiction a "poetry" of the quotidian, where the resources of myth are put to work to infuse the commonplace with spiritual glory. *The Adventures of Augie March* is Bellow's largest and most impressive defense of the idea of America; it is a contemporary epic, and its hero, a young second-generation Jew in whom lives the indestructible spirit of Franklin, Emerson, Mark Twain, and William James. "Though unable to go along one hundred percent with a man like the Reverend Beecher," says Augie, "telling his congregation, 'Ye are Gods, you are crystalline, your faces are radiant!' I am not," Augie continues, "an optimist of that degree. . . . But I was and have always been ready to venture as far as possible."[17] How far Bellow, like Salinger and Malamud, has been willing to venture to redeem the American idea with a Jewish sense of the fundamental beauty of the commonplace is suggested by Augie's vision when adrift in a lifeboat. It is a dream of an ugly old woman "almost like a dwarf," who begs the price of a beer. "In kindness," says Augie, "I touched her on the crown of her old head and a great thrill passed through me from it. 'Why old woman,' I said, 'You've got the hair of an angel!' 'Why shouldn't I have,' she said gently, 'like other daughters of men?' "[18]

Augie's dream vision is followed by the last experience, the final episode in Bellow's picaresque hymn to the controlling idea of his culture. Augie, stranded in northern France, walks over frozen fields toward a ruined Dunkerque, where the "white anger coming from the savage grey . . . was like eternity opening up right beside destructions of the modern world." Augie laughs—not the hyena laugh of Melville, Barth,

Pynchon, Vonnegut—but the laugh of undefeated hope: "Look at me, going everywhere!" he exults. "Why, I am a sort of Columbus of those near-at-hand and believe you can come to them in this immediate *terra incognita* that spreads out in every gaze. I may well be a flop at this line of endeavor. Columbus too thought he was a flop, probably, when they sent him back in chains. Which doesn't prove there was no America."[19]

Bellow is the most recent, and most accomplished, of the "Columbuses" of the "near-at-hand" in American literature who have come to the ordinary reader and have spoken to him in images consonant with his idea of the world and its value and meaning. Compared to the achievements of the artists who have found their inspiration in a rejection of their culture's controlling beliefs, the novelists and poets who have celebrated the quotidian may appear at the moment lesser artists, though scarcely "flops." The current evaluation does not mean that there was no America, no organizing concept that created a context of reality and made sense of history. Quite the reverse. The idea of America was a point of departure for most of our writers. When American artists felt the tragic failure of their culture's vision of reality, they created new controlling visions of people, places, events, metaphors, verbal structures to reflect their doubt, their abandonment of empirical certainties, their quest after transcendent meanings, or their attempts to make a self-sufficient world of art. When American novelists and poets concurred in the way their culture made sense of the universe, they made similar sense in their art and created significant forms that embodied their affirmation.

Notes

CHAPTER I

1. Vernon Louis Parrington, *Main Currents in American Thought*.

2. A selection of works that have wedded Parrington's approach to aesthetics by their concern with the form of the literary artifact as it engages itself with the forms of history and society are: F. O. Matthiessen, *American Renaissance*; Harry Levin, *Contexts of Criticism* and *The Gates of Horn*; Perry Miller, *The New England Mind*; Roy Harvey Pearce, *Historicism Once More*; Raymond Williams, *The Long Revolution*; Lucien Goldmann, *Pour une sociologie du roman*; Kenneth Burke, *The Philosophy of Literary Form*; Howard Mumford Jones, *The Theory of American Literature*; Frederic Ives Carpenter, *American Literature and the Dream*.

3. J. B. Bury, *The Idea of Progress*, esp. pp. 202–349.

4. Richard Foster Jones, *Ancients and Moderns*, pp. 45–46.

5. Marquis de Condorcet, *Outlines of an Historical View of the Progress of the Human Mind*, p. 11.

6. Morris Ginsberg, *The Idea of Progress*, p. 2.

7. Herbert Spencer, *Principles of Sociology*, 3:610.

8. Perry Miller, "The Romantic Dilemma in American Nationalism and the Concept of Nature," p. 241.

9. Abe C. Ravitz, "Timothy Dwight: Professor of Rhetoric," p. 68.

10. Thomas Jefferson, *The Works of Thomas Jefferson*, 12:89–90.

11. Ralph Waldo Emerson, "English Traits," in *The Complete Works of Ralph Waldo Emerson*, 5:286–87.

12. Henry Nash Smith, introduction to James Fenimore Cooper, *The Prairie*.

13. Harvey Gates Townsend, *Philosophical Ideas in the United States*, p. 96; Isaac Woodbridge Riley, *American Thought*, pp. 118–19.

14. Adam Ferguson, *An Essay on the History of Civil Society*, p. 13.

15. R. W. B. Lewis, *The American Adam*, has admirably suggested the influence of the idea of primitive innocence on American literature but has erred, I believe, in seeing this innocence as a goal rather than as a symbolic faith that makes possible a belief in progress. Henry Nash Smith, in *Virgin Land*, analyzed the association of the myth of innocence with the American West. Charles L. Sanford, in *The Quest for Paradise*, described the European backgrounds of the combination of regressive longings and progressive hopes.

CHAPTER II

1. Perry Miller, *The New England Mind*, p. 40.

2. Walter Abell, *The Collective Dream in Art*, p. 234.

3. Perry Miller, ed., *The American Puritans*, p. 95.

4. Nathaniel Ward, "The Simple Cobler of Aggawam," in ibid., p. 95.

5. Thomas Hooker, "A True Sight of Sin," in *The Puritans*, ed. Perry Miller and Thomas H. Johnson, 1:292–95.

6. Anne Bradstreet, "The Flesh and the Spirit," in ibid., 2:571.

7. Bradstreet, "Contemplation," in ibid., 2:570.

8. Edward Taylor, "Meditation Eight," in ibid., 2:656.

9. Jonathan Edwards, "Personal

Narrative," in *Jonathan Edwards*, ed. Clarence H. Faust and Thomas H. Johnson, p. 62.

10. Ibid., pp. 63–64.

11. Ibid., p. 68.

12. Ibid., p. 70.

13. Jonathan Edwards, *Images or Shadows of Divine Things*, p. 79.

14. Ibid., p. 136.

15. Edwards, "Personal Narrative," p. 62.

16. Edwards, *Images or Shadows*, p. 102.

17. Edwards, "The Nature of True Virtue," in *Jonathan Edwards*, p. 355.

18. Edwards, "Personal Narrative," pp. 65–66.

19. Ibid., p. 57.

20. Ibid., p. 69.

21. Ibid., p. 62.

22. Ibid., p. 70.

23. Ibid., p. 71.

24. Ibid., p. 61.

25. Ibid., pp. 69–70.

26. Edwards, "Sinners in the Hands of an Angry God," in *Jonathan Edwards*, pp. 164–65.

27. Roger Williams, "The Bloody Tenent," in *The Complete Writings of Roger Williams*, 3:249.

28. Ibid., p. 250.

29. Ibid.

30. John Wise, "A Vindication of the Government of New England Churches," in *Colonial American Writing*, ed. Roy Harvey Pearce, p. 211.

31. Ibid.

32. Ibid., p. 216.

33. Ibid.

34. William Penn, "Letter from William Penn to the Committee of the Free Society of Traders," in *Narratives of Early Pennsylvania, West Jersey, and Delaware, 1630–1707*, p. 228.

35. Ibid., p. 233.

36. John Woolman, *The Journal*, p. 125.

37. Ibid., p. 99.

38. John Smith, *Travels and Works of Captain John Smith*, 1:208.

39. William Byrd, *The Secret Diary of William Byrd of Westover, 1709–12*, 23 December 1711, p. 458.

40. Ibid., 6 January 1712, p. 465.

41. William Byrd, "History of the Dividing Line," in *The Prose Works*, p. 160.

42. Leon Howard, "The American Revolt Against Pope," p. 65.

43. Philip Freneau, "On the Universality and Other Attributes of the God of Nature," in *Poems of Freneau*, p. 422.

44. Ibid.

45. Freneau, "On the Uniformity and Perfection of Nature," in ibid., p. 424.

46. Freneau, "On the Religion of Nature," in ibid., p. 425.

47. Hector St. John de Crèvecoeur, from *Letters from an American Farmer*, in *Literature of the Early Republic*, ed. E. H. Cady, p. 258.

48. Ibid., pp. 291–92.

49. Ibid., p. 262.

50. Jefferson to Henry Lee, 8 May 1825, in *The Life and Selected Writings of Thomas Jefferson*, ed. Adrienne Koch and William Peden, p. 719.

51. The text is from Julian P. Boyd, *The Declaration of Independence*, plate 10.

52. Boyd, *The Declaration*, plate 9.

53. Boyd, *The Declaration*, plate 1.

54. Jefferson wrote that "the sentiments were of all America" and that they were a "genuine effusion of the soul of our country at that time." Jefferson to Joseph Delaplaine, 12 April 1817, and Jefferson to Dr. James Mease, 26 September 1825, in *The Life and Selected Writings*, pp. 680, 722.

55. Carl L. Becker, *The Declaration of Independence*, p. 142, says the hand appears to be Franklin's.

56. I. Bernard Cohen, *Benjamin Franklin*, pp. 59–60.

57. Ibid., p. 51.

58. Benjamin Franklin, *The Autobiography of Benjamin Franklin*, p. 43.

59. Ibid., p. 45.

60. Ibid., pp. 178–79.

61. Ibid., p. 207.

62. Ibid., p. 117.

63. Ibid., p. 127.

64. Ibid.

CHAPTER III

1. James Fenimore Cooper, *The Prairie*, p. 449.

2. Ibid.

3. James Fenimore Cooper, *The Complete Works of James Fenimore Cooper*, vol. 4, *The Pioneers*, p. 215.

4. Cooper, *The Prairie*, p. 450.

5. Cooper, *Complete Works of*, vol. 2, *The Last of the Mohicans*, p. 321.

6. Cooper, *The Prairie*, p. 8.

7. Ibid., p. v.

8. Ibid., p. 451.

9. Cooper, *The Last of the Mohicans*, p. 3.

10. Ibid., p. 188.

11. William Cullen Bryant, "Inscription for the Entrance to a Wood," in *The Poetical Works of William Cullen Bryant*, 1:23.

12. Ibid.

13. Bryant, "The Disinterred Warrior," in ibid., p. 191.

14. Bryant, "The Ages," in ibid., p. 53.

15. Ibid.

16. Ibid.

17. Ibid., p. 55.

18. Ibid.

19. Ibid.

20. Ibid., p. 56.

21. Ibid., p. 57.

22. Ibid., p. 66.

23. Ibid.

24. Ibid., p. 67.

25. Ibid.

26. Ibid.

27. Bryant, "To a Waterfowl," in ibid., p. 27.

28. Bryant, "Thanatopsis," in ibid., pp. 19–20.

29. Henry Wadsworth Longfellow, "My Cathedral," in *The Complete Poetical Works of Longfellow*, p. 348.

30. Longfellow, "Wapentake: To Alfred Tennyson," in ibid., p. 323.

31. Longfellow, "My Cathedral," in ibid., p. 348.

32. Longfellow, "The Day Is Done," in ibid., p. 64.

33. Ibid.

34. Ibid.

35. Longfellow, "The Bells of San Blas," in ibid., p. 359.

36. Stith Thompson, "The Indian Legend of Hiawatha," *PMLA* 31 (1916): 161–80.

37. Henry Wadsworth Longfellow, notes to *The Song of Hiawatha*, in *The Works of Henry Wadsworth Longfellow*, 2:351.

38. Longfellow, *The Song of Hiawatha*, in *Complete Poetical Works*, p. 114.

39. Ibid., p. 114.

40. Ibid., pp. 124–26.

41. Ibid., pp. 162–64.

42. Quoted in Henry Adams, *The Education of Henry Adams*, p. 33.

43. James Russell Lowell, "On Board the '76: Written for Mr. Bryant's Seventieth Birthday," in *The Writings of James Russell Lowell*, 10:16.

44. Lowell to C. F. Briggs, December 1848, in *Letters of James Russell Lowell*, 1:148.

45. Lowell, "Prometheus," in *Writings of*, 7:116.

46. Ibid.

47. Lowell, "Under the Willows," in ibid., 9:160.

48. Quoted in Richmond Croom Beatty, *James Russell Lowell*, p. 34.

49. Lowell, "Prometheus," in *Writings of*, 7:111.

50. Lowell, *The Vision of Sir Launfal*, in ibid., p. 298.

51. Lowell, "On the Death of a Friend's Child," in ibid., p. 239.

52. Lowell, "Under the Willows," in ibid., 9:160.

53. Lowell, "Ode," in ibid., 7:36.

54. Lowell, "Thoreau," in ibid., 1:375.

55. Ibid., p. 376.

56. Lowell, "The Street," in ibid., p. 71.

57. Lowell, *Ode Recited at the Harvard Commemoration*, in ibid., 10:17.

58. Ibid., p. 27.

59. Ibid., p. 28.

60. Ibid., p. 23.

61. Lowell, "Ode to France," in ibid., 7:257.

62. Ibid., p. 258.

63. Quoted in Harry Hayden Clark, "Lowell's Criticism of Romantic Literature," p. 222.

64. Lowell, *The Cathedral*, in *Writings of*, 10:45.

65. Ibid.

66. Ibid., p. 49.

67. Ibid., p. 55.

68. Ibid., p. 56.

69. Ibid., p. 58.

70. Ibid., p. 63.

71. Ibid.

72. Lowell, "Sonnet XVIII," in ibid., 7:67.

73. Lowell, "Sonnet XXV," in ibid., p. 71.

74. Lowell, Introduction to *The Biglow Papers*, 2d series, in ibid., 8:155.

75. Ibid., p. 156.

76. Ibid., p. 159.

77. Lowell, "The Courtin'," in ibid., pp. 211–14.

78. Lowell, *The Biglow Papers*, in ibid., p. 47.

79. Ibid., p. 77.

80. Ibid., p. 112.

81. Lowell, *A Fable for Critics*, in ibid., 9:85. Lowell puts these words in the mouth of Apollo, but the self-criticism is clear.

82. Lowell, "Prefatory Note," in ibid., p. [3].

83. Ibid., p. 52.

84. Ibid., p. 72.

85. Ibid., p. 84.

86. Ibid., p. 42.

87. Ibid., p. 61.

88. Ibid., p. 59.

89. Oliver Wendell Holmes, *The Writings of Oliver Wendell Holmes*, vol. 2, *The Professor at the Breakfast-Table*, p. 4.

90. Ibid., p. 109.

91. Ibid., p. 111.

92. Ibid., vol. 1, *The Autocrat of the Breakfast-Table*, p. 42.

93. Ibid.

94. Holmes, *The Professor*, p. 209.

95. Ibid., p. 114.

96. Ibid., p. 106.

97. Ibid., p. 114.

98. Ibid.

99. Ibid.

100. Ibid., p. 113.

101. Ibid., p. 39.

102. Holmes, *The Autocrat*, p. 290.

103. Holmes, *The Professor*, p. 15.

104. Holmes, *The Autocrat*, p. 113.

105. Holmes, *The Professor*, p. 117.

106. Ibid.

107. Ibid., p. 113.

108. Holmes, *The Autocrat*, p. 9.

109. Holmes, *The Professor*, pp. 124–25.

110. Holmes, *The Autocrat*, p. 231.

111. Ibid.

112. Ibid., p. 204.

113. Ibid., p. 23.

114. Holmes, *Writings of*, vol. 5, *Elsie Venner*, pp. 322–23.

115. Holmes, *The Autocrat*, pp. 220–21.

116. Ibid., p. 238.

117. Holmes, *The Professor*, pp. 35–36.

118. Ibid., p. 122.

119. Holmes, *The Autocrat*, p. 314.

120. Holmes, *The Professor*, p. 23.

121. Ibid., pp. 82–83.

122. Holmes, *The Autocrat*, pp. 132–34.

123. Holmes, "My Aunt," in *Writings of*, 11:12.

124. Ibid., p. 14.

125. Holmes, "At the Atlantic Dinner," in ibid., 13:14.

126. Ibid., p. 15.

127. Holmes, "The Moral Bully," in ibid., 11:205–7.

128. Holmes, *The Professor*, p. 114.

129. Holmes, "The Deacon's Masterpiece," in *Writings of*, 12:131–35.

130. Holmes, "Wind-Clouds and Star-Drifts," in ibid., p. 169.

131. Ibid., p. 170.

132. Ibid., p. 171.

133. Ibid.

134. Ibid., p. 172.

135. Ibid., p. 173.

136. Ibid., p. 175.

137. Ibid., p. 181–82.

138. Ibid., p. 190.

139. Holmes, *The Professor*, p. 125.

140. Holmes, "Wind-Clouds and Star-Drifts," p. 195.

141. Ibid., p. 186.

142. The occasion for the writing of the poem, after seeing "a figure of one of these shells and a section of it," is reported in *The Autocrat of the Breakfast-Table*, p. 97.

143. Holmes, "The Chambered Nautilus," in *Writings of*, 12:107–8.

CHAPTER IV

1. Alexander H. Everett, "History of Intellectual Philosophy," in *The Transcendentalists*, ed. Perry Miller, p. 29.

2. Perry Miller, "Jonathan Edwards to Emerson," p. 601.

3. Ralph Waldo Emerson, "Nature," in *The Complete Works of Ralph Waldo Emerson*, 1:25.

4. Journal of Ralph Waldo Emerson, 7 April 1840, in ibid., 7:342.

5. Emerson, "Nature," in ibid., 1:9–10.

6. Emerson, "The Tragic," in ibid., 12:408.

7. Emerson, "Experience," in ibid., 3:48.

8. Emerson, "Threnody," in ibid., 9:151, 155.

9. Emerson, "Swedenborg," in *Complete Works*, 3:48.

10. Ibid., 4:138.

11. Emerson, "Nature," in ibid., 1:12.

12. Emerson, "Address," in ibid., p. 129.

13. Emerson, "Illusion," in ibid., 9:287–88.

14. James Russell Lowell, "Emerson the Lecturer," in *The Writings of James Russell Lowell*, 2:3.

15. Journal of Emerson, 1825, no day or month, in *The Journals and Miscellaneous Notebooks of Ralph Waldo Emerson*, 2:316.

16. Emerson, "Memory," in *Complete Works*, 12:97–98.

17. Emerson, "Civilization," in ibid., 7:28–29.

18. Emerson, "The American Scholar," in ibid., 1:111–12.

19. Journal of Emerson, 19 December 1834, *The Journals and Miscellaneous Notebooks*, 4:363.

20. Henry Adams, *The Education of Henry Adams*, p. 451.

21. Emerson, "The Poet," in *Complete Works*, 3:8.

22. Ibid., p. 25.

23. Ibid., p. 9.

24. Quoted in F. O. Matthiessen, *American Renaissance*, p. 150.

25. Emerson, "Self-Reliance," in *Complete Works*, 2:82–83.

26. Emerson, "Beauty," in ibid., 6:290.

27. Emerson, "The American Scholar," in ibid., 1:82.

28. Emerson, "Address," in ibid., p. 128.

29. Emerson, "The Poet," in ibid., 3:6.

30. Emerson, "Bacchus," in ibid., 9:125.

31. Emerson, "The Poet," in ibid., 3:37–38.

32. Journal of Emerson, 1841, no day or month, in *The Journals and Miscellaneous Notebooks*, 8:96.

33. Henry David Thoreau, *The Writings of Henry David Thoreau*, vol. 1, *A Week on the Concord and Merrimack Rivers*, p. 74.

34. Ibid., p. 133.

35. Journal of Henry David Thoreau, 11 August 1856, in *Writings of*, 9:48.

36. Henry David Thoreau, *Walden*, p. 171.

37. Journal of Thoreau, 25 January 1841, in *Writings of*, 7:176.

38. Journal of Thoreau, 30 April 1851, in ibid., p. 185.

39. Thoreau, *A Week*, p. 56.

40. Thoreau, *Walden*, p. 204.

41. Ibid., p. 207.

42. Ibid., p. 168.

43. Thoreau, *A Week*, p. 153.

44. Thoreau, *Walden*, p. 91.

45. Ibid., p. 179.

46. Thoreau, *A Week*, pp. 266–67.

47. Thoreau, *Walden*, p. 179.

48. Ibid., p. 298.

49. Ibid., p. 22.

50. Ibid., p. 44.

51. Ibid., p. 140.

52. Ibid., p. 311.

53. Ibid., p. 326.

54. Ibid., p. 90.

55. Ibid., p. 93.

56. Ibid., p. 98.

57. Thoreau, *A Week*, p. 138.

58. Thoreau, *Walden*, p. 147.

59. Ibid., p. 153.

60. Journal of Thoreau, 15 November 1851, in *The Writings*, 3:119.

61. Thoreau, *A Week*, p. 193.

62. Thoreau, *Walden*, p. 323.

63. Ibid., p. 40.

64. Ibid., p. 16.

65. Ibid., pp. 230–31.

66. Thoreau, *A Week*, p. 195.

67. The allusions to business are in *Walden*, pp. 19–20, 90.

68. Thoreau, "Civil Disobedience," in *The Writings*, 4:368.

69. Thoreau, *Walden*, p. 330.

70. The changing attitudes are in *Walden*, pp. 114–22.

71. The descriptions of the railroad embankment are in *Walden*, pp. 304–9.

72. Ibid., p. 311.

73. Ibid., p. 320.

74. Ibid., p. 321.

75. Ibid., p. 49.

76. Quoted in Gay Wilson Allen, *The Solitary Singer*, p. 205.

77. Ibid., p. 52.

78. Esther Shephard, *Walt Whitman's Pose*.

79. Emerson, "The Poet," in *Complete Works*, 3:41.

80. Ibid., p. 40.

81. Walt Whitman, *Song of Myself*, in *Leaves of Grass*, p. 55.

82. Ibid., p. 29.

83. Emerson, "The Poet," in *Complete Works*, 3:37.

84. Whitman, *Song of Myself*, p. 61.

85. Emerson, "The Poet," p. 41.

86. Whitman, *Song of Myself*, p. 47.

87. Whitman, "Starting from

Paumanok," in *Leaves of Grass*, p. 18.

88. Whitman, *Song of Myself*, p. 77.

89. Ibid., p. 85.

90. Whitman, "When I Heard the Learn'd Astronomer," in *Leaves of Grass*, p. 271.

91. Whitman, *Song of Myself*, p. 88.

92. Whitman, "One's-Self I Sing," in *Leaves of Grass*, p. 88.

93. Emerson, "The Poet," p. 38.

94. Ibid., p. 37.

95. Whitman, "Give Me the Splendid Silent Sun," in *Leaves of Grass*, p. 314.

96. Emerson, "The Poet," p. 21.

97. Ibid., p. 26.

98. Whitman, *Song of Myself*, p. 33.

99. Whitman, "Out of the Cradle Endlessly Rocking," in *Leaves of Grass*, p. 249.

100. Whitman, *Song of Myself*, p. 49.

101. Whitman, "I Sing the Body Electric," in *Leaves of Grass*, p. 96.

102. Whitman, *Song of Myself*, p. 33.

103. Whitman, "So Long!" in *Leaves of Grass*, p. 505.

104. Whitman, *Song of Myself*, p. 52.

105. Ibid., p. 75.

106. Walt Whitman, "Preface, 1855, to *Leaves of Grass*," in *Prose Works 1892*, 2:454.

107. Whitman, "A Backward Glance O'er Travel'd Roads," in ibid., p. 714.

108. Whitman, "One's-Self I Sing," p. 1.

109. Whitman, "To a Historian," in *Leaves of Grass*, p. 4.

110. Whitman, *Song of Myself*, p. 29.

111. Ibid., p. 34.

112. Ibid., p. 43.

113. Ibid., p. 52.

114. Ibid., p. 29.

115. Ibid., p. 42.

116. Ibid., p. 41.

117. Ibid., p. 34.

118. Ibid., p. 43.

119. Ibid., p. 61.

120. Ibid., p. 75.

121. The case has been well made by James E. Miller, Jr., *A Critical Guide to Leaves of Grass*, pp. 6–35.

122. Whitman, *Song of Myself*, p. 88.

123. Ibid., p. 29.

124. Siegfried Kracauer, *Theory of Film*, pp. 10–11.

125. Emerson, "Brahma," in *The Complete Works*, 9:195.

126. Whitman, "Democratic Vistas," in *Prose Works*, 2:369–70.

127. Whitman, "To a Locomotive in Winter," in *Leaves of Grass*, p. 472.

128. Whitman, *Song of Myself*, p. 51.

CHAPTER V

1. Ralph Waldo Emerson, *The Heart of Emerson's Journals*, p. 305.

2. "Without all the deeper trust in the comprehensive sympathy above us, we might . . . be led to suspect the insult of a sneer, as well as an immitigable frown, on the iron countenance of fate." Nathaniel Hawthorne, *The House of the Seven Gables*, p. 41.

3. William James, "Varieties of Religious Experience," in F. O. Matthiessen, *The James Family*, p. 232.

4. Ibid., p. 234.

5. Nathaniel Hawthorne, "The Celestial Railroad," in *The Writings of Nathaniel Hawthorne*, 4:260.

6. Ibid., p. 263.

7. Ibid., p. 265.

8. Ibid., p. 283.

9. Ibid., p. 275.

10. Ibid.

11. Ibid., p. 277.

12. Ibid., p. 287.

13. Hawthorne, "Earth's Holocaust," in ibid., 4:222–23.

14. Hawthorne, "Dr. Heidegger's Experiment," in ibid., 1:319.

15. Ibid., p. 321.

16. Ibid., p. 323.

17. Nathaniel Hawthorne, *The Blithedale Romance*, p. 7.

18. Hawthorne, "The Gentle Boy," in *The Writings*, 1:118.

19. Ibid., p. 119.

20. Nathaniel Hawthorne, *The Scarlet Letter*, p. 197.

21. Ibid., p. 195.

22. George B. Loring, "Hawthorne's Scarlet Letter," in *The Transcendentalists*, ed. Perry Miller, pp. 475–82.

23. Hawthorne, *Scarlet Letter*, p. 203.

24. Ibid., p. 27.

25. Hawthorne, *House of the Seven Gables*, p. 319.

26. Ibid., pp. 65–66.

27. Ibid., p. 316.

28. Ibid., p. 184.

29. Ibid., p. 182.

30. Ibid., p. 158.

31. Hawthorne, *Scarlet Letter*, p. 37.

32. Hawthorne, *House of the Seven Gables*, p. 250.

33. Ibid., p. 267.

34. Ibid., p. 181.

35. Ibid., p. 180.

36. Hawthorne, *Blithedale Romance*, p. 9.

37. Ibid., p. 20.

38. Ibid., pp. 18–19.

39. Ibid., p. 179.

40. Nathaniel Hawthorne, *The Marble Faun*, p. 166.

41. Hawthorne, *House of the Seven Gables*, p. 131.

42. Ibid., pp. 205–6.

43. Ibid., p. 82.

44. Ibid., p. 161.

45. Hawthorne, *Scarlet Letter*, p. 10.

46. Hawthorne, *Marble Faun*, p. 466.

47. Hawthorne, *Scarlet Letter*, p. 37.

48. Hawthorne, *Marble Faun*, p. 3.

49. Erich Auerbach, *Mimesis*, pp. 1–20.

50. Emerson, "The Rhodora," in *The Complete Works*, 9:48.

51. Hawthorne, *Scarlet Letter*, p. 48.

52. Hawthorne, *Marble Faun*, p. 40.

53. Ibid., p. 27.

54. Hawthorne, *Scarlet Letter*, p. 174.

55. Ibid., p. 56.

56. Ibid., p. 164.

57. Ibid., p. 260.

58. Ibid., p. 195.

59. Ibid., p. 87.

60. Hawthorne, *Marble Faun*, pp. 92–93.

61. Hawthorne, *Scarlet Letter*, p. 31.

62. Hawthorne, *Marble Faun*, p. 461.

63. Hawthorne, *House of the Seven Gables*, p. 220.

64. Ibid., p. 26.

65. Clarence P. Oberndorf, *A History of Psychoanalysis in America*, pp. 23–30.

66. Hawthorne, *Scarlet Letter*, p. 124.

67. Ibid., p. 260.

68. Ibid., p. 142.

69. Ibid., p. 264.

70. Edgar Allan Poe, "The Colloquy of Monos and Una," in *The Complete Poems and Stories of Edgar Allan Poe*, 1:359.

71. Ibid., p. 360.

72. Ibid.

73. Ibid., p. 359.

74. Ibid., p. 360.

75. Ibid.

76. Edgar Allan Poe, "The Conqueror Worm," in *Collected Works of Edgar Allan Poe*, 1:326.

77. Poe, "The Poetic Principle," in *Complete Poems and Stories*, 2:1026.

78. Ibid.

79. Poe, "Morning on the Wissahiccon," in ibid., 1:495.

80. Poe, "Bryant's Poems," in ibid., 2:890.

81. Poe, "Sonnet—To Science," in *Collected Works*, 1:91.

82. Poe, "Mellonta Tauta," in *Complete Poems and Stories*, 2:688.

83. Poe, "Ballads and Other Poems," in ibid., p. 937.

84. Poe, "The Poetic Principle," in ibid., p. 1026.

85. Poe, "A Dream Within a Dream," in *Collected Works*, 1:452.

86. Poe, *Al Aaraaf*, in ibid., pp. 99–115.

87. Poe, "The Purloined Letter," in *Complete Poems and Stories*, 2:597.

88. Quoted in Arthur Hobson Quinn, *Edgar Allan Poe*, pp. 210–12.

89. Ibid., p. 289.

90. As Roger Asselineau has written: "presque aucun lecteur ne peut ajouter foi au retour et à la survie du héros," Roger Asselineau, *Les aventures d'Arthur Gordon Pym*, p. 31.

91. Poe, *Narrative of A. Gordon Pym*, in *Complete Poems and Stories*, 2:732–33.

92. Ibid., p. 791.

93. Ibid., p. 738.

94. Ibid., p. 776.

95. Ibid., p. 783.

96. Ibid.

97. Poe, "M.S. Found in a Bottle," in ibid., 1:135–36.

98. Poe, "Ligeia," in ibid., p. 225.

99. Ibid., p. 233.

100. Edgar Allan Poe, "Letter to B———," in ibid., 2:860.

101. Nathaniel Hawthorne, *The English Notebooks of Nathaniel Hawthorne*, pp. 432–33.

102. Herman Melville, *White-Jacket*, p. 151.

103. Herman Melville, *Moby-Dick*, p. 114.

104. Herman Melville, Preface to "Battle Pieces," in *The Works of Herman Melville*, 16:187.

105. Melville, *White-Jacket*, p. 150.

106. Melville to Duyckinck, 3 March 1849, in *The Letters of Herman Melville*, p. 79.

107. Melville, *Moby-Dick*, p. 193.

108. Herman Melville, *Typee*, p. 124.

109. Ibid., p. 201.
110. Ibid., p. 124.
111. Ibid., p. 195.
112. Ibid., pp. 219–21.
113. Herman Melville, *Omoo*, p. 27.
114. Herman Melville, *The Works*, vol. 11, *Israel Potter*, p. 82. Modern studies of criminology link tattooing to criminality and emotional immaturity. See Walter Bromberg, *The Mold of Murder*.
115. Melville, *Typee*, p. 252.
116. Herman Melville, "Benito Cereno," in *Piazza Tales*, p. 87.
117. Melville, *Israel Potter*, p. 198.
118. Ibid., p. 62.
119. Ibid., p. 49.
120. Ibid., p. 52.
121. Ibid., p. 55.
122. Ibid., p. 69.
123. Melville, "The Bell-Tower," in *Piazza Tales*, p. 208.
124. Ibid., p. 220.
125. Herman Melville, *Clarel*, pp. 476, 480.
126. Melville, *Typee*, p. 172.
127. Ibid., p. 173.
128. Herman Melville, *Mardi and a Voyage Thither*, p. 557.
129. Ibid., p. 654.
130. Ibid., p. 42.
131. Ibid., p. 357.
132. Melville, *Moby-Dick*, p. 236.
133. Ibid., p. 345.
134. Ibid., p. 432.
135. Ibid., p. 491.
136. Ibid., p. 525.
137. Ibid., p. 463.
138. Melville to Hawthorne, 16 April 1851, in *The Letters*, pp. 124–25.
139. Melville, *Mardi*, p. 390.
140. Melville, *Moby-Dick*, p. 3.
141. Ibid., p. 185.
142. Ibid., p. 193.
143. Ibid., p. 194.
144. A. C. Bradley, "Hegel's Theory of Tragedy," in *Oxford Lectures on Poetry*, pp. 71–73.
145. Emerson, "The Tragic," in *The Complete Works*, 12:408.
146. Melville, *Moby-Dick*, p. 566.
147. Herman Melville, "Billy Budd," in *The Works*, 13:108.
148. Melville, *Moby-Dick*, pp. 486–87.
149. Ibid., p. 225.
150. Herman Melville, *The Confidence-Man*, p. 75.
151. Ibid., p. 16

152. Ibid., p. 1.
153. Ibid., p. 15.

CHAPTER VI
1. Henry Adams, *The Education of Henry Adams*, p. 33.
2. Quoted in Ralph Barton Perry, *The Thought and Character of William James*, 1:331.
3. Ibid., 2:258.
4. James to Henry James, 6 June 1903, in *The Letters of William James*, 2:195.
5. William James, "Address at the Emerson Centenary in Concord," in *The James Family*, ed. F. O. Matthiessen, p. 458.
6. James, "What Makes Life Significant," in ibid., p. 412.
7. James, Preface to *Psychology*, in ibid., p. 372.
8. James, "Louis Agassiz," in ibid., p. 542.
9. James to Henri Bergson, 13 June 1907, in *The Letters*, 2:292.
10. James, "What Makes Life Significant," p. 415.
11. Ibid., p. 417.
12. James, "The Will to Believe," in *The James Family*, p. 393.
13. James, "What Makes Life Significant," p. 416.
14. Quoted in Perry, *The Thought and Character*, 1:723–24.
15. James, "What Makes Life Significant," p. 410.
16. Ibid., pp. 405–12.
17. Ibid., p. 409.
18. William Dean Howells, *Their Wedding Journey*, p. 42.
19. William Dean Howells, *Literary Friends and Acquaintance*, p. 56.
20. William Dean Howells, *A Foregone Conclusion*, p. 262.
21. William Dean Howells, *Years of My Youth*, p. 200, wrote of "our faith in the good ending, as if our national story were a tale that must end well."
22. William Dean Howells, *Indian Summer*, p. 269.
23. Thomas Mann, "Goethe and Tolstoi," in *Essays of Three Decades*, pp. 118–19; Mann to Stephen Zweig, 28 July 1920, in *Letters of Thomas Mann*, pp. 106–7.
24. James to W. D. Howells, 17 May 1890, in *The Letters of Henry James*, 1:167.
25. William Dean Howells, *A Hazard of New Fortunes*, 2:240.

26. Ibid., p. 319.

27. DeLancey Ferguson, *Mark Twain*, p. 146.

28. Mark Twain, *The Writings of Mark Twain*, vol. 1, *The Innocents Abroad*, p. 37.

29. Ibid., p. 142.

30. Ibid., p. 82.

31. Ibid., p. 276.

32. Ibid., p. 235.

33. Ibid., 2:265.

34. Ibid., p. 362–63.

35. Ibid., vol. 12, *The Adventures of Tom Sawyer*, p. 322.

36. Samuel Langhorne Clemens, *A Connecticut Yankee in King Arthur's Court*, p. 390.

37. Louis Budd amply demonstrates that Twain was a middle-class liberal in his social philosophy. Louis Budd, *Mark Twain*.

38. Twain, *Tom Sawyer*, p. 318.

39. Ibid., pp. 161–63.

40. Ibid., p. 327.

41. Ibid., p. 62.

42. Samuel Langhorne Clemens, *Adventures of Huckleberry Finn*, p. 30. Edgar M. Branch, in *The Literary Apprenticeship of Mark Twain*, pointed out the importance of the "two providences."

43. Clemens, *Huckleberry Finn*, pp. 49–50.

44. Clemens, *A Connecticut Yankee*, p. 387.

45. Mark Twain, *The Writings*, vol. 2, *Joan of Arc*, p. 66.

46. Ibid., p. 280.

47. Twain, *Innocents Abroad*, 2:135.

48. Twain, *The Writings*, vol. 9, *Life on the Mississippi*, p. 85.

49. Ibid., p. 140.

50. Ibid., p. 309.

51. Ibid., p. 347.

52. Ibid., p. 421.

53. Ibid., p. 426.

54. Ibid., p. 343.

55. Twain to Howells, 22 November 1889, in *Mark Twain-Howells Letters, 1872–1910*, 2:621.

56. Coleman O. Parsons, "Mark Twain in Australia," p. 459.

57. Clinton S. Burhans, Jr. in "The Sober Affirmation of Mark Twain's Hadleyburg," p. 384, has demonstrated how the story "shows . . . that experience of living can determine man to his salvation as well as to his perdition."

58. Twain, *The Writings*, vol. 21, *The American Claimant and Other Stories and Sketches*, p. 22.

59. Clemens, *Huckleberry Finn*, p. 365.

60. J. C. Levenson, *The Mind and Art of Henry Adams*, p. 88.

61. Hamlin Garland, *Crumbling Idols*, p. 43.

62. Oliver Wendell Holmes, "Mechanism in Thought and Morals," in *The Writings of Oliver Wendell Holmes*, 8:310.

63. John DeForest, *Miss Ravenel's Conversion from Secession to Loyalty*, p. 217.

64. Ibid., p. 5.

65. Ibid.

66. William Dean Howells, *Dr. Breen's Practice*, p. 91.

67. William Dean Howells, *An Imperative Duty*, p. 39.

68. Twain, *The Writings*, vol. 15, *The Prince and the Pauper*, p. 125.

69. Clemens, *Huckleberry Finn*, p. 33.

70. Jacques Ellul, *The Technological Society*, p. 25.

71. Clemens, *A Connecticut Yankee*, p. 20.

72. Twain, *The Writings*, vol. 14, *Pudd'nhead Wilson and Those Extraordinary Twins*, p. 20.

73. Ibid., p. 304.

74. Harold Frederic, *The Damnation of Theron Ware*, pp. 229–30.

75. Henry Steele Commager, *The American Mind*, p. 41.

76. Leo Marx, "The Machine in the Garden," *New England Quarterly* 29 (March 1956): 30.

77. DeForest, *Miss Ravenel's Conversion*, p. 64.

78. Clemens, *A Connecticut Yankee*, p. 513.

79. Ibid., p. 120.

80. Twain to Howells, 21 October 1889, *Twain-Howells Letters*, 2:615. This was five months after he finished *A Connecticut Yankee*.

81. Frederic, *The Damnation*, p. 333.

82. Ibid., p. 345.

83. Stephen Crane, "Poem Six," in *The Black Riders and Other Lines*, p. 6.

84. Frederic, *The Damnation*, p. 262.

85. Ibid., p. 233.

86. Harry Levin, *Contexts of Criticism*, p. 75.

87. Twain to Howells, 22 January 1898, in *Twain-Howells Letters*, 2:669.

88. Mark Twain, "No. 44, the Mysterious Stranger," in *The Mysterious Stranger*, p. 405.

89. Henry Adams, *The Education of Henry Adams*, p. 4.

90. Ibid., p. 33.

91. Ibid.

92. Ibid., p. 127.

93. Ibid., p. 261.

94. Ibid., p. 289.

95. Ibid., p. 433.

96. Ibid., p. 451.

97. Ibid., p. 472.

98. Ibid., p. 90.

99. Ibid., p. 328.

100. Ibid., p. 360.

101. Henry James, *The Notebooks of Henry James*, p. 68.

102. Henry James, *The Portrait of a Lady*, 1:68.

103. Ibid.

104. Ibid., 1:322.

105. Ibid., 1:130–31.

106. Ibid., 2:435.

107. Ibid., 2:188.

108. Ibid., 2:405.

109. Quoted in F. W. Dupee, *Henry James*, p. 29.

110. Henry James, *The Ambassadors*, 1:193–94.

111. Ibid., 2:273.

112. Quoted in F. O. Matthiessen, *American Renaissance*, p. 247.

113. James, *The Portrait of a Lady*, 1:72.

114. Henry James, Preface to *The Wings of the Dove*, 1:xi.

115. Ibid., 1:xiv.

116. Ibid., 1:xi.

CHAPTER VII

1. Saul Bellow, *Herzog*, p. 75

2. Ibid., pp. 75, 106. Moses Herzog goes on to say that "no philosopher . . . has fallen" into the ordinary "deeply enough," p. 106.

3. Ibid., p. 304.

4. Ibid., pp. 316–17.

5. Saul Bellow, quoted in *Fiction of the Fifties*, ed. Herbert Gold, p. 19.

6. Bellow, *Herzog*, p. 272.

7. Ibid., p. 243.

8. Ibid., pp. 272–73.

9. Ibid., p. 160.

10. Ibid., pp. 74–75.

11. Saul Bellow, *Henderson the Rain King*, p. 199.

12. Ibid., p. 276.

13. Ibid., p. 277.

14. Ibid., p. 156.

15. Ibid., p. 269.

16. Ibid., p. 232.

17. Saul Bellow, *The Adventures of Augie March*, p. 76.

18. Ibid., p. 507.

19. Ibid., p. 536.

Bibliography

Abell, Walter. *The Collective Dream in Art: A Psycho-historical Theory of Culture Based on Relations between the Arts, Psychology, and the Social Sciences*. Cambridge: Harvard University Press, 1957.

Adams, Henry. *The Education of Henry Adams*. Edited by Ernest Samuels. Boston: Houghton Mifflin Co., 1973.

Allen, Gay Wilson. *The Solitary Singer: A Critical Biography of Walt Whitman*. New York: Macmillan Co., 1955.

Auerbach, Erich. *Mimesis: The Representation of Reality in Western Literature*. Translated by Willard R. Trask. Princeton, N.J.: Princeton University Press, 1953.

Beatty, Richmond Croom. *James Russell Lowell*. Nashville: Vanderbilt University Press, 1942.

Becker, Carl L. *The Declaration of Independence: A Study in the History of Political Ideas*. New York: Harcourt, Brace & Co., 1922.

Bellow, Saul. *The Adventures of Augie March, A Novel*. New York: Viking Press, 1953.

———. *Henderson the Rain King, A Novel*. New York: Viking Press, 1959.

———. *Herzog*. New York: Viking Press, 1964.

Boorstin, Daniel. *The Americans: The Colonial Experience; The National Experience; The Democratic Experience*. 3 vols. New York: Random House, 1958, 1965, 1973.

Boyd, Julian P., ed. *The Declaration of Independence: The Evolution of the Text*. Washington, D.C.: Library of Congress, 1943.

Bradley, A. C. *Oxford Lectures on Poetry*. London: Macmillan & Co., 1909.

Branch, Edgar M. *The Literary Apprenticeship of Mark Twain, with Selections from His Apprentice Writing*. Urbana: University of Illinois Press, 1950.

Bromberg, Walter. *The Mold of Murder: A Psychiatric Study of Homicide*. New York: Grune and Stratton, 1961.

Bryant, William Cullen. *The Poetical Works of William Cullen Bryant*. Edited by Parke Goodwin. 2 vols. New York: Russell and Russell, 1967.

Budd, Louis. *Mark Twain: Social Philosopher*. Bloomington: Indiana University Press, 1962.

Burhans, Clinton S., Jr. "The Sober Affirmation of Mark Twain's Hadleyburg." *American literature* 34 (1962): 375–84.

Burke, Kenneth. *The Philosophy of Literary Form: Studies in Symbolic Action*. Baton Rouge: Louisiana State University Press, 1941.

Bury, J. B. *The Idea of Progress: An Inquiry into Its Origin and Growth*. New York: Dover, 1932.

Byrd, William. *The Prose Works of William Byrd of Westover*. Edited by Louis B. Wright. Cambridge: Harvard University Press, 1966.

————. *The Secret Diary of William Byrd of Westover, 1709–12*. Edited by Louis B. Wright and Marion Tinling. Richmond, Va.: Dietz Press, 1941.

Cady, Edwin H., ed. *Literature of the Early Republic*. New York: Rinehart and Co., 1969.

Cargill, Oscar. *Intellectual America: Ideas on the March*. New York: Macmillan Co., 1941.

Carpenter, Frederic Ives. *American Literature and the Dream*. New York: Philosophical Library, 1955.

Clark, Harry Hayden, "Lowell's Criticism of Romantic Literature." *PMLA* 41 (1926): 209–28.

Clemens, Samuel Langhorne. *Adventures of Huckleberry Finn*. Facsimile of the First Edition. San Francisco: Chandler Publishing Co., 1962.

————. *A Connecticut Yankee in King Arthur's Court*. Facsimile of the First Edition with introduction by Hamlin Hill. San Francisco: Chandler Publishing Co., 1963.

Cohen, I. Bernard. *Benjamin Franklin: His Contributions to the American Tradition*. Indianapolis: Bobbs-Merrill, 1953.

Commager, Henry Steele. *The American Mind: An Interpretation of American Thought and Character since the 1880's*. New Haven: Yale University Press, 1950.

Condorcet, Marie Jean Antoine Nicholas Caritat, marquis de. *Outlines of an Historical View of the Progress of the Human Mind: Being a Posthumous Work of the Late M. de Condorcet*. Translated from the French. Philadelphia: M. Carey, H. and P. Rice and Co., J. Ormrod, B. F. Bache, and J. Fellows, 1796.

Cooper, James Fenimore. *The Prairie*. Edited by Henry Nash Smith. New York: Rinehart and Co., 1950.

————. *The Complete Works of James Fenimore Cooper*. 32 vols. New York: G. P. Putnam's Sons, n.d.

Crane, Stephen. *The Black Riders and Other Lines*. Boston: Copeland and Day, 1896.

Curti, Merle Eugene. *The Growth of American Thought*. New York: Harper and Brothers, 1943.

DeForest, John. *Miss Ravenel's Conversion from Secession to Loyalty*. New York: Harper and Brothers, 1939.

Dupee, F. W. *Henry James*. New York: Sloane, 1951.

Edwards, Jonathan. *Images or Shadows of Divine Things*. Edited by Perry Miller. New Haven: Yale University Press, 1948.

Ekirch, Arthur Alphonse. *The Idea of Progress in America*. New York: Columbia University Press, 1944.

Ellul, Jacques. *The Technological Society*. Translated by John Wilkinson. New York: Alfred A. Knopf, 1965.

Emerson, Ralph Waldo. *The Complete Works of Ralph Waldo Emerson*. Edited by Edward W. Emerson. 12 vols. Boston: Houghton Mifflin Co., 1903.

————. *The Heart of Emerson's Journals*. Edited by Bliss Perry. Boston: Houghton Mifflin Co., 1926.

————. *The Journal and Miscellaneous Notebooks of Ralph Waldo Emerson*. Edited by William H. Gilman, Alfred R. Ferguson et al. 10 vols. Cambridge: Harvard University Press, 1960–73.

Faust, Clarence H., and Johnson, Thomas H., eds. *Jonathan Edwards*. New York: American Book Co., 1935.

Ferguson, Adam. *An Essay on the History of Civil Society*. London: T. Cadell, 1793.

Ferguson, DeLancey. *Mark Twain: Man and Legend*. Indianapolis: Bobbs-Merrill, 1943.

Franklin, Benjamin. *The Autobiography of Benjamin Franklin*. Edited by Leonard W. Labaree et al. New Haven: Yale University Press, 1964.

Frederic, Harold. *The Damnation of Theron Ware*. Edited by Everett Carter. Cambridge: Harvard University Press, 1960.

Freneau, Philip. *Poems of Freneau*. Edited by Harry Hayden Clark. New York: Harcourt, Brace & Co., 1929.

Gabriel, Ralph Henry. *The Course of American Democratic Thought: An Intellectual History Since 1815*. New York: Ronald Press Co., 1940.

Garland, Hamlin. *Crumbling Idols: Twelve Essays on Art Dealing Chiefly with Literature, Painting and the Drama*. Edited by Jane Johnston. Cambridge: Harvard University Press, 1960.

Ginsberg, Morris. *The Idea of Progress: A Revaluation*. Boston: Beacon Press, 1953.

Gold, Herbert, ed. *Fiction of the Fifties: A Decade of American Writing*. New York: Doubleday & Co., 1959.

Goldmann, Lucien. *Pour une sociologie du roman*. Paris: Gallimard, 1964.

Hawthorne, Nathaniel. *The Blithedale Romance*. Columbus: Ohio State University Press, 1964.

———. *The English Notebooks of Nathaniel Hawthorne*. Edited by Randall Stewart. New York: Russell and Russell, 1962.

———. *The House of the Seven Gables*. Columbus: Ohio State University Press, 1965.

———. *The Marble Faun*. Columbus: Ohio State University Press, 1968.

———. *The Scarlet Letter*. Columbus: Ohio State University Press, 1962.

———. *The Writings of Nathaniel Hawthorne*. 16 vols. Boston: Houghton Mifflin Co., 1900.

Holmes, Oliver Wendell. *The Writings of Oliver Wendell Holmes*. 13 vols. Boston: Houghton Mifflin Co., 1891–93.

Howard, Leon. "The American Revolt Against Pope." *Studies in Philology* 49 (1952): 48–65.

Howells, William Dean. *Doctor Breen's Practice*. Boston: James R. Osgood and Co., 1881.

———. *A Foregone Conclusion*. Boston: James R. Osgood and Co., 1875.

———. *A Hazard of New Fortunes*. 2 vols. New York: Harper and Brothers, 1890.

———. *An Imperative Duty*. New York: Harper and Brothers, 1892.

———. *Indian Summer*. Edited by Scott Bennett. Bloomington: Indiana University Press, 1971.

———. *Literary Friends and Acquaintance: A Personal Retrospect of American Authorship*. Edited by David F. Hiatt and Edwin H. Cady. Bloomington: Indiana University Press, 1968.

———. *Their Wedding Journey*. Edited by John K. Reeves. Bloomington: Indiana University Press, 1968.

———. *Years of My Youth*. Edited by David J. Nordloh. Bloomington: Indiana University Press, 1975.

James, Henry. *The Ambassadors*. 2 vols. New York: Charles Scribner's Sons, 1909.

———. *The Letters of Henry James*. Edited by Percy Lubbock. 2 vols. London: Macmillan & Co., 1920.

———. *The Notebooks of Henry James*. Edited by F. O. Matthiessen and Kenneth B. Murdock. New York: Oxford University Press, 1947.

———. *The Portrait of a Lady*. 2 vols. New York: Charles Scribner's Sons, 1908.

———. *The Wings of the Dove*. 2 vols. New York: Charles Scribner's Sons, 1909.

James, William. *The Letters of William James*. Edited by Henry James. 2 vols. Boston: Little, Brown & Co., 1920.

Jefferson, Thomas. *The Works of Thomas Jefferson*. Edited by Paul Leicester Ford. 12 vols. New York: G. P. Putnam's Sons, 1904–5.

Jones, Howard Mumford. *The Theory of American Literature*. Ithaca, N. Y.: Cornell University Press, 1948.

Jones, Richard Foster. *Ancients and Moderns: A Study of the Rise of the Scientific Movement in Seventeenth-Century England*. St. Louis: Washington University, 1961.

Koch, Adrienne and Peden, William, eds. *The Life and Selected Writings of Thomas Jefferson*. New York: Modern Library, 1944.

Kracauer, Siegfried. *Theory of Film: The Redemption of Physical Reality*. New York: Oxford University Press, 1960.

Lerner, Max. *America as a Civilization*. 2 vols. New York: Simon and Schuster, 1957.

Levenson, J. C. *The Mind and Art of Henry Adams*. Boston: Houghton Mifflin Co., 1957.

Levin, Harry. *Contexts of Criticism*. Cambridge: Harvard University Press, 1957.

———. *The Gates of Horn: A Study of Five French Realists*. New York: Oxford University Press, 1963.

Lewis, R. W. B. *The American Adam: Innocence, Tragedy and Tradition in the Nineteenth Century*. Chicago: University of Chicago Press, 1955.

Longfellow, Henry Wadsworth. *The Complete Poetical Works of Longfellow*. Boston: Houghton Mifflin Co., 1893.

———. *The Works of Henry Wadsworth Longfellow*. 14 vols. Boston: Houghton Mifflin Co., 1886.

Lowell, James Russell. *Letters of James Russell Lowell*. Edited by Charles Eliot Norton. 2 vols. New York: Harper and Brothers, 1894.

———. *The Writings of James Russell Lowell*. 12 vols. Boston: Houghton Mifflin Co., 1894–95.

Marx, Leo. "The Machine in the Garden." *New England Quarterly* 29 (1956): 27–42.

Mann, Thomas. *Essays of Three Decades*. Translated by H. T. Lowe-Porter. New York: Alfred A. Knopf, 1947.

———. *Letters of Thomas Mann: 1889–1955*. Selected and Translated by Richard and Clara Winston. New York: Alfred A. Knopf, 1971.

Matthiessen, F. O. *American Renaissance: Art and Expression in the Age of Emerson and Whitman*. New York: Oxford University Press, 1941.

———. *The James Family, Including Selections from the Writings of Henry James, Senior, William, Henry, and Alice James*. New York: Alfred A. Knopf, 1947.

Melville, Herman. *Clarel: A Poem and Pilgrimage in the Holy Land*. Edited by Walter E. Bezanson. New York: Hendricks House, 1960.

_____. *The Confidence-Man: His Masquerade*. Edited by Elizabeth S. Foster. New York: Hendricks House, 1954.

_____. *The Letters of Herman Melville*. Edited by Merrell R. Davis and William H. Gilman. New Haven: Yale University Press, 1960.

_____. *Mardi and a Voyage Thither*. Edited by Harrison Hayford, Herschel Parker, and G. Thomas Tanselle. Evanston, Ill.: Northwestern University Press, 1970.

_____. *Moby-Dick or, The Whale*. Edited by Luther S. Mansfield and Howard P. Vincent. New York: Hendricks House, 1962.

_____. *Omoo: A Narrative of Adventures in the South Seas*. Edited by Harrison Hayford, Herschel Parker, and G. Thomas Tanselle. Evanston, Ill.: Northwestern University Press, 1968.

_____. *Piazza Tales*. Edited by Egbert S. Oliver. New York: Hendricks House, 1962.

_____. *Typee: A Peep at Polynesian Life*. Edited by Harrison Hayford, Herschel Parker, and G. Thomas Tanselle. Evanston, Ill.: Northwestern University Press, 1968.

_____. *White-Jacket or, The World in a Man-of-War*. Edited by Harrison Hayford, Herschel Parker, and G. Thomas Tanselle. Evanston, Ill.: Northwestern University Press, 1970.

_____. *The Works of Herman Melville*. 16 vols. New York: Russell and Russell, 1963.

Miller, James E., Jr. *A Critical Guide to Leaves of Grass*. Chicago: University of Chicago Press, 1957.

Miller, Perry. "Jonathan Edwards to Emerson." *New England Quarterly* 13 (1940): 589–617.

_____. *The New England Mind: The Seventeenth Century*. Cambridge: Harvard University Press, 1963.

_____. "The Romantic Dilemma in American Nationalism and the Concept of Nature." *The Harvard Theological Review* 48 (1955): 239–53.

_____, ed. *The American Puritans: Their Prose and Poetry*. New York: Doubleday & Co., 1956.

_____. *The Transcendentalists: An Anthology*. Cambridge: Harvard University Press, 1950.

_____, and Johnson, Thomas H., eds. *The Puritans*. 2 vols. New York: Harper and Row, 1963.

Oberndorf, Clarence P. *A History of Psychoanalysis in America*. New York: Grune and Stratton, 1953.

Parkes, Henry Bamford. *The American Experience: An Interpretation of the History and Civilization of the American People*. New York: Alfred A. Knopf, 1955.

Parrington, Vernon Louis. *Main Currents in American Thought*. 3 vols. in one. New York: Harcourt Brace and Co., 1930.

Parsons, Coleman O. "Mark Twain in Australia." *Antioch Review* 21 (Winter 1961–62): 455–68.

Pearce, Roy Harvey, ed. *Colonial American Writing*. New York: Rinehart and Co., 1969.

_____. *The Continuity of American Poetry*. Princeton, N.J.: Princeton University Press, 1961.

_____. *Historicism Once More: Problems and Occasions for the American Scholar*. Princeton, N.J.: Princeton University Press, 1969.

Penn, William. "Letter from William Penn to the Committee of the Free Society of Traders." *Narratives of Early Pennsylvania, West Jersey, and*

Delaware, 1630–1707. Edited by A. C. Myers. New York: Charles Scribner's Sons, 1912.

Perry, Ralph Barton. *The Thought and Character of William James As Revealed in Unpublished Correspondence and Notes, Together with His Unpublished Writings*. 2 vols. Boston: Little, Brown & Co., 1935.

Poe, Edgar Allan. *The Complete Poems and Stories of Edgar Allan Poe*. Edited by Arthur Hobson Quinn and Edward O'Neill. 2 vols. New York: Alfred A. Knopf, 1964.

————. *Collected Works of Edgar Allan Poe*. Edited by Thomas O. Mabbott. 2 vols. Cambridge: Harvard University Press, 1969.

————. *Les aventures d'Arthur Gordon Pym*. Edited by Thomas O. Mabbott. 2 vols. Cambridge: Harvard University Press, 1969.

Quinn, Arthur Hobson. *Edgar Allan Poe: A Critical Biography*. New York: D. Appleton-Century Co., 1941.

Ravitz, Abe C. "Timothy Dwight: Professor of Rhetoric." *New England Quarterly* 29 (March 1956): 63–72.

Riley, Isaac Woodbridge. *American Thought: From Puritanism to Pragmatism and Beyond*. Gloucester, Mass.: Smith, 1959.

Shephard, Esther. *Walt Whitman's Pose*. New York: Harcourt, Brace & Co., 1938.

Smith, John. *Travels and Works of Captain John Smith*. Edited by Edward Arber and A. G. Bradley. 2 vols. Edinburgh: J. Grant, 1910.

Sanford, Charles L. *The Quest for Paradise: Europe and the American Moral Imagination*. Urbana: University of Illinois Press, 1961.

Smith, Henry Nash. *Virgin Land: The American West as Symbol and Myth*. Cambridge: Harvard University Press, 1950.

Spencer, Herbert. *Principles of Sociology*. 3 vols. New York: D. Appleton and Co., 1904.

Thoreau, Henry David. *Walden*. Edited by J. Lyndon Shanley. Princeton, N.J.: Princeton University Press, 1971.

————. *The Writings of Henry David Thoreau*. Edited by Bradford Torrey. 20 vols. Boston: Houghton Mifflin Co., 1906.

Townsend, Harvey Gates. *Philosophical Ideas in the United States*. New York: American Book Co., 1934.

Twain, Mark. *The Mysterious Stranger*. Edited by William M. Gibson. Berkeley and Los Angeles: University of California Press, 1969.

————. *The Writings of Mark Twain*. 25 vols. New York: Harper and Brothers, 1899.

————. and Howells, William Dean. *Mark Twain–Howells Letters, 1872–1910*. Edited by Henry Nash Smith and William M. Gibson. 2 vols. Cambridge: Harvard University Press, 1960.

Wagar, W. Warren. *Good Tidings: the Belief in Progress from Darwin to Marcuse*. Bloomington: Indiana University Press, 1972.

Whitman, Walt. *Leaves of Grass*. Edited by H. W. Blodgett and Sculley Bradley. New York: New York University Press, 1965.

————. *Prose Works 1892*. Edited by Floyd Stovall. 2 vols. New York: New York University Press, 1963.

Williams, Raymond. *The Long Revolution*. London: Chatto and Windus, 1961.

Williams, Roger. *The Complete Writings of Roger Williams*. 7 vols. New York: Russell and Russell, 1963.

Woolman, John. *The Journal and Major Essays of John Woolman*. Edited by Phillips P. Moulton. New York: Oxford University Press, 1971.

Index

Malraux, André, 241
Mann, Thomas, 210
Marvell, Andrew, 16
Marx, Karl, 6
Marx, Leo, 237
Mason, George: and the Virginia Bill of Rights, 32
Mather, Cotton, 24
Matthiessen, F. O., 3, 90, 255 (chap. I, n. 2)
Maturin, Charles, 170
Melville, Herman, viii, 3, 18, 30, 36, 82, 101, 125–27, 135, 157, 176–96, 202, 204 232, 253; "The Bell-Tower," 182–83; "Benito Cereno," 177, 181, 186, 191; "Billy Budd," 181, 186, 191–92; *Clarel*, 183–84; *The Confidence-Man*, 178, 181, 183, 193–95, 239; *Israel Potter*, 180, 182; "The Lightning-Rod Man," 182; *Mardi*, 178, 184–85, 188–89; *Moby-Dick*, 177, 186–94, 241; *Omoo*, 180; *Pierre*, 177, 191; *Redburn*, 14, 179; *Typee*, 178–81, 184, 189; *White-Jacket*, 177–78, 233
Mill, John Stuart, 6, 163, 202
Miller, Henry, 161
Miller, James E., Jr., 119, 260 (n. 121)
Miller, Perry, 3, 12, 80, 255 (chap. I, n. 2)
Milton, John, 13, 147, 190; *Paradise Lost*, 153
Mimesis, 149–50
Modernism, viii, 3
Montage, 123
Montesquieu, Charles Louis, 31
Mumford, Lewis, 88
Mysticism, 81, 92, 94–95, 117–18, 121, 134
Mythology, 31, 64, 66, 77, 88, 91–92, 94, 99, 115, 127, 253

N
Natural rights of man, 7, 32
Nature, 4, 8–9, 24, 42, 45, 47–48, 50, 53, 55, 57, 67, 95–96, 107, 113, 135, 139–40, 244
Negative mythology, 13
Neoclassicism, 27, 31, 43, 46, 61, 70
Newman, John Cardinal, 197
Newton, Sir Isaac, 18–19, 26
Niebuhr, Reinhold, 23
Norris, Frank, 240
Norton, Andrews, 79

O
Oberndorf, Clarence, 157
Objective style, 11, 21, 36–37

Official faith, 3, 6, 30–31, 36–37, 43, 79–80, 83, 196–97, 220, 222, 229, 232, 237
Open universe, 198, 200, 209
Optimism, viii, 5, 8, 11–12, 23, 25–26, 32, 41, 43–45, 50, 52–53, 56–57, 59, 62–63, 69, 71, 74–75, 81, 100, 107, 112, 116, 122, 128–29, 133–34, 136, 138, 141, 177–78, 183, 188, 192, 196, 198, 202, 205, 208–11, 216, 226, 229, 232, 242, 251

P
Paine, Thomas, 110
Parkes, Henry Bamford, ix
Parrington, Vernon Louis, 3, 5, 23, 232, 255 (chap. I, n. 1)
Past *vs.* present, 5, 28, 64, 89, 127; in Hawthorne, 140–44, 147, 150; in Melville, 177, 198–99
Pearce, Roy Harvey, 3, 255 (chap. I, n. 2)
Penn, William, 25, 27
Pessimism, 6, 28, 63–64, 126, 134, 194, 202–3, 209, 226
Plato, 88, 94, 117
Pluralism, 201
Poe, Edgar, Allen, 3, 5, 18, 30, 61, 77, 89, 101, 125–27, 135, 157, 159–76, 182, 204; conception of Beauty, 160–65, 167–68, 170, 174–75; *Al Aaraaf*, 163, 165–69, 173–74; "Berenice," 171; "City in the Sea," 14; "The Colloquy of Monos and Una," 159–61; "Ligeia," 173–75; "Mellonta Tauta," 163; "Morning on the Wissahiccon," 162; "M.S. Found in a Bottle," 173; *The Narrative of A. Gordon Pym*, 171–73, 239; "The Poetic Principle," 161–62, 164; "The Purloined Letter," 168; "The Raven," 169; "To Helen," 169–70, 173–74; "To Science," 77, 163
Polysensua, 185–86
Pomfret, John, 28
Pope, Alexander, 35, 52; *An Essay on Man*, 28, 31
Pragmatism, 33, 36, 62, 66, 197–200, 202–7
Primitivism, 8–10, 13, 26, 30, 37–41, 43, 45, 49, 50, 53, 66–67, 79, 81, 101–2, 136, 138–40, 159–61, 177, 179, 181, 213, 217–18, 221–22, 243
Prior, Matthew, 28
Private man, 81, 94
Progress, idea of, ix, 5–13, 17, 19, 33, 35, 37–41, 43, 45, 49–51, 55–56, 66, 68, 71, 78–79, 81, 97, 101, 110, 130–33, 142–43, 145, 160, 162, 167, 169,

177–78, 182, 194, 202, 213, 222–23, 237–38, 243, 250
Psychoanalysis, 157–58
Puritanism, 11–19, 22, 24, 26, 63, 71–72, 79, 136, 147, 153–54
Pynchon, Thomas, 254

Q
Quakers, 11, 24–26, 111

R
Rabelais, François, 190
Ransom, John Crowe, 233
Realism, 33, 35, 58, 197, 200–201, 207–10, 227, 232, 240, 249, 252–53
Reason, 24, 36, 43, 45, 47, 51, 56, 62, 65, 67, 78, 80, 84–85, 91, 117, 134, 159, 163, 172, 174, 182, 194, 228
Reason, higher, 84–85
Reformation, 23, 79
Renaissance, 5, 27, 55, 132, 171, 182
Romance, 147–50, 153
Romanticism, 43–44, 47, 56, 80, 88, 112, 134, 159, 168–69, 204, 224
Rousseau, Jean Jacques, 26, 31, 80, 179
Royal Society, 7

S
St. Augustine, 147, 197
Salinger, J. D., 253
Sanford, Charles L., 255 (n. 15)
Satiric modes: in Lowell, 52, 60–61; in Holmes, 69–71; in Thoreau, 104; in Twain, 213–14
Schoolcraft, Henry, 49
Schopenhauer, Arthur, 202
Scientific method, 5–7, 33, 35, 62, 64–65, 76–77, 163, 197, 200–202, 232, 235
Scott, Sir Walter, 224
Sentimentalism, 204–6, 224, 228
Shaftesbury, Anthony Ashley Cooper, third earl of, 26
Shakespeare, 29, 190; Henry IV, 39
Shelley, Percy Bysshe, 169; Prometheus Unbound, 186
Shenstone, William, 28
Smith, Henry Nash, 255 (n. 15)
Smith, John, 27, 171
Sophocles: Antigone, 191
Spatial form, 122, 248
Spencer, Herbert, 6, 241
Spenser, Edmund, 190
Steele, Richard, 68
Steinbeck, John, 30, 249
Stewart, Dugald, 8
Structural analysis, 4

Structure of feeling, 4, 10, 136, 147–48, 176
Subjective style, 11, 37
Swedenborg, Emanuel, 83
Symbolism, 4, 14, 41, 64, 240–41; Emerson's concept of, 80–81, 84, 93–95; Thoreau's use of, 97, 100, 102–3, 108; Whitman's use of, 109, 111, 113–14, 122, 133; Hawthorne's use of, 148, 150; Poe's use of, 168; Melville's use of, 185

T
Taylor, Edward, 16–17, 19–20, 148; "Huswifery,"16; "Meditation Six," 16; "Meditation Eight," 17
Tennyson, Alfred Lord, 198
Thoreau, Henry David, viii, 20, 54–55, 61, 81, 88, 93–109, 114, 116, 121, 129, 150; "Civil Disobedience," 105; Walden 94, 96–109; A Week on the Concord and Merrimack Rivers, 94, 97
Tolstoi, Leo, 204, 209–10
Tragedy, 81–82, 190–93
Transcendentalism, 54, 98–99, 104, 116, 128, 131–33, 136, 175
Twain, Mark, viii, 30, 59, 62, 91, 150, 193, 196, 199, 208, 212–31, 234–42, 247, 253; The Adventures of Huckleberry Finn, 58, 212–13, 217–22, 227, 229–31, 234–35, 238; The Adventures of Tom Sawyer, 213, 217–19, 222; The American Claimant, 229; "The Celebrated Jump-ing Frog of Calaveras County," 213; A Connecticut Yankee in King Arthur's Court, 213, 218, 221, 224–26, 235–36, 238–39; The Innocents Abroad, 212–16, 222, 227; Joan of Arc, 221–22; Life on the Mississippi, 213, 220, 222–24, 227; The Mysterious Stranger, 212, 240, 242; The Prince and the Pauper, 234; Pudd'nhead Wilson, 227, 236; "What is Man?" 226–27; and Charles Dudley Warner, The Gilded Age, 183, 213, 228, 234
Types; Puritan concept of, 19–20

U
Unitarianism, 17, 52, 79, 136
Utilitarianism, 6, 73, 88, 169, 202, 243

V
Vaughan, Henry, 16
Vernacular, 57–59, 72–73, 213, 235
Voltaire, 80
Vonnegut, Kurt, 254